One in thine hand

The Stick of *Judah* and the Stick of *Joseph*

One in thine hand

The Stick of *Judah* and the Stick of *Joseph*

Lynn F. Price

Horizon Publishers
Springville, Utah

ISBN 13: 978-0-88290-816-8
ISBN 10: 0-88290-816-2

Published by Horizon Publishers, an imprint of Cedar Fort, Inc., 2373 W. 700 S., Springville, UT, 84663
Distributed by Cedar Fort, Inc. www.cedarfort.com

LIBRARY OF CONGRESS CATALOGING-IN-PUBLICATION DATA

Price, Lynn F.
One in Thine Hand / Lynn F. Price.
p. cm.
ISBN-13: 978-0-88290-816-8
1. Church of Jesus Christ of Latter-day Saints--Apologetic works. 2. Mormon Church--Apologetic works. 3. Bible--Criticism, interpretation, etc. 4. Book of Mormon--Criticism, interpretation, etc. 5. Mormon Church--Doctrines. [1. Church of Jesus Christ of Latter-Day Saints--Doctrines.] I. Title.
BX8635.5.P75 2007
289.3--dc22
2006034232

Cover design by Nicole Williams
Edited and typeset by Annaliese B. Cox
Cover design © 2006 by Lyle Mortimer

Printed in the United States of America

10 9 8 7 6 5 4 3 2 1

Printed on acid-free paper

And join them one to another into one stick;
and they shall become one in thine hand.

Ezekiel 37:15-17

Table of Contents

Foreword

Periodically, various evangelists display signs in downtown Salt Lake City (or wherever Mormons are gathered) that proclaim: "Read the Bible! Not the Book of Mormon!" In response to that statement, I did just that—I read the Bible, but I also read the Book of Mormon. It was exciting to see how completely they support each other. I discovered doctrine taught in the Old Testament that I had no idea was contained therein. As I then read the New Testament, the Doctrine and Covenants, and the Pearl of Great Price, I experienced quite a thrill as one truth after another was taught in each of the books of scripture.

Like the evangelists, I urge everyone to read the Bible—but don't stop there! Read the Book of Mormon and the other scriptures too, and learn for yourselves that they all teach the same doctrines. This book is a compilation of scriptures from the Old Testament, New Testament, Book of Mormon, Doctrine and Covenants, and Pearl of Great Price that will help you discover how consistently they all teach the same truths relative to any doctrinal tenet.

Preface

One in Thine Hand: The Stick of Judah and the Stick of Joseph is a compilation of verses from each of the standard works that provide scriptural evidence that the Old Testament, New Testament, Book of Mormon, Doctrine and Covenants, and Pearl of Great Price all teach the same truths.

The Lord instructed his children that the stick of Judah and the stick of Joseph should be used as "one in thine hand" to understand the truths of his doctrine. The stick of Judah is the Bible, and the stick of Joseph is the Book of Mormon: Another Testament of Jesus Christ. Many different religions use the Bible as the basis for their beliefs, and yet the doctrine varies from church to church. *One in Thine Hand: The Stick of Judah and the Stick of Joseph* explores what the scriptures actually say about various tenets: (1) The stick of Judah and the stick of Joseph; (2) Apostasy and restoration; (3) The Church as organized by Christ; (4) The Godhead; (5) The need for a Redeemer: The birth, death, and Second Coming of Christ foretold; (6) Death and resurrection; (7) Grace, faith, works, and exaltation; (8) Repentance and forgiveness; (9) Christ's grace impacts us in this life as well as in the next; (10) God communicates with his children; (11) Born again; (12) Baptism; (13) One must have authority to act in God's name; (14) Tithing; (15) Priesthood: Aaronic Priesthood/ Melchizedek Priesthood; (16) Marraige, homosexuality, and plural marriage; (17) The plan of salvation; and (18) The Sabbath day.

Following the Lord's instructions to use the stick of Judah (the Bible) and the stick of Joseph (the Book of Mormon: Another Testament of Jesus Christ) together as one provides greater knowledge of the truths Christ taught and puts the follower of the doctrine on the path to a more perfect understanding of the gospel.

Christ said, "Come unto me." A more perfect understanding of the gospel can bring one unto Christ.

Acknowledgments

I extend a special word of thanks to my husband for his unwavering encouragement and support as I have worked on this project; to Duane Crowther for encouraging me to finish and submit the manuscript; to Dianne Richards and the women of the Monument Park 15th Ward Relief Society who expressed their appreciation and desire for more when I presented some of this information in a few Relief Society lessons, giving me reason to believe that others would also find this information valuable; and, finally, to the personnel and publishers at Cedar Fort who have found this work worth publishing, and to Annaliese B. Cox, specifically, for her help in editing this work.

Chapter 1

The Stick of Judah and the Stick of Joseph

TENET: The Bible is the word of God as far as it is translated correctly; the Book of Mormon is also the word of God. The Bible is the stick of Judah, and the Book of Mormon is the stick of Joseph. The Bible indicates that these two sticks should be joined together and used as one.

Both the Bible and the Book of Mormon make reference to additional scriptures, some of which have been lost; others were prophesied to come forth later. Both books also record the Lord's promise to raise up additional prophets to guide the people.

(A) Lost scriptures

Old Testament

The Old Testament refers to the book of the covenant, the book of the wars of the Lord, the book of Jasher, the book of the acts of Solomon, among others. These scriptures have been lost.

Exodus 24:4, 7	And Moses wrote all the words of the Lord, and rose up early in the morning, and builded an altar under the hill, and twelve pillars, according to the twelve tribes of Israel. . . . And he took the book of the covenant, and read in the audience of the people: and they said, All that the Lord hath said will we do, and be obedient.
Numbers 21:14	Wherefore it is said in the book of the wars of the Lord,

	What he did in the Red sea, and in the brooks of Arnon.
Joshua 10:13	And the sun stood still, and the moon stayed, until the people had avenged themselves upon their enemies. Is not this written in the book of Jasher?
1 Samuel 10:25	Then Samuel told the people the manner of the kingdom, and wrote it in a book, and laid it up before the Lord.
2 Samuel 1:18	Also he bade them teach the children of Judah the use of the bow: behold, it is written in the book of Jasher.
1 Kings 11:41	And the rest of the acts of Solomon, and all that he did, and his wisdom, are they not written in the book of the acts of Solomon?
1 Chronicles 29:29	Now the acts of David the king, first and last, behold, they are written in the book of Samuel the seer, and in the book of Nathan the prophet, and in the book of Gad the seer.
2 Chronicles 9:29	Now the rest of the acts of Solomon, first and last, are they not written in the book of Nathan the prophet, and in the prophecy of Ahijah the Shilonite, and in the visions of Iddo the seer against Jeroboam the son of Nebat?
2 Chronicles 12:15	Now the acts of Rehoboam, first and last, are they not written in the book of Shemaiah the prophet, and of Iddo the seer concerning genealogies?
2 Chronicles 13:22	And the rest of the acts of Abijab, and his ways, and his sayings, are written in the story of the prophet Iddo.
2 Chronicles 20:34	Now the rest of the acts of Jehoshaphat, first and last, behold, they are written in the book of Jehu the son of Hanani, who is mentioned in the book of the kings of Israel.
2 Chronicles 33:18–19	Now the rest of the acts of Manasseh, and his prayer

unto his God, and the words of the seers that spake to him in the name of the Lord God of Israel, behold, they are written in the book of the kings of Israel.

His prayer also, and how God was intreated of him, and all his sin, and his trespass, and the places wherein he built high places, and set up groves and graven images, before he was humbled: behold, they are written among the sayings of the seers.

New Testament

The New Testament also makes reference to scriptures that have been lost.

Matthew 2:23 — And he came and dwelt in a city called Nazareth: that it might be fulfilled which was spoken by the prophets, He shall be called a Nazarene.

The scriptures, or words of the prophets, in Matthew 2:23 that refer to the Savior as a Nazarene have been lost.

1 Corinthians 5:9 — I wrote unto you in an epistle not to company with fornicators.

This previous epistle referred to in 1 Corinthians 5:9 is lost.

Ephesians 3:1–3 — For this cause I Paul, the prisoner of Jesus Christ for you Gentiles,

If ye have heard of the dispensation of the grace of God which is given me to you-ward: How that by revelation he made known unto me the mystery; (as I wrote afore in few words,

Whereby, when ye read, ye may understand my knowledge in the mystery of Christ).

The words that Paul wrote "afore" are missing.

Colossians 4:16 — And when this epistle is read among you, cause that it be read also in the church of the Laodiceans; and that ye likewise read the epistle from Laodicea.

The epistle to the Laodiceans has been lost.

Jude refers to prophesies of Enoch (Jude 1:14) that the early saints obviously had, but we do not.

Nonbiblical scriptures also make reference to scriptures we don't have; for instance, the Book of Mormon refers to the writings of the prophets Zenos, Zenock, and Neum (1 Nephi 19:10; Jacob 6:1; Alma 33:3, 12–13; Alma 34:7; Helaman. 8:19–20; 15:11).

Book of Mormon

Ether, a descendant of Coriantor, records in the Book of Mormon:

Ether 1:3–5 And as I suppose that the first part of this record, which speaks concerning the creation of the world, and also of Adam, and an account from that time even to the great tower, and whatsoever things transpired among the children of men until that time, is had among the Jews—

Therefore I do not write those things which transpired from the days of Adam until that time; but they are had upon the plates; and whoso findeth them, the same will have power that he may get the full account.

But behold, I give not the full account, but a part of the account I give, from the tower down until they were destroyed.

The plates that Ether refers to contain additional scripture that apparently duplicates some of what is contained in the Old Testament.

Moroni, the last prophet of the Book of Mormon, abridged the records kept by Ether and said:

Ether 15:33 And the hundredth part I have not written.

The unabridged part has yet to come forth.

Doctrine and Covenants

The resurrected Savior revealed certain information to Joseph Smith regarding Adam and his posterity.

D&C 107:57 These things were all written in the book of Enoch, and are to be testified of in due time.

Again, the book of Enoch referred to by the Lord in the Doctrine and Covenants is still lost to mankind.

Pearl of Great Price

The Lord informed Moses in ancient times, as recorded in the Pearl of Great Price, that scriptures would be lost due to the wickedness of men.

Moses 1:41	And in a day when the children of men shall esteem my words as naught and take many of them from the book which thou shalt write, behold, I will raise up another like unto thee; and they shall be had again among the children of men—among as many as shall believe.

The Bible, Book of Mormon, Doctrine and Covenants, and Pearl of Great Price are consistent in revealing that there are records (scriptures) that we no longer have. The scriptures we do have, as we will see, are also consistent in prophesying about additional scriptures to come forth "even as one speaking out of the dust" (Moroni 10:27).

(B) Indications of other scriptures to eventually come forth

Old Testament

Isaiah foretold of a time of destruction but said the voices of those destroyed will:

Isaiah 29:4	Speak out of the ground, and thy speech shall be low out of the dust, and thy voice shall be, as of one that hath a familiar spirit, out of the ground, and thy speech shall whisper out of the dust.

Isaiah continued prophesying:

Isaiah 29:10–11	For the Lord hath poured out upon you the spirit of deep sleep, and hath closed your eyes: the prophets and your rulers, the seers hath he covered. And the vision of all is become unto you as the words of a book that is sealed, which men deliver to one that is learned, saying, read this, I pray thee: and he saith, I cannot; for it is sealed.

The fulfillment of this prophecy is recorded in the Pearl of Great Price (see Joseph Smith—History 1:64–65).

Isaiah 29:18	And in that day shall the deaf hear the words of

the book, and the eyes of the blind shall see out of obscurity, and out of darkness.

The Lord instructed the Prophet Ezekiel, saying:

Ezekiel 37:16–17 Moreover, thou son of man, take thee one stick, and write upon it, For Judah, and for the children of Israel his companions: then take another stick, and write upon it, For Joseph, the stick of Ephraim, and for all the house of Israel his companions.

And join them one to another into one stick; and they shall become one in thine hand.

Book of Mormon

Sometime between 600 and 592 B.C., here on the American continent, the Lord told Nephi, son of the Prophet Lehi:

1 Nephi 13:35–36 I will manifest myself unto thy seed, that they shall write many things which I shall minister unto them, which shall be plain and precious; and after thy seed shall be destroyed, and dwindle in unbelief, and also the seed of thy brethren, behold, these things shall be hid up, to come forth unto the Gentiles, by the gift and power of the Lamb. And in them shall be written my gospel, saith the Lamb.

The Lord also said:

2 Nephi 28:29–30 Wo be unto him that shall say: We have received the word of God, and we need no more of the word of God, for we have enough!

For behold, thus saith the Lord God: I will give unto the children of men line upon line, precept upon precept, here a little and there a little; and blessed are those who hearken unto my precepts, and lend an ear unto my counsel, for they shall learn wisdom; for unto him that receiveth I will give more; and from them that shall say, We have enough, from them shall be taken away even that which they have.

2 Nephi 29: 3–4, 6–8, 10–12

And because my words shall hiss forth—many of the Gentiles shall say: A Bible! A Bible! We have got a Bible, and there cannot be any more Bible.

But thus saith the Lord God: O fools, they shall have a Bible; and it shall proceed forth from the Jews, mine ancient covenant people. And what thank they the Jews for the Bible which they received from them? Yea, what do the Gentiles mean? . . .

Thou fool, that shall say: A Bible, we have got a Bible, and we need no more Bible. Have ye obtained a Bible save it were by the Jews?

Know ye not that there are more nations than one? Know ye not that I, the Lord your God, have created all men, and that I remember those who are upon the isles of the sea; and that I rule in the heavens above and in the earth beneath; and I bring forth my word unto the children of men, yea, even upon all the nations of the earth?

Wherefore murmur ye, because that ye shall receive more of my word? Know ye not that the testimony of two nations is a witness unto you that I am God, that I remember one nation like unto another? Wherefore, I speak the same words unto one nation like unto another. And when the two nations shall run together the testimony of the two nations shall run together also. . . .

Wherefore, because that ye have a Bible ye need not suppose that it contains all my words; neither need ye suppose that I have not caused more to be written.

For I command all men, both in the east and in the west, and in the north, and in the south, and in the islands of the sea, that they shall write the words which I speak unto them; for out of the books which shall be written I will judge the world, every man according to their works, according to that which is written.

For behold, I shall speak unto the Jews and they shall write it; and I shall also speak unto the Nephites and they shall write it; and I shall also speak unto the other tribes of the house of Israel, which I have led away, and they shall write it; and I shall also speak unto all nations of the earth and they shall write it.

Doctrine and Covenants

The Lord also revealed to Joseph Smith that there would be additional scriptures:

D&C 45:15–17 Wherefore, hearken and I will reason with you, and I will speak unto you and prophesy, as unto men in days of old.

And I will show it plainly as I showed it unto my disciples as I stood before them in the flesh, and spake unto them, saying: As ye have asked of me concerning the signs of my coming, in the day when I shall come in my glory in the clouds of heaven, to fulfil the promises that I have made unto your fathers,

For as ye have looked upon the long absence of your spirits from your bodies to be a bondage, I will show unto you how the day of redemption shall come, and also the restoration of the scattered Israel.

In a revelation given to Joseph Smith in 1831, the Lord said:

D&C 68:4 Whatsoever they shall speak when moved upon by the Holy Ghost shall be scripture, shall be the will of the Lord, shall be the mind of the Lord, shall be the word of the Lord, shall be the voice of the Lord, and the power of God unto salvation.

D&C 76:7–8 And to them will I reveal all mysteries, yea, all the hidden mysteries of my kingdom from days of old, and for ages to come, will I make known unto them the good pleasure of my will concerning all things pertaining to my kingdom.

Yea, even the wonders of eternity shall they know, and things to come will I show them, even the things of many generations.

D&C 104:58 — And for this purpose I have commanded you to organize yourselves, even to print my words, the fulness of my scriptures, the revelations which I have given unto you, and which I shall, hereafter, from time to time give unto you.

Pearl of Great Price

Isaiah's prophecy (see Isaiah 29:10–11) was fulfilled in 1828 as reported by Martin Harris:

JS—H 1:64–65 — I went to the city of New York, and presented the characters which had been translated, with the translation thereof, to Professor Charles Anthon, a gentleman celebrated for his literary attainments. Professor Anthon stated that the translation was correct, more so than any he had before seen translated from the Egyptian. I then showed him those which were not yet translated, and he said that they were Egyptian, Chaldaic, Assyriac, and Arabic; and he said they were true characters. He gave me a certificate, certifying to the people of Palmyra that they were true characters, and that the translation of such of them as had been translated was also correct. I took the certificate and put it into my pocket, and was just leaving the house, when Mr. Anthon called me back, and asked me how the young man found out that there were gold plates in the place where he found them. I answered that an angel of God had revealed it unto him.

He then said to me, "Let me see that certificate." I accordingly took it out of my pocket and gave it to him, when he took it and tore it to pieces, saying that there was no such thing now as ministering of angels, and that if I would bring the plates to him he would translate them. I informed him that part of the plates were sealed, and that I was forbidden to bring them. He replied, "I cannot read a sealed book."

(C) The stick of Judah and the stick of Joseph

The scriptures make reference to the stick of Judah and the stick of Joseph (the stick of Joseph is also called the stick of Ephraim). The Bible Dictionary states: "A book in ancient times was usually written on parchment of papyrus in a series of parallel columns, which answered to the pages of a modern book. At each end, and parallel to the columns, was a stick around which the skin or papyrus was rolled, the reader as he went along unrolling one end and rolling of the other."[1]

The stick of Judah (the Bible) is the record of the Lord's dealings with the house of Judah. The stick of Joseph (the Book of Mormon), or the stick of Ephraim, is the record of the Lord's dealings with "one portion of the tribe of Ephraim that was led from Jerusalem to America about 600 B.C."[2] These two sticks, or books, complement each other and the Lord gave instruction that they were to be used together to present a unified testimony of the divinity of Jesus Christ.

Old Testament

JST, Genesis 50:31 Wherefore the fruit of thy loins shall write, and the fruit of the loins of Judah shall write; and that which shall be written by the fruit of thy loins, and also that which shall be written by the fruit of the loins of Judah, shall grow together unto the confounding of false doctrines, and laying down of contentions, and establishing peace among the fruit of thy loins, and bringing them to a knowledge of their fathers in the latter days; and also to the knowledge of my covenants, saith the Lord.

In the King James version of the Bible, Genesis only goes to 50:26. However, Joseph Smith's translation of the Bible shows that some verses had been lost. His translation restores and corrects those verses (see JST, Genesis 50:24–38).

The Lord stressed that truth must be verified by more than one witness.

Deuteronomy 17:6 At the mouth of two witnesses, or three witnesses, shall he that is worthy of death be put to death; but at the mouth of one witness he shall not be put to death.

The stick of Judah and the stick of Joseph provide two witnesses to the truth of God's teachings: one alone is not sufficient.

Ezekiel 37:15–19 The word of the Lord came again unto me, saying,

Moreover, thou son of man, take thee one stick and write upon it, For Judah, and for the children of Israel his companions: then take another stick, and write upon it, For Joseph, the stick of Ephraim, and for all the house of Israel his companions:

And join them one to another into one stick; and they shall become one in thine hand.

And when the children of thy people shall speak unto thee, saying, Wilt thou not shew us what thou meanest by these?

Say unto them, Thus saith the Lord God; Behold, I will take the stick of Joseph, which is in the hand of Ephraim, and the tribes of Israel his fellows, and will put them with him even with the stick of Judah, and make them one stick, and they shall be one in mine hand.

New Testament

The New Testament does not make specific reference to the stick of Judah nor to the stick of Joseph, but Christ told the people:

Matthew 18:16 In the mouth of two or three witnesses every word may be established.

He also reminded the people about his "other sheep," saying:

John 10:16 Other sheep I have, which are not of this fold: them also I must bring, and they shall hear my voice; and there shall be one fold, and one shepherd.

These "other sheep" also kept records of their interaction with the Lord. The people to whom Jesus spoke did not understand the significance of what he was telling them. The Lord knew there would be additional scriptures. The Savior told the Nephites that they were the other sheep to whom he referred (see 3 Nephi 15:21–24). Their record is the Book of Mormon, or the stick of Joseph.

Book of Mormon

Lehi, the first prophet of the Book of Mormon, explained to his son Joseph that Joseph who was sold into Egypt was told by the Lord that his posterity should keep a record of God's word, and that it would be combined with the stick of Judah to bring people to the truth.

2 Nephi 3:11–12 But a seer will I raise up out of the fruit of thy loins; and unto him will I give power to bring forth my word unto the seed of thy loins—and not to the bringing forth my word only, saith the Lord, but to the convincing them of my word, which shall have already gone forth among them.

Wherefore, the fruit of thy loins shall write; and the fruit of the loins of Judah shall write; and that which shall be written by the fruit of thy loins, and also that which shall be written by the fruit of the loins of Judah, shall grow together, unto the confounding of false doctrines and laying down of contentions, and establishing peace among the fruit of thy loins, and bringing them to the knowledge of their fathers in the latter days, and also to the knowledge of my covenants, saith the Lord.

Nephi, the son of Lehi, also prophesied that the testimony, or records, kept by Joseph's descendants (the Book of Mormon) and the testimony kept by the Jews (the Bible) would be combined to testify of the truthfulness of God's teachings.

2 Nephi 29: 7–8, 10, 12–13

Know ye not that there are more nations than one? Know ye not that I, the Lord your God, have created all men, and that I remember those who are upon the isles of the sea; and that I rule in the heavens above and in the earth beneath; and I bring forth my word unto the children of men, yea, even upon all the nations of the earth?

Wherefore murmur ye, because that ye shall

receive more of my word? Know ye not that the testimony of two nations is a witness unto you that I am God, that I remember one nation like unto another? Wherefore, I speak the same words unto one nation like unto another. And when the two nations shall run together the testimony of the two nations shall run together also. . . .

Wherefore, because that ye have a Bible ye need not suppose that it contains all my words . . . For behold, I shall speak unto the Jews and they shall write it; and I shall also speak unto the Nephites and they shall write it. . . .

And it shall come to pass that the Jews shall have the words of the Nephites, and the Nephites shall have the words of the Jews.

Doctrine and Covenants

D&C 27:5 Behold, this is wisdom in me; wherefore, marvel not, for the hour cometh that I will drink of the fruit of the vine with you on the earth, and with Moroni, whom I have sent unto you to reveal the Book of Mormon, containing the fulness of my everlasting gospel, to whom I have committed the keys of the record of the stick of Ephraim.

D&C 42:12 And again, the elders, priests and teachers of this church shall teach the principles of my gospel, which are in the Bible and the Book of Mormon, in the which is the fulness of the gospel.

Pearl of Great Price

Articles of Faith 1:8 We believe the Bible to be the word of God as far as it is translated correctly; we also believe the Book of Mormon to be the word of God.

Articles of Faith 1:9 We believe all that God has revealed, all that He does now reveal, and we believe that He will yet reveal many great and important things pertaining to the Kingdom of God.

(D) Other prophets and other sheep

Old Testament

The Prophet Amos reminded the people:

Amos 3:7 — Surely the Lord God will do nothing, but he revealeth his secrets unto his servants the prophets.

Those secrets revealed by the Lord through his prophets are recorded as scripture.

New Testament

In the New Testament, Jesus taught the people that "his sheep [his followers] know his voice" and indicated that there were yet other sheep that he had.

John 10:16 — And other sheep I have, which are not of this fold: them also I must bring, and they shall hear my voice; and there shall be one fold, and one shepherd.

These "other sheep" have also kept records of the Lord's instructions to them. Because the Lord is no respecter of persons and is the same yesterday, today, and tomorrow, those instructions—those scriptures—parallel the truths taught in the Bible.

Book of Mormon

When the Prophet Lehi realized that his days here on earth were growing short, he called his children together and gave them each a blessing. To his youngest son, Joseph, he said:

2 Nephi 3:3–9, 11–12, 15, 18–20

> And now, Joseph, my last-born . . . may the Lord bless thee forever, for thy seed shall not utterly be destroyed.
>
> For behold, thou art the fruit of my loins; and I am a descendant of Joseph who was carried captive into Egypt. And great were the covenants of the Lord which he made unto Joseph.
>
> Wherefore, Joseph truly saw our day. And he obtained a promise of the Lord, that out of the fruit of his loins the Lord God would raise up a righteous

branch unto the house of Israel; not the Messiah, but a branch which was to be broken off, nevertheless, to be remembered in the covenants of the Lord that the Messiah should be made manifest unto them in the latter days, in the spirit of power, unto the bringing of them out of darkness unto light—yea, out of hidden darkness and out of captivity unto freedom.

For Joseph truly testified, saying: A seer shall the Lord my God raise up, who shall be a choice seer unto the fruit of my loins. . . . [Note: the Old Testament record of God's promise to Joseph regarding this seer is found in JST, Genesis 50:33.]

And unto him will I give commandment that he shall do a work for the fruit of thy loins, his brethren, which shall be of great worth unto them, even to the bringing of them to the knowledge of the covenants which I have made with thy fathers.

And I will give unto him a commandment that he shall do none other work, save the work which I shall command him. And I will make him great in mine eyes; for he shall do my work.

And he shall be great like unto Moses, whom I have said I would raise up unto you, to deliver my people, O house of Israel. . . .

But a seer will I raise up out of the fruit of thy loins; and unto him will I give power to bring forth my word unto the seed of thy loins—and not to the bringing forth my word only, saith the Lord, but to the convincing them of my word, which shall have already gone forth among them.

Wherefore, the fruit of thy loins shall write; and the fruit of the loins of Judah shall write; and that which shall be written by the fruit of thy loins, and also that which shall be written by the fruit of the loins of Judah, shall grow together, unto the confounding of false doctrines and laying down of contentions, and establishing peace among the fruit of thy loins, and bringing them to the knowledge of

> their father in the latter days, and also to the knowledge of my covenants, saith the Lord. . . .
>
> And his name shall be called after me; and it shall be after the name of his father. [Note: Joseph Smith, Jr., the son of Joseph Smith, Sr., called after the name of Joseph who was sold into Egypt, is that prophet.] And he shall be like unto me; for the thing, which the Lord shall bring forth by his hand, by the power of the Lord shall bring my people unto salvation. . . .
>
> And I, behold, I will give unto him that he shall write the writing of the fruit of thy loins, unto the fruit of thy loins. . . .
>
> And the words which he shall write shall be the words which are expedient in my wisdom should go forth unto the fruit of thy loins. And it shall be as if the fruit of thy loins had cried unto them from the dust; for I know their faith.
>
> And they shall cry from the dust; yea, even repentance unto their brethren, even after many generations have gone by them.

Following the Savior's resurrection, he appeared to the Nephites here in America. He said:

3 Nephi 15:21–24, 16:1–4

> And verily I say unto you, that ye are they of whom I said: Other sheep I have which are not of this fold; them also I must bring, and they shall hear my voice; and there shall be one fold, and one shepherd.
>
> And they understood me not, for they supposed it had been the Gentiles; for they understood not that the Gentiles should be converted through their preaching.
>
> And they understood me not that I said they shall hear my voice; and they understood me not that the Gentiles should not at any time hear my voice—that I should not manifest myself unto them save it were by the Holy Ghost.

> But behold, ye have both heard my voice, and seen me; and ye are my sheep, and ye are numbered among those whom the Father hath given me.
>
> And verily, verily, I say unto you that I have other sheep, which are not of this land, neither of the land of Jerusalem, neither in any parts of that land round about whither I have been to minister.
>
> For they of whom I speak are they who have not as yet heard my voice; neither have I at any time manifested myself unto them.
>
> But I have received a commandment of the Father that I shall go unto them, and that they shall hear my voice, and shall be numbered among my sheep, that there may be one fold and one shepherd; therefore I go to show myself unto them.
>
> And I command you that ye shall write these sayings after I am gone, that if it so be that my people at Jerusalem, they who have seen me and been with me in my ministry, do not ask the Father in my name, that they may receive a knowledge of you by the Holy Ghost, and also of the other tribes whom they know not of, that these sayings which ye shall write shall be kept and shall be manifested unto the Gentiles, that through the fulness of the Gentiles, the remnant of their seed, who shall be scattered forth upon the face of the earth because of their unbelief, may be brought in, or may be brought to a knowledge of me, their Redeemer.

The record the Lord commanded these "sheep" to write is contained in the Book of Mormon. The "other sheep" to which he referred will undoubtedly have their own records (scriptures) when they are eventually reunited with the House of Israel.

Pearl of Great Price

In Moses 1:41, the Lord promised Moses that he would raise up another prophet like unto him. In Acts 3:19–24, Peter indicates that Christ is the prophet Moses referred to in Moses. The Lord also promised Joseph, son of Jacob, that he would raise up Moses (JST, Genesis 50:29) and that he would raise up still another prophet.

JST, Genesis 50:33 And that seer will I bless, and they that seek to destroy him shall be confounded; for this promise I give unto you; for I will remember you from generation to generation; and his name shall be called Joseph, and it shall be after the name of his father; and he shall be like unto you; for the thing which the Lord shall bring forth by his hand shall bring my people unto salvation.

Of this seer, the Lord said:

JST, Genesis 50:30–31

And again, a seer will I raise up out of the fruit of thy loins, and unto him will I give power to bring forth my word unto the seed of thy loins; and not to the bringing forth of my word only, saith the Lord, but to the convincing them of my word, which shall have already gone forth among them in the last days;

Wherefore the fruit of thy loins shall write, and the fruit of the loins of Judah shall write; and that which shall be written by the fruit of thy loins, and also that which shall be written by the fruit of the loins of Judah, shall grow together unto the confounding of false doctrines, and laying down of contentions, and establishing peace among the fruit of thy loins, and bringing them to a knowledge of their fathers in the latter days; and also to the knowledge of my covenants, saith the Lord.

(E) The scriptures and the word of the Lord will be rejected

Old Testament

Isaiah prophesied that the earth would be defiled "because they have transgressed the laws, changed the ordinance, broken the everlasting covenant" (Isaiah 24:5).

Jeremiah 8:9 The wise men are ashamed, they are dismayed and taken: lo, they have rejected the word of the Lord; and what wisdom is in them?

The Prophet Amos prophesied that the Lord God would send a famine "of hearing the words of the Lord" (Amos 8:11).

NEW TESTAMENT

In the New Testament, Christ chastised the Pharisees and scribes for putting tradition ahead of truth:

Mark 7:6–7	Well hath Esaias prophesied of you hypocrites, as it is written, This people honoureth me with their lips, but their heart is far from me. Howbeit in vain do they worship me, teaching for doctrines the commandments of men.
Luke 9:21–22	And he straitly charged them, and commanded them to tell no man that thing; Saying, The Son of man must suffer many things, and be rejected of the elders and chief priests and scribes, and be slain, and be raised the third day.

John records that Christ's disciples rejected his teachings:

John 6:66	From that time many of his disciples went back, and walked no more with him.

In Paul's second epistle to the Thessalonians, he reminded the people that there would be an apostasy before Christ came a second time and that the people would reject or alter the scriptures.

2 Thessalonians 2:3	Let no man deceive you by any means: for that day shall not come, except there come a falling away first, and that man of sin be revealed, the son of perdition.

BOOK OF MORMON

Speaking of our day, the Lord told Nephi that:

2 Nephi 29:1–3, 6–8, 10–11

At that day when I shall proceed to do a marvelous work among them, that I may remember my covenants which I have made unto the children of men, that I may set my hand again the second time to recover my people, which are of the house of Israel;

And also, that I may remember the promises which I have made unto thee, Nephi, and also unto thy father, that I would remember your seed; and that the words of your seed should proceed forth out of my mouth unto your seed; and my words shall hiss forth unto the ends of the earth, for a standard unto my people, which are of the house of Israel;

And because my words shall hiss forth—many of the Gentiles shall say: A Bible! A Bible! We have got a Bible, and there cannot be any more Bible. . . .

Thou fool, that shall say: A Bible, we have got a Bible, and we need no more Bible. Have ye obtained a Bible save it were by the Jews?

Know ye not that there are more nations than one? Know ye not that I, the Lord your God, have created all men, and that I remember those who are upon the isles of the sea; and that I rule in the heavens above and in the earth beneath; and I bring forth my word unto the children of men, yea, even upon all the nations of the earth:

Wherefore murmur ye, because that ye shall receive more of my word? Know ye not that the testimony of two nations is a witness unto you that I am God, that I remember one nation like unto another? Wherefore, I speak the same words unto one nation like unto another. And when the two nations shall run together the testimony of two nations shall run together also. [Note: the Bible, or the stick of Judah, and the Book of Mormon, or the stick of Joseph, are two testimonies that serve as witnesses of the divinity of Jesus Christ.]

Wherefore, because that ye have a Bible ye need not suppose that it contains all my words; neither need ye suppose that I have not caused more to be written.

For I command all men, both in the east and in the west, and in the north, and in the south, and in the islands of the sea, that they shall write the words which

I speak unto them; for out of the books which shall be written I will judge the world, every man according to their works, according to that which is written.

Helaman 6:2 — For behold, there were many of the Nephites who had become hardened and impenitent and grossly wicked, insomuch that they did reject the word of God and all the preaching and prophesying which did come among them.

3 Nephi 16:10 — And thus commandeth the Father that I should say unto you: At that day when the Gentiles shall sin against my gospel, and shall reject the fulness of my gospel, and shall be lifted up in the pride of their hearts above all nations, and above all the people of the whole earth, and shall be filled with all manner of lyings, and of deceits, and of mischiefs, and all manner of hypocrisy, and murders, and priestcrafts, and whoredoms, and of secret abominations; and if they shall do all those things, and shall reject the fulness of my gospel, behold, saith the Father, I will bring the fulness of my gospel from among them.

Doctrine and Covenants

Knowing people would continue to reject his word, the Savior reminded modern-day prophets that if people reject the word today, it is no different than their having rejected him in other times. Blessed are those who keep the word. In a revelation given to Joseph Smith the prophet and Oliver Cowdery in April 1829, the Lord said:

D&C 6:29–31 — Verily, verily, I say unto you, if they reject my words, and this part of my gospel and ministry, blessed are ye, for they can do no more unto you than unto me.

And even if they do unto you even as they have done unto me, blessed are ye, for you shall dwell with me in glory.

But if they reject not my words, which shall be established by the testimony which shall be given, blessed are they, and then shall ye have joy in the fruit of your labors.

Pearl of Great Price

Moses 5:25–26	And it shall be said in time to come—That these abominations were had from Cain; for he rejected the greater counsel which was had from God; and this is a cursing which I will put upon thee, except thou repent. And Cain was wroth, and listened not any more to the voice of the Lord, neither to Abel, his brother, who walked in holiness before the Lord.

Notes

1. Bible Dictionary, "Roll," 763.
2. Ibid., "Ephraim, Stick of," 666.

Chapter 2

Apostasy and Restoration

TENET: Long before the birth of Christ, Isaiah and Amos, prophets of the Old Testament, prophesied that a great apostasy would occur, as would an eventual restoration of the truth.

(A) The Apostasy was foretold

Old Testament

Isaiah 24:5	The earth also is defiled under the inhabitants thereof; because they have transgressed the laws, changed the ordinance, broken the everlasting covenant.
Isaiah 29:13–14	Wherefore the Lord said, Forasmuch as this people draw near me with their mouth, and with their lips do honour me, but have removed their heart far from me, and their fear toward me is taught by the precept of men: Therefore, behold, I will proceed to do a marvellous work among this people, even a marvellous work and a wonder: for the wisdom of their wise men shall perish, and the understanding of their prudent men shall be hid.
Isaiah 60:2–3	For, behold, the darkness shall cover the earth, and gross darkness the people: but the Lord shall arise

upon thee, and his glory shall be seen upon thee.

And the Gentiles shall come to thy light, and kings to the brightness of thy rising.

Amos spoke with equal boldness:

Amos 8:11–12 Behold, the days come, saith the Lord God, that I will send a famine in the land, not a famine of bread, nor a thirst for water, but of hearing the words of the Lord:

And they shall wander from sea to sea, and from the north even to the east, they shall run to and fro to seek the word of the Lord, and shall not find it.

New Testament

When Christ was upon the earth, he warned the people (using the parable of the wheat and tares) about an apostasy that would occur and continue clear up until the last days—until the end of the world. He taught:

Matthew 13:24–25 The kingdom of heaven is likened unto a man which sowed good seed in his field;

But while men slept, his enemy came and sowed tares among the wheat, and went his way.

Christ then explained the parable to his disciples.

Matthew 13:37–39 He that soweth the good seed is the Son of man;

The field is the world; the good seed are the children of the kingdom; but the tares are the children of the wicked one;

The enemy that sowed them is the devil; the harvest is the end of the world; and the reapers are the angels.

Christ warned that apostasy would occur.

Matthew 24:24 For there shall arise false Christs, and false prophets, and shall shew great signs and wonders; insomuch that, if it were possible, they shall deceive the very elect.

This apostasy began even during Christ's lifetime.

John 6:66	From that time many of his disciples went back, and walked no more with him.

Paul predicted that apostasy would occur.

Acts 20:29–30	For I know this, that after my departing shall grievous wolves enter in among you, not sparing the flock. Also of your own selves shall men arise, speaking perverse things, to draw away disciples after them.

Paul chastised the Corinthians because there were "divisions" and "heresies" among the people in the church (see 1 Corinthians 11:18–19).

Apostasy was also occurring among the Galatians at the same time.

Galatians 1:6–7	I marvel that ye are so soon removed from him that called you into the grace of Christ unto another gospel: Which is not another; but there be some that trouble you, and would pervert the gospel of Christ.
Galatians 3:1	O foolish Galatians, who hath bewitched you, that ye should not obey the truth, before whose eyes Jesus Christ hath been evidently set forth, crucified among you?

Paul taught the Thessalonians that apostasy would precede the Second Coming of the Savior.

2 Thessalonians 2:3	Let no man deceive you by any means; for that day shall not come, except there come a falling away first, and that man of sin be revealed, the son of perdition.

Paul described the apostate condition of the world in the latter days:

2 Timothy 3:1–5	This know also, that in the last days perilous times shall come. For men shall be lovers of their own selves, covetous, boasters, proud, blasphemers, disobedient to parents, unthankful, unholy,

Without natural affection, trucebreakers, false accusers, incontinent, fierce, despisers of those that are good,

Traitors, heady, highminded, lovers of pleasures more than lovers of God;

Having a form of godliness; but denying the power thereof.

Paul continued:

2 Timothy 4:3–4 For the time will come when they will not endure sound doctrine; but after their own lusts shall they heap to themselves teachers, having itching ears;

And they shall turn away their ears from the truth, and shall be turned unto fables.

In his epistle to Titus, Paul wrote:

Titus 1:15–16 Unto the pure all things are pure: but unto them that are defiled and unbelieving is nothing pure; but even their mind and conscience is defiled.

They profess that they know God; but in works they deny him, being abominable, and disobedient, and unto every good work reprobate.

The Apostle Peter also wrote regarding apostasy.

2 Peter 2:1–2 But there were false prophets also among the people, even as there shall be false teachers among you, who privily shall bring in damnable heresies, even denying the Lord that bought them, and bring upon themselves swift destruction.

And many shall follow their pernicious ways; by reason of whom the way of truth shall be evil spoken of.

Book of Mormon

Just as the prophets of the Old and New Testaments prophesied of the apostasy that would occur, the prophets of the Book of Mormon also prophesied of such an apostasy.

1 Nephi 13:24–29 And the angel of the Lord said unto me: Thou hast

beheld that the book [the Bible] proceeded forth from the mouth of a Jew; and when it proceeded forth from the mouth of a Jew it contained the fulness of the gospel of the Lord, of whom the twelve apostles bear record; and they bear record according to the truth which is in the Lamb of God.

Wherefore, these things go forth from the Jews in purity unto the Gentiles, according to the truth which is in God.

And after they go forth by the hand of the twelve apostles of the Lamb, from the Jews unto the Gentiles, thou seest the formation of that great and abominable church, which is most abominable above all other churches; for behold, they have taken away from the gospel of the Lamb many parts which are plain and most precious; and also many covenants of the Lord have they taken away.

And all this have they done that they might pervert the right ways of the Lord, that they might blind the eyes and harden the hearts of the children of men.

Wherefore, thou seest that after the book hath gone forth through the hands of the great and abominable church, that there are many plain and precious things taken away from the book, which is the book of the Lamb of God.

And after these plain and precious things were taken away it goeth forth unto all the nations of the gentiles; and after it goeth forth unto all the nations of the Gentiles, yea, even across the many waters which thou hast seen with the Gentiles which have gone forth out of captivity, thou seest—because of the many plain and precious things which have been taken out of the book, which were plain unto the understanding of the children of men, according to the plainness which is in the Lamb of God—because of these things which are taken away out of the gospel of the Lamb, an exceedingly great many do stumble, yea, insomuch that Satan hath great power over them.

2 Nephi 26:19–21 And it shall come to pass, that those who have dwindled in unbelief shall be smitten by the hand of the Gentiles.

And the Gentiles are lifted up in the pride of their eyes, and have stumbled, because of the greatness of their stumbling block, that they have built up many churches; nevertheless, they put down the power and miracles of God, and preach up unto themselves their own wisdom and their own learning, that they may get gain and grind upon the face of the poor.

And there are many churches built up which cause envyings, and strifes, and malice.

2 Nephi 27:1, 4–5 But, behold, in the last days, or in the days of the Gentiles—yea, behold all the nations of the Gentiles and also the Jews, both those who shall come upon this land and those who shall be upon other lands, yea, even upon all the lands of the earth, behold, they will be drunken with iniquity and all manner of abominations. . . .

For behold, all ye that doeth iniquity, stay yourselves and wonder, for ye shall cry out, and cry; yea, ye shall be drunken but not with wine, ye shall stagger but not with strong drink.

For behold, the Lord hath poured out upon you the spirit of deep sleep. For behold, ye have closed your eyes, and ye have rejected the prophets; and your rulers, and the seers hath he covered because of your iniquity.

Four hundred years after Christ's birth, death, and resurrection, Moroni, the last prophet of the Book of Mormon, lamented that his people had been destroyed because of wickedness and that total apostasy prevailed in the land.

Mormon 8:9–10 And now, behold, I say no more concerning them [his people, the Nephites] for there are none save it be the Lamanites and robbers that do exist upon the face of the land.

And there are none that do know the true God save it be the disciples of Jesus, who did tarry in the land until the wickedness of the people was so great that the Lord would not suffer them to remain with the people.

Doctrine and Covenants

We are reminded of the pervasiveness of the apostasy in a revelation given to Joseph Smith by the Lord on November 1, 1831:

D&C 1:15–16 For they have strayed from mine ordinances, and have broken mine everlasting covenant;

They seek not the Lord to establish his righteousness, but every man walketh in his own way, and after the image of his own god, whose image is in the likeness of the world, and whose substance is that of an idol, which waxeth old and shall perish in Babylon, even Babylon the great, which shall fall.

More than a year later, on December 6, 1832, the Lord explained the meaning of the parable of the wheat and tares to Joseph Smith: the field was the world, the apostles were the sowers of the seed, and Satan was the sower of the tares.

D&C 86:3 And after they have fallen asleep the great persecutor of the church, the apostate, the whore, even Babylon, that maketh all nations to drink of her cup, in whose hearts the enemy, even Satan, sitteth to reign—behold he soweth the tares; wherefore, the tares choke the wheat and drive the church into the wilderness.

Underscoring the tremendous need for the restoration of the gospel, on July 23, 1837, the Lord revealed the following to the Prophet Joseph Smith:

D&C 112:23 Verily, verily, I say unto you, darkness covereth the earth, and gross darkness the minds of the people, and all flesh has become corrupt before my face.

Pearl of Great Price

When Joseph Smith was just a young boy of 14 years, he desired to know which of all the churches he should join. A religious revival occurred in the early 1800s in the area where Joseph lived, and his family was somewhat divided on the matter of religion; Some family members attended one church and some attended another, and various religious leaders all claimed to have the true gospel. Joseph knew they could not all be right, and following the admonition given by James in the New Testament, "If any of you lack wisdom, let him ask of God, that giveth to all men liberally, and upbraideth not; and it shall be given him" (James 1:5), Joseph sought a place to pray and inquired of God as to which church he should join.

In answer to his prayer, the Father and the Son appeared to him.

JS—H 1:19 — I was answered that I must join none of them, for they were all wrong; and the Personage who addressed me said that all their creeds were an abomination in his sight; that those professors were all corrupt; that: "they draw near to me with their lips, but their hearts are far from me, they teach for doctrines the commandments of men, having a form of godliness, but they deny the power thereof."

(B) Restoration of the true Church in latter days was also foretold

Old Testament

Along with prophecies regarding apostasy that would repeatedly occur, the Prophet Isaiah prophesied of the restoration of truth in the latter days:

Isaiah 2:2–3 — And it shall come to pass in the last days, that the mountain of the Lord's house shall be established in the top of the mountains, and shall be exalted above the hills; and all nations shall flow unto it.

And many people shall go and say, Come ye, and let us go up to the mountain of the Lord, to the house of the God of Jacob; and he will teach us of his ways, and we will walk in his paths: for out of Zion [the new Jerusalem rather than the old

Jerusalem] shall go forth the law, and the word of the Lord from Jerusalem.

Jeremiah also prophesied of the restoration:

Jeremiah 31:31–34 Behold, the days come, saith the Lord, that I will make a new covenant with the house of Israel, and with the house of Judah:

Not according to the covenant that I made with their fathers in the day that I took them by the hand to bring them out of the land of Egypt; which my covenant they brake, although I was an husband unto them, saith the Lord:

But this shall be the covenant that I will make with the house of Israel; After those days, saith the Lord, I will put my law in their inward parts, and write it in their hearts; and will be their God, and they shall be my people.

And they shall teach no more every man his neighbour, and every man his brother, saying, Know the Lord: for they shall all know me, from the least of them unto the greatest of them, saith the Lord: for I will forgive their iniquity, and I will remember their sin no more.

Referring to the everlasting covenant that the Lord said he would make with his people in the last days, Ezekiel recorded:

Ezekiel 37:26 Moreover I will make a covenant of peace with them; it shall be an everlasting covenant with them: and I will place them, and multiply them: and will set my sanctuary in the midst of them for evermore.

King Nebuchadnezzar had a dream that Daniel interpreted for him. The dream reveals events that will take place in the last days, including the millennial reign of the Savior.

Daniel 2:44–45 And in the days of these kings shall the God of heaven set up a kingdom [establish his church], which shall never be destroyed: and the kingdom shall not be left to other people, but it shall break in

> pieces and consume all these kingdoms, and it shall stand for ever.
>
> Forasmuch as thou sawest that the stone was cut out of the mountain without hands, and that it brake in pieces the iron, the brass, the clay, the silver, and the gold; the great God hath made known to the king what shall come to pass hereafter: and the dream is certain, and the interpretation thereof sure.

The Lord revealed to the Prophet Joel events that would transpire in the last days:

Joel 2:28–32

> And it shall come to pass afterward, that I will pour out my spirit upon all flesh; and your sons and your daughters shall prophesy, your old men shall dream dreams, your young men shall see visions:
>
> And also upon the servants and upon the handmaids in those days will I pour out my spirit.
>
> And I will shew wonders in the heavens and in the earth, blood, and fire, and pillars of smoke.
>
> The sun shall be turned into darkness, and the moon into blood, before the great and the terrible day of the Lord come.
>
> And it shall come to pass, that whosoever shall call on the name of the Lord shall be delivered: for in mount Zion and in Jerusalem shall be deliverance, as the Lord hath said, and in the remnant whom the Lord shall call.

A sign of the restoration of the Lord's church is the restoration of the same organization that the Lord established when he was upon the earth, namely, with apostles, prophets, pastors, teachers, evangelists and other priesthood leaders. The Prophet Amos reminded the people that:

Amos 3:7

> Surely the Lord God will do nothing, but he revealeth his secret unto his servants the prophets.

It therefore stands to reason that when there were no prophets upon the earth because of the apostasy, God did not reveal his secrets to anyone. Churches taught the precepts of men.

Micah also prophesied that the house of the Lord would be established in the tops of the mountains in the last days.

Micah 4:1–2	But in the last days it shall come to pass, that the mountain of the house of the Lord shall be established in the top of the mountains, and it shall be exalted above the hills: and people shall flow unto it. And many nations shall come, and say, Come, and let us go up to the mountain of the Lord, and to the house of the God of Jacob; and he will teach us of his ways, and we will walk in his paths: for the law shall go forth of Zion [the New Jerusalem], and the word of the Lord from Jerusalem.

The Lord revealed to Malachi that he would send his messenger to prepare the way before he came the second time.

Malachi 3:1	Behold, I will send my messenger, and he shall prepare the way before me: and the Lord, whom ye seek, shall suddenly come to his temple, even the messenger of the covenant, whom ye delight in: behold, he shall come, saith the Lord of hosts.

Had there not been an apostasy, a falling away from Christ's teachings, the Lord would not have had to send a messenger to prepare the way for his coming.

With the apostasy came the loss of the priesthood and its attendant blessings. The restoration required a return of all the priesthood blessings by the hands of those prophets who held the keys of the various dispensations. The Lord told Malachi:

Malachi 4:5–6	Behold, I will send you Elijah the prophet [who held the keys of the sealing power of the priesthood] before the coming of the great and dreadful day of the Lord: And he shall turn the heart of the fathers to the children, and the heart of the children to their fathers, lest I come and smite the earth with a curse.

New Testament

Christ himself prophesied that angels would come and restore all truth:

JST, Matthew 17:10–14

> And Jesus answered and said unto them, Elias truly shall first come, and restore all things, as the prophets have written.
>
> And again I say unto you that Elias has come already, concerning whom it is written, Behold, I will send my messenger, and he shall prepare the way before me; and they knew him not, and have done unto him, whatsoever they listed.
>
> Likewise shall also the Son of Man suffer of them.
>
> But I say unto you, Who is Elias? Behold, this is Elias, whom I send to prepare the way before me.
>
> Then the disciples understood that he spake unto them of John the Baptist, and also of another who should come and restore all things, as it is written by the prophets.

Christ taught that his true gospel would be restored and missionaries would carry it throughout the world prior to his Second Coming:

Matthew 24:14

> And this gospel of the kingdom shall be preached in all the world for a witness unto all nations; and then shall the end come.

Peter's teachings reflect an acknowledgment that an apostasy would occur and that truth would eventually be restored. He taught:

Acts 3:20–21

> And he shall send Jesus Christ, which before was preached unto you:
>
> Whom the heaven must receive until the times of restitution of all things, which God hath spoken by the mouth of all his holy prophets since the world began.

Paul, in his epistle to the Ephesians, referred to the restoration that would occur in the latter day:

Ephesians 1:10

> That in the dispensation of the fulness of times he

might gather together in one all things in Christ, both which are in heaven, and which are on earth; even in him.

John the Revelator saw in vision events that would occur in the latter days, including the restoration of the gospel.

Revelation 14:6–7 And I saw another angel fly in the midst of heaven, having the everlasting gospel to preach unto them that dwell on the earth, and to every nation, and kindred, and tongue, and people,

Saying with a loud voice, Fear God, and give glory to him; for the hour of his judgment is come: and worship him that made heaven, and earth, and the sea, and the fountains of waters.

Book of Mormon

Just as both the apostasy and the restoration of the gospel were foretold in the Old and New Testaments, both are foretold in the Book of Mormon. Nephi recounted:

1 Nephi 13:34–40 And it came to pass that the angel of the Lord spake unto me saying: Behold, saith the Lamb of God, after I have visited the remnant of the house of Israel—and this remnant of whom I speak is the seed of thy father—wherefore, after I have visited them in judgment, and smitten them by the hand of the Gentiles, and after the Gentiles do stumble exceedingly, because of the most plain and precious parts of the gospel of the Lamb which have been kept back by that abominable church, which is the mother of harlots, saith the Lamb—I will be merciful unto the Gentiles in that day, insomuch that I will bring forth unto them, in mine own power, much of my gospel, which shall be plain and precious, saith the Lamb.

For behold, saith the Lamb: I will manifest myself unto thy seed, that they shall write many things which I shall minister unto them, which shall be plain and precious; and after thy seed shall be destroyed, and dwindle in unbelief, and also the seed of thy brethren, behold, these things shall be hid up, to come forth unto the Gentiles, by the gift and power of the Lamb.

And in them shall be written my gospel, saith the Lamb, and my rock and my salvation.

And blessed are they who shall seek to bring forth my Zion at that day, for they shall have the gift and the power of the Holy Ghost; and if they endure unto the end they shall be lifted up at the last day. . . .

And it came to pass that I beheld the remnant of the seed of my brethren, and also the book of the Lamb of God, which had proceeded forth from the mouth of the Jew, that it came forth from the Gentiles unto the remnant of the seed of my brethren.

And after it had come forth unto them I beheld other books, which came forth by the power of the Lamb, from the Gentiles unto them, unto the convincing of the Gentiles and the remnant of the seed of my brethren, and also the Jews who were scattered upon all the face of the earth, that the records of the prophets and of the twelve apostles of the Lamb are true.

And the angel spake unto me, saying: These last records, which thou hast seen among the Gentiles, shall establish the truth of the first, which are of the twelve apostles of the Lamb, and shall make known the plain and precious things which have been taken away from them; and shall make known to all kindreds, tongues, and people, that the Lamb of God is the Son of the Eternal Father, and the Savior of the world; and that all men must come unto him, or they cannot be saved.

Nephi looked into the last days:

1 Nephi 15:13 And now, the thing which our father meaneth concerning the grafting in of the natural branches

> through the fulness of the Gentiles, is, that in the latter days, when our seed shall have dwindled in unbelief, yea, for the space of many years, and many generations after the Messiah shall be manifested in body unto the children of men, then shall the fulness of the gospel of the Messiah come unto the Gentiles, and from the Gentiles unto the remnant of our seed.

Lehi taught his son Joseph that Joseph who was sold into Egypt prophesied concerning the restoration:

2 Nephi 3:24

> And there shall rise up one mighty among them, who shall do much good, both in word and in deed, being an instrument in the hands of God, with exceeding faith, to work mighty wonders, and do that thing which is great in the sight of God, unto the bringing to pass much restoration unto the house of Israel, and unto the seed of thy brethren.

Jacob, Nephi's brother, prophesied that the Jews would be "restored to the true church" (2 Nephi 9:2) as would his descendants:

2 Nephi 10:2

> God will be merciful unto many; and our children shall be restored, that they may come to that which will give them the true knowledge of their Redeemer.

The Lord also revealed:

2 Nephi 27:6–7, 14, 24–26, 28–30

> And it shall come to pass that the Lord God shall bring forth unto you the words of a book [the Book of Mormon], and they shall be the words of them which have slumbered.
>
> And behold the book shall be sealed; and in the book shall be a revelation from God, from the beginning of the world to the ending thereof. . . .
>
> Wherefore, the Lord God will proceed to bring forth the words of the book; and in the mouth of as many witnesses as seemeth him good will he establish

his word; and wo be unto him that rejecteth the word of God!

And again it shall come to pass that the Lord shall say unto him that shall read the words that shall be delivered him:

Forasmuch as this people draw near unto me with their mouth, and with their lips do honor me, but have removed their hearts far from me, and their fear towards me is taught by the precepts of men—

Therefore, I will proceed to do a marvelous work among this people, yea, a marvelous work and a wonder, for the wisdom of their wise and learned shall perish, and the understanding of their prudent shall be hid.

But behold, saith the Lord of Hosts: I will show unto the children of men that it is yet a very little while and Lebanon shall be turned into a fruitful field; and the fruitful field shall be esteemed as a forest.

And in that day shall the deaf hear the words of the book, and the eyes of the blind shall see out of obscurity and out of darkness.

And the meek also shall increase, and their joy shall be in the Lord, and the poor among men shall rejoice in the Holy One of Israel.

2 Nephi 30:5 — And the gospel of Jesus Christ shall be declared among them; wherefore, they shall be restored unto the knowledge of their fathers, and also to the knowledge of Jesus Christ, which was had among their fathers.

Moroni, the last prophet of the Book of Mormon, also spoke of the eventual restoration of the truth:

Mormon 8:23, 28, 32–33

Search the prophecies of Isaiah. Behold, I cannot write them. Yea, behold I say unto you, that those saints who have gone before me, who have possessed this land, shall cry, yea, even from the dust will they cry unto the Lord; and as the Lord liveth he will remember the covenant which he hath made with them.

Yea, it shall come in a day when the power of God shall be denied, and churches become defiled and be lifted up in the pride of their hearts; yea, even in a day when leaders of churches and teachers shall rise in the pride of their hearts, even to the envyings of them who belong to their churches.

Yea, it shall come in a day when there shall be churches built up that shall say: Come unto me, and for your money you shall be forgiven of your sins.

O ye wicked and perverse and stiffnecked people, why have ye built up churches unto yourselves to get gain? Why have ye transfigured the holy word of God, that ye might bring damnation upon your souls? Behold, look ye unto the revelations of God; for behold, the time cometh at that day when all these things must be fulfilled.

Doctrine and Covenants

On November 1, 1831, the Lord reminded the people that he had begun the restoration and said:

D&C 1:17, 20–23 Wherefore, I the Lord . . . called upon my servant Joseph Smith, Jun., and spake unto him from heaven, and gave him commandments. . . .

That every man might speak in the name of God the Lord, even the Savior of the world;

That faith also might increase in the earth;

That mine everlasting covenant might be established;

That the fulness of my gospel might be proclaimed by the weak and the simple unto the ends of the world, and before kings and rulers.

Referring to the "stone cut out of the mountain without hands" (Daniel 2:45), the Lord revealed to the Prophet Joseph Smith the following:

D&C 65:2 The keys of the kingdom of God are committed unto

man on the earth, and from thence shall the gospel roll forth unto the ends of the earth, as the stone which is cut out of the mountain without hands shall roll forth, until it has filled the whole earth.

On September 22 and 23, 1832, the Lord confirmed in a revelation given to Joseph Smith that the restoration had begun:

D&C 84:2 Yea, the word of the Lord concerning his church, established in the last days for the restoration of his people, as he has spoken by the mouth of his prophets, and for the gathering of his saints to stand upon Mount Zion, which shall be the city of New Jerusalem.

The parable of the wheat and the tares, which the Lord explained to Joseph Smith, also pointed to the restoration which would eventually occur. In the last days, the righteous people (the wheat) will be gathered out and the tares (the wicked people who refuse to accept the Savior) will be destroyed (D&C 86).

On April 3, 1836, the keys of this dispensation—the dispensation of the fulness of times—were conferred upon Joseph Smith and Oliver Cowdery. Moses committed "the keys of the gathering of Israel from the four parts of the earth, and the leading of the ten tribes from the land of the north" (D&C 110:11); Elias "committed the dispensation of the gospel of Abraham, saying that in us and our seed all generations after us should be blessed" (110:12); Elijah appeared unto them in fulfillment of Malachi's prophecy:

D&C 110:14–16 That he [Elijah] should be sent, before the great and dreadful day of the Lord come—

To turn the hearts of the fathers to the children, and the children to the fathers, lest the whole earth be smitten with a curse—

Therefore, the keys of this dispensation are committed into your hands; and by this ye may know that the great and dreadful day of the Lord is near, even at the doors.

Pearl of Great Price

On September 21, 1823, as Joseph was engaged in prayer, an angel appeared unto him with instructions from the Lord. He called him by name and said that:

JS—H 1:33–34

> His name was Moroni; that God had a work for me to do; and that my name should be had for good and evil among all nations, kindreds, and tongues, or that it should be both good and evil spoken of among all people.
>
> He said there was a book deposited, written upon gold plates, giving an account of the former inhabitants of this continent, and the source from whence they sprang. He also said that the fulness of the everlasting Gospel was contained in it, as delivered by the Savior to the ancient inhabitants.

After four years and more visits by the Angel Moroni, Joseph Smith was finally given the gold plates to translate (September 22, 1827), and thus began the restoration of the gospel which had been prophesied by the prophets of the Old Testament, New Testament, and the Book of Mormon. The Doctrine and Covenants and Pearl of Great Price are additional testaments that an apostasy had been prophesied along with prophecies regarding the restoration of all truth.

As one views the condition of the world today, there is no question that an apostasy took place: evil is rampant, sin is portrayed as virtue, church attendance is very low in many countries, and many preachers even deny the divinity of the Savior. However, any sincere scholar of the scriptures should know of the prophesied restoration. A diligent search for the truth will reveal that the restoration has begun.

Chapter 3

The Church as Organized by Christ

TENET: Christ organized his church when he was upon the earth, with specific offices. Those same offices were present among worshipers who followed the Lord in Old Testament times and in Book of Mormon times and were instituted again when Christ restored his church in 1830. Those offices included prophets, apostles, priests, elders, and teachers. Worthy men were "called" and "anointed" and ordained to these offices by one having authority to do so. The same holds true today. To be Christ's true church, it must have the same offices as in ancient times, and men must be called and ordained to those offices by one having authority from God.

Old Testament

The following Old Testament scriptures identify the offices of priest, elder, member of the Seventy, prophet, and the twelve disciples. They also point out that people were called and anointed to these positions by someone having authority to call and anoint them.

Genesis 14:18	And Melchizedek king of Salem brought forth bread and wine: and he was the priest of the most high God.

Moses was authorized, indeed commanded, by God to call people to be leaders over the Israelites. These leaders did not just appoint themselves to these leadership positions.

Exodus 18:21–23 Moreover thou shalt provide out of all the people able men, such as fear God, men of truth, hating covetousness; and place such over them, to be rulers of thousands, and rulers of hundreds, rulers of fifties, and rulers of tens:

And let them judge the people at all seasons: and it shall be, that every great matter they shall bring unto thee, but every small matter they shall judge: so shall it be easier for thyself, and they shall bear the burden with thee.

If thou shalt do this thing, and God command thee so, then thou shalt be able to endure, and all this people shall also go to their place in peace.

Exodus 24:9 Then went up Moses, and Aaron, Nadah, and Abihu, and seventy of the elders of Israel.

Numbers 11:16–17, 25

And the Lord said unto Moses, Gather unto me seventy men of the elders of Israel, whom thou knowest to be the elders of the people, and officers over them; and bring them unto the tabernacle of the congregation, that they may stand there with thee.

And I will come down and talk with thee there: and I will take of the spirit which is upon thee, and will put it upon them; and they shall bear the burden of the people with thee, that thou bear it not thyself alone. . . .

And the Lord came down in a cloud, and spake unto him, and took of the spirit that was upon him, and gave it unto the seventy elders: and it came to pass, that, when the spirit rested upon them, they prophesied, and did not cease.

Numbers 27:15–20 And Moses spake unto the Lord, saying,

Let the Lord, the God of the spirits of all flesh, set a man over the congregation,

Which may go out before them, and which may go in before them, and which may lead them out, and which may bring them in; that the congregation of the Lord be not as sheep which have no shepherd.

And the Lord said unto Moses, Take thee Joshua the son of Nun, a man in whom is the spirit, and lay thine hand upon him;

And set him before Eleazar the priest, and before all the congregation; and give him a charge in their sight.

And thou shalt put some of thine honour upon him, that all the congregation of the children of Israel may be obedient.

Deuteronomy 27:1 And Moses with the elders of Israel commanded the people, saying, Keep all the commandments which I command you this day.

Deuteronomy 31:9 And Moses wrote this law, and delivered it unto the priests the sons of Levi, which bare the ark of the covenant of the Lord, and unto the elders of Israel.

Deuteronomy 34:9–10

And Joshua the son of Nun was full of the spirit of wisdom; for Moses had laid his hands upon him, and the children of Israel hearkened unto him, and did as the Lord commanded Moses.

And there arose not a prophet since in Israel like unto Moses, whom the Lord knew face to face,

Joshua 4:4 Then Joshua called the twelve men, whom he had prepared of the children of Israel, out of every tribe a man.

New Testament

The New Testament mentions the same offices: President of the Church (who receives the keys of the kingdom), the quorum of the Twelve Apostles, seven Presidents of the Seventy, quorum of the Seventy (missionaries), prophets, high priests, evangelists, pastors, bishops, priests, teachers, and deacons. The Lord himself called and anointed men to these positions and gave them authority to act in his name. People were ordained to their callings by the laying on of hands, as evidenced in Acts 6:6.

The apostles were called by Christ.

Matthew 16:17–19 And Jesus answered and said unto him, Blessed art thou, Simon Bar-jona: for flesh and blood hath not revealed it unto thee, but my Father which is in heaven.

And I say also unto thee, That thou art Peter, and upon this rock [the rock of revelation and Christ, the bedrock, or foundation, of the Church] I will build my church; and the gates of hell shall not prevail against it.

And I will give unto thee the keys of the kingdom of heaven: and whatsoever thou shalt bind on earth shall be bound in heaven: and whatsoever thou shalt loose on earth shall be loosed in heaven.

The apostles did not choose themselves—they were chosen by Christ.

Luke 6:13 And when it was day, he called unto him his disciples: and of them he chose twelve, whom also he named apostles.

Christ also appointed missionaries.

Luke 10:1 After these things the Lord appointed other seventy also, and sent them two and two before his face into every city and place, whither he himself would come.

John 15:16 Ye have not chosen me, but I have chosen you, and ordained you, that ye should go and bring forth fruit, and that your fruit would remain: that whatsoever ye shall ask of the Father in my name, he may give it you.

The pattern for filling vacancies in the Quorum of the Twelve Apostles was established from the very beginning.

Acts 1:22–26 Beginning from the baptism of John, unto that same day that he was taken up from us, must one be ordained to be a witness with us of his resurrection.

And they appointed two, Joseph called Barsabas, who was surnamed Justus, and Matthias.

And they prayed, and said, Thou, Lord, which

knowest the hearts of all men, shew whether of these two thou hast chosen,

That he may take part of this ministry and apostleship, from which Judas by transgression fell, that he might go to his own place.

And they gave forth their lots; and the lot fell upon Matthias; and he was numbered with the eleven apostles.

Those called to serve were ordained by the laying on of hands.

Acts 6:3–7

Wherefore, brethren, look ye out among you seven men of honest report, full of the Holy Ghost and wisdom, whom we may appoint over this business.

But we will give ourselves continually to prayer, and to the aministry of the word.

And the saying pleased the whole multitude: and they chose. . . . [seven men named in Acts 6:5]

Whom they set before the apostles: and when they had prayed, they laid their hands on them.

And the word of God increased; and the number of the disciples multiplied in Jerusalem greatly; and a great company of the priests were obedient to the faith.

One of the offices in the Melchizedek priesthood is that of elder.

Acts 11:27–30

And in these days came prophets from Jerusalem unto Antioch.

And there stood up one of them named Agabus, and signified by the Spirit that there should be great dearth throughout all the world: which came to pass in the days of Claudius Cæsar.

Then the disciples, every man according to his ability, determined to send relief unto the brethren which dwelt in Judæa:

Which also they did, and sent it to the elders by the hands of Barnabas and Saul.

Acts 13:1

Now there were in the church that was at Antioch certain prophets and teachers.

Acts 14:23	And when they had ordained them elders in every church, and had prayed with fasting, they commended them to the Lord, on whom they believed.
Acts 15:4, 6	And when they were come to Jerusalem, they were received of the church, and of the apostles and elders. . . . And the apostles and elders came together for to consider of this matter.

The foundation of the true church is apostles and prophets, with Christ as the head.

Ephesians 2:19–20	Now therefore ye are no more strangers and foreigners, but fellow citizens with the saints, and of the household of God And are built upon the foundation of the apostles and prophets, Jesus Christ himself being the chief corner stone.
Ephesians 4:11–12	And he gave some apostles; and some, prophets, and some, evangelists; and some, pastors and teachers; For the perfecting of the saints, for the work of the ministry, for the edifying of the body of Christ.

Other offices in the priesthood are mentioned.

Philippians 1:1	Paul and Timotheus, the servants of Jesus Christ, to all the saints in Christ Jesus which are at Philippi, with the bishops and deacons.
1 Timothy 2:7	Whereunto I am ordained a preacher, and an apostle.
2 Timothy 1:11	Whereunto I am appointed a preacher, and an apostle, and a teacher of the Gentiles.
Titus 1:5, 7	For this cause left I thee in Crete, that thou shouldest set in order the things that are wanting, and ordain elders in every city, as I had appointed thee. . . . For a bishop must be blameless, as the steward of God.

There is the office of high priest in the Melchizedek priesthood, and the office of priest in the lesser or Aaronic priesthood.

Hebrews 5:1, 4–6 — For every high priest taken from among men is ordained for men in things pertaining to God, that he may offer both gifts and sacrifices for sins. . . .

And no man taketh this honour unto himself, but he that is called of God, as was Aaron.

So also Christ glorified not himself to be made an high priest; but he that said unto him, Thou art my Son, to day have I begotten thee.

As he saith also in another place, Thou art a priest for ever after the order of Melchisedec.

James 5:14 — Is any sick among you? let him call for the elders of the church; and let them pray over him, anointing him with oil in the name of the Lord.

Book of Mormon

The Book of Mormon also refers to offices in the Church that Christ established among the Nephites: prophet, twelve disciples, high priest, elder, priest, and teacher. Again, people did not take these positions of their own choosing, but were called to them and were consecrated (ordained) by someone having authority to do so, by the laying on of hands (see Alma 6:1).

1 Nephi 1:10 — And he also saw twelve other following him, and their brightness did exceed that of the stars in the firmament.

2 Nephi 5:26 — And it came to pass that I, Nephi, did consecrate Jacob and Joseph, that they should be priests and teachers over the land of my people.

Mosiah 12:1 — And it came to pass . . . that Abinadi . . . began to prophesy among them, saying: Thus has the Lord commanded me, saying—Abinadi, go and prophesy unto this my people.

Mosiah 18:18 — And it came to pass that Alma, having authority from God, ordained priests; even one priest to every fifty of their number did he ordain to preach unto them.

Mosiah 25:19 — And it came to pass that king Mosiah granted unto Alma that he might establish churches throughout all the land of Zarahemla; and gave him power to ordain priests and teachers over every church.

Alma 4:7 — Now this was the cause of much affliction to Alma, yea, and to many of the people whom Alma had consecrated to be teachers, and priests, and elders over the church.

Alma 6:1 — And now it came to pass that after Alma had made an end of speaking unto the people of the church, which was established in the city of Zarahemla, he ordained priests and elders, by laying of his hands according to the order of God, to preside and watch over the church.

Alma 13:1–2, 8–9, 14

And again, my brethren, I would cite your minds forward to the time when the Lord God gave these commandments unto his children; and I would that ye should remember that the Lord God ordained priests, after his holy order, which was after the order of his Son, to teach these things unto the people.

And those priests were ordained after the order of his Son, in a manner that thereby the people might know in what manner to look forward to his Son for redemption.

Now they were ordained after this manner—being called with a holy calling, and ordained with a holy ordinance, and taking upon them the high priesthood of the holy order, which calling, and ordinance, and high priesthood, is without beginning or end—

Thus they become high priests forever, after the order of the Son, the Only Begotten of the Father. . . .

Yea, humble yourselves even as the people in the days of Melchizedek, who was also a high priest

	after this same order which I have spoken, who also took upon him the high priesthood forever.
3 Nephi 12:1	And it came to pass that when Jesus had spoken these words unto Nephi, and to those who had been called, (now the number of them who had been called, and received power and authority to baptize, was twelve) and behold, he stretched forth his hand unto the multitude, and cried unto them, saying: Blessed are ye if ye shall give heed unto the words of these twelve whom I have chosen from among you to minister unto you, and to be your servants; and unto them I have given power that they may baptize you with water, and after that ye are baptized with water, behold, I will baptize you with fire and with the Holy Ghost.
3 Nephi 13:25	And now it came to pass that when Jesus had spoken these words he looked upon the twelve whom he had chosen, and said unto them. . . . ye are they whom I have chosen to minister unto this people.
3 Nephi 15:11–12	And now it came to pass that when Jesus had spoken these words, he said unto those twelve whom he had chosen: Ye are my disciples; and ye are a light unto this people, who are a remnant of the house of Joseph.
3 Nephi 18:5	And when the multitude had eaten and were filled, he said unto the Disciples: Behold there shall one be ordained among you, and to him will I give power that he shall break bread and bless it and give it unto the people of my church.
4 Nephi 1:14	And it came to pass that . . . the disciples of Jesus, whom he had chosen, had all gone to the paradise of God, save it were the three who should tarry; and there were other disciples ordained in their stead.
Moroni 3: 1–4	The manner which the disciples, who were called the elders of the church, ordained priests and teachers—

After they had prayed unto the Father in the name of Christ, they laid their hands upon them, and said:

In the name of Jesus Christ I ordain you to be a priest, (or, if he be a teacher) I ordain you to be a teacher, to preach repentance and remission of sins through Jesus Christ, by endurance of faith on his name to the end. Amen.

And after this manner did they ordain priests and teachers, according to the gifts and callings of God unto men; and they ordained them by the power of the Holy Ghost, which was in them.

Moroni 4:1 — The manner of their elders and priests administering the flesh and blood of Christ unto the church; and they administered it according to the commandments of Christ; wherefore we know the manner to be true; and the elder or priest did minister it.

Doctrine and Covenants

The Doctrine and Covenants reveals that in these latter days the Lord again established his Church with these same offices: prophet, the Presidency of the Church, seer, the Twelve Apostles, the quorum of the Seventy, bishop, high priest, elder, priest, teacher, deacon, and translator with instructions that people be called and ordained to the various positions by the "laying on of hands" (see D&C 53:3, 84:6).

D&C 1:14 — And the arm of the Lord shall be revealed; and the day cometh that they who will not hear the voice of the Lord, neither the voice of his servants, neither give heed to the words of the prophets and apostles, shall be cut off from among the people.

D&C 18:26–27 — And now, behold, there are others who are called to declare my gospel, both unto Gentile and unto Jew;

Yea, even twelve; and the Twelve shall be my disciples, and they shall take upon them my name.

D&C 20:2 — Which commandments were given to Joseph Smith, Jun., who was called of God, and ordained an apostle of Jesus Christ, to be the first elder of this church;

And to Oliver Cowdery, who was also called of God, an apostle of Jesus Christ, to be the second elder of this church, and ordained under his hand.

D&C 20:38, 60 The duty of the elders, priests, teachers, deacons, and members of the church of Christ—An apostle is an elder. . . .

Every elder, priest, teacher, or deacon is to be ordained according to the gifts and callings of God unto him; and he is to be ordained by the power of the Holy Ghost, which is in the one who ordains him.

D&C 21:1 Behold, there shall be a record kept among you; and in it thou shalt be called a seer, a translator, a prophet, an apostle of Jesus Christ, an elder of the church through the will of God the Father, and the grace of your Lord Jesus Christ,

D&C 27:5, 7–8, 12 Behold, this is wisdom in me; wherefore, marvel not, for the hour cometh that I will drink of the fruit of the vine with you on the earth, and with Moroni. . . .

And also John the son of Zacharias. . . .

Which John I have sent unto you, my servants, Joseph Smith, Jun., and Oliver Cowdery, to ordain you unto the first priesthood which you have received, that you might be called and ordained even as Aaron. . . .

And also with Peter, and James, and John, whom I have sent unto you, by whom I have ordained you and confirmed you to be apostles, and especial witnesses of my name, and bear the keys of your ministry and of the same things which I revealed unto them.

D&C 53:3–4 Take upon you mine ordination, even that of an elder, to preach faith and repentance and remission of sins, according to my word, and the reception of the Holy Spirit by the laying on of hands;

And also to be an agent unto this church in the place which shall be appointed by the bishop, according to commandments which shall be given hereafter.

D&C 84:6 And the sons of Moses, according to the Holy Priesthood which he received under the hand of his father-in-law, Jethro.

D&C 84:29–30 And again, the offices of elder and bishop are necessary appendages belonging unto the high priesthood.

And again, the offices of teacher and deacon are necessary appendages belonging to the lesser priesthood, which priesthood was confirmed upon Aaron and his sons.

D&C 84:63 And as I said unto mine apostles, even so I say unto you, for you are mine apostles, even God's high priests; ye are they whom my Father hath given me; ye are my friends.

D&C 84:111 And behold, the high priests should travel, and also the elders, and also the lesser priests; but the deacons and teachers should be appointed to watch over the church, to be standing ministers unto the church.

D&C 102:30 There is a distinction between the high council or traveling high priests abroad, and the traveling high council composed of the twelve apostles, in their decisions.

D&C 107:1, 3, 7–10, 18, 20, 22–23, 25, 73, 85–89, 91–92

There are . . . two priesthoods, namely, the Melchizedek and Aaronic, including the Levitical Priesthood. . . .

Before his [Melchizedek's] day it was called the Holy Priesthood, after the Order of the Son of God. . . .

The office of an elder comes under the priesthood of Melchizedek.

The Melchizedek Priesthood holds the right of

presidency, and has power and authority over all the offices in the church in all ages of the world, to administer in spiritual things.

The Presidency of the High Priesthood, after the order of Melchizedek, have a right to officiate in all the offices in the church.

High priests after the order of the Melchizedek Priesthood have a right to officiate in their own standing, under the direction of the presidency, in administering spiritual things, and also in the office of an elder, priest (of the Levitical order), teacher, deacon, and member. . . .

The power and authority of the higher, or Melchizedek Priesthood, is to hold the keys of all the spiritual blessings of the church. . . .

The power and authority of the lesser, or Aaronic Priesthood, is to hold the keys of the ministering of angels, and to administer in outward ordinances, the letter of the gospel, the baptism of repentance for the remission of sins, agreeable to the covenants and commandments.

Of the Melchizedek Priesthood, three Presiding High Priests, chosen by the body, appointed and ordained to that office, and upheld by the confidence, faith, and prayer of the church, form a quorum of the Presidency of the Church.

The twelve traveling councilors are called to be the Twelve Apostles. . . .

The Seventy are also called to preach the gospel, and to be especial witnesses unto the Gentiles and in all the world. . . .

This is the duty of a bishop. . . .

And again, verily I say unto you, the duty of a president over the office of a deacon is to preside over twelve deacons. . . .

And also the duty of the president over the office of the teachers is to preside over twenty-four of the teachers. . . .

Also the duty of the president over the Priesthood of Aaron is to preside over forty-eight priests. . . .

This president is to be a bishop; for this is one of the duties of this priesthood.

Again, the duty of the president over the office of elders is. . . .

And again, the duty of the President of the office of the High Priesthood is to preside over the whole church, and to be like unto Moses—

Behold, here is wisdom; yea, to be a seer, a revelator, a translator, and a prophet, having all the gifts of God which he bestows upon the head of the church.

Pearl of Great Price

In the Pearl of Great Price, God calling Moses to do a work is recorded. Abraham's desire to obtain the High Priesthood is recorded. The account of Joseph Smith and Oliver Cowdery receiving the priesthood is also reported. The fifth and sixth articles of faith of The Church of Jesus Christ of Latter-day Saints, as given by Joseph Smith, state that men must be called of God by one in authority, and indicate that the same offices should be in place today as in the early church.

Moses 1:3, 6, 25

And God spake unto Moses, saying: Behold, I am the Lord God Almighty, and Endless is my name. . . .

And I have a work for thee, Moses, my son. . . .

Blessed art thou, Moses, for I, the Almighty, have chosen thee, and thou shalt be made stronger than many waters; for they shall obey thy command as if thou wert God.

Abraham 1:1–4

In the land of the Chaldeans, at the residence of my fathers, I, Abraham, saw that it was needful for me to obtain another place of residence;

And, finding there was greater happiness and peace and rest for me, I sought for the blessings of the fathers, and the right whereunto I should be ordained to administer the same; having been myself a follower of righteousness, desiring also to be one who possessed great knowledge, and to be a greater follower of righteousness, and to possess a greater knowledge, and to be a father of many nations, a prince of peace, and desiring to receive instructions, and to keep the commandments of God, I became a rightful heir, a High Priest, holding the right belonging to the fathers.

It was conferred upon me from the fathers; it came down from the fathers, from the beginning of time, yea, even from the beginning or before the foundation of the earth, down to the present time. I sought for mine appointment unto the Priesthood according to the appointment of God unto the fathers concerning the seed.

JS—H 1:68–69 We on a certain day went into the woods to pray and inquire of the Lord respecting baptism for the remission of sins, that we found mentioned in the translation of the plates. While we were thus employed, praying and calling upon the Lord, a messenger from heaven descended in a cloud of light, and having laid his hands upon us, he ordained us, saying:

Upon you my fellow servants, in the name of Messiah, I confer the Priesthood of Aaron.

Articles of Faith 1:5 We believe that a man must be called of God, by prophecy, and by the laying on of hands by those who are in authority, to preach the Gospel and administer in the ordinances thereof.

Articles of Faith 1:6 We believe in the same organization that existed in the Primitive Church, namely, apostles, prophets, pastors, teachers, evangelists, and so forth.

Chapter 4

The Godhead

TENET: (A) There are multiple Gods. The Godhead is composed of God the Father, his Son Jesus Christ, and the Holy Ghost. (B) The Godhead is composed of three separate Beings who are one in purpose. (C) God the Father and Jesus Christ have tangible, albeit immortal, bodies. The Holy Ghost is a personage of spirit.

(A) There are multiple Gods. The Godhead is composed of God the Father, his Son Jesus Christ, and the Holy Ghost.

Old Testament

As the creation of the earth is recounted in the Old Testament, when Adam and Eve partook of the forbidden fruit and when people tried to build a tower to heaven, God repeatedly used plural pronouns indicating that there are multiple Gods.

Genesis 1:26	And God said, Let us make man in our image, after our likeness.
Genesis 3:22	And the Lord God said, Behold, the man is become as one of us, to know good and evil.
Genesis 11:7	Go to, let us go down, and there confound their language, that they may not understand one another's speech.

God was obviously speaking to someone, not to himself. He would have had no need to speak if the plural pronoun referred to himself. He spoke to someone other than himself. He didn't just think, "Me, myself, and I will go down and make man in my multiple image."

New Testament

Following the Savior's resurrection, he sent his apostles into the world to preach the Gospel, indicating the makeup of the Godhead.

Matthew 28:19 — Go ye therefore, and teach all nations, baptizing them in the name of the Father, and of the Son, and of the Holy Ghost.

All three members of the Godhead were represented at Christ's own baptism.

Mark 1:10–11 — And straightway coming up out of the water, he [Jesus Christ] saw the heavens opened, and the Spirit like a dove descending upon him:

And there came a voice from heaven, saying, Thou art my beloved Son, in whom I am well pleased.

It is implausible to think Christ would have used ventriloquism, and that it was Christ himself who said, "Thou art my beloved Son, in whom I am well pleased."

Jesus, in defending himself before the Jews when they accused him of breaking the Sabbath by healing a man, repeatedly points out that he and the Father are separate Beings. The Father sent his Son to do a job. God the Father did not come to do the job himself; he remained in heaven.

John 5:19–20 — Then answered Jesus and said unto them, Verily, verily, I say unto you, The Son can do nothing of himself, but what he seeth the Father do: for what things soever he doeth, these also doeth the Son likewise.

For the Father loveth the Son, and sheweth him all things that himself doeth: and he will shew him greater works than these, that ye may marvel.

John 5: 26–27 — For as the Father hath life in himself; so hath he given to the Son to have life in himself;

And hath given him authority to execute judgment also, because he is the Son of man.

All three members of the Godhead were evident when Stephen was martyred.

Acts 7:55–56 But he [Stephen], being full of the Holy Ghost, looked up stedfastly into heaven, and saw the glory of God, and Jesus standing on the right hand of God,

And said, Behold, I see the heavens open, and the Son of man standing on the right hand of God.

A person cannot stand on one's own right-hand side.

Book of Mormon

These same truths are echoed in additional scriptures of The Church of Jesus Christ of Latter-day Saints. The Book of Mormon testifies that God the Father and his Son are separate Beings.

2 Nephi 31:15 And I heard a voice from the Father, saying: Yea, the words of my Beloved are true and faithful.

Doctrine and Covenants

The Doctrine and Covenants states these same truths.

D&C 76:23 For we saw him, even on the right hand of God; and we heard the voice bearing record that he is the Only Begotten of the Father.

D&C 137:2–3 I saw the transcendent beauty of the gate through which the heirs of that kingdom will enter. . . .

Also the blazing throne of God, whereon was seated the Father and the Son.

Pearl of Great Price

The creation is recounted in the Pearl of Great Price, with the same use of plural pronouns as used in the Old Testament.

Abraham 4:1 And then the Lord said: Let us go down. And they went down at the beginning, and they, that is the Gods, organized and formed the heavens and the earth.

Joseph Smith's account of the vision he received in answer to his prayer is consistent with the scriptures.

JS—H 1:17	When the light rested upon me I saw two Personages, whose brightness and glory defy all description, standing above me in the air. One of them spake unto me, calling me by name and said, pointing to the other: This is my Beloved Son, Hear Him!

(B) The Godhead is one: One in Purpose

Jesus told the people that he and the Father are one and that those who have seen him have also seen the Father. He also said that the Father, the Word and the Holy Ghost are one. However, other scriptures make it clear that they are separate individuals but one in purpose.

Webster's New World Dictionary defines *oneness* as: "(1) The quality or state of being one, singleness, unity; (2) Unity of mind, feeling, or purpose; (3) Sameness, identity."[1] The word *one* is defined as "characterized by unity, forming a whole, united, undivided, with one accord" and "single in kind, the same, all of one mind."[2]

Webster's Third New International Dictionary's definition of *one* includes "actually or virtually the same as something else . . . identical with or substantially the same as something else" and "single in kind, quite the same, equal . . . amounts to the same thing."[3]

It is in this sense that the Father, the Son, and the Holy Ghost are one: they are one in purpose.

In the Old Testament, the Lord used the word *one* to signify unity and sameness.

Old Testament

Ezekiel 37:15–17	The word of the Lord came again unto me, saying, Moreover, thou son of man, take thee one stick, and write upon it, For Judah [the Bible], and for the children of Israel his companions: then take another stick, and write upon it, For Joseph, the stick of Ephraim [the Book of Mormon], and for all the house of Israel his companions: And join them one to another into one stick;

and they shall become one in thine hand.

New Testament

The New Testament repeatedly uses the word *one* in the same sense.

Matthew 19:5–6 For this cause shall a man leave father and mother, and shall cleave to his wife: and they twain shall be one flesh?

Wherefore they are no more twain, but one flesh.

Obviously, when a couple get married, they do not become one physical body but are admonished to be united and have singleness of purpose in their marriage. Likewise, the scriptures, or sticks, referred to in Ezekiel were two separate sticks—two separate sets of scriptures—that were to be used together to serve a common purpose: to teach the same truths, to be one in the hand of those seeking to know the Lord.

Christ's intercessory prayer for his disciples further illustrates that Christ uses the word *one* to signify "unity of purpose."

John 17:9–11, 21–23 I pray for them: I pray not for the world, but for them which thou hast given me; for they are thine.

And all mine are thine, and thine are mine; and I am glorified in them.

And now I am no more in the world, but these are in the world, and I come to thee. Holy Father, keep through thine own name those whom thou hast given me, that they may be one, as we are. . . .

That they all may be one; as thou, Father, art in me, and I in thee, that they also may be one in us: that the world may believe that thou hast sent me.

And the glory which thou gavest me I have given them; that they may be one, even as we are one:

I in them, and thou in me, that they may be made perfect in one; and that the world may know that thou hast sent me, and has loved them, as thou hast loved me.

Christ was not praying that his disciples would suddenly all be combined into one physical body. He was praying that they would be united—be of one mind in doing what the Lord would have them do. He was praying that their desires would be the same as his and as those of God the Father—that they would be one, "even as we are one" (John 17:22).

Christ also taught his disciples:

John 5:30–31, 37	I can of mine own self do nothing: as I hear, I judge: and my judgment is just; because I seek not mine own will, but the will of the Father which hath sent me. If I bear witness of myself, my witness is not true. And the Father himself, which hath sent me, hath borne witness of me.

Note that Jesus pointed out that if he bore witness of himself, that witness would not be valid. In the Jewish law of Christ's day, just as in our laws today, truth must be established by the mouths of two or more witnesses.

John 8:17–18	It is also written in your law, that the testimony of two men is true. I am one that bear witness of myself, and the Father that sent me beareth witness of me.

No court would accept as two separate testimonies a man speaking in behalf of himself as the father of his child and in behalf of himself as the son of his father. Testimony has to come from two separate beings as Christ testified.

Because Christ did only what the Father commanded him to do and what the Father himself would do, he and the Father are one—in purpose. It is in this same context that he reminded Philip that he and the Father are one.

John 10:30	I and my Father are one.
John 14:9–10	Jesus saith unto him, Have I been so long with you, and yet hast thou not known me, Philip? He that hath seen me hath seen the Father; and how sayest thou then, Shew us the Father? Believest thou not that I am in the Father, and the Father in me? the words that I speak unto you I speak not of myself: but the Father that dwelleth in me, he doeth the works.

When Jesus spoke to Mary as she mourned outside the empty tomb, she went to touch him. Again, Jesus pointed out that he and his Father are two separate Beings.

John 20:17	Jesus saith unto her, Touch me not; for I am not yet ascended to my Father: but go to my brethren, and say unto them, I ascend unto my Father, and your Father; and to my God, and your God.

In Acts 4:32 we read that the "multitude of them that believed were of one heart and of one soul." It would be ludicrous to think they were literally combined into one physical heart and one single soul. Obviously, they were united and one in purpose.

The Apostle Paul wrote to the Corinthians and reminded them that:

1 Corinthians 6:17	He that is joined unto the Lord is one spirit.

Later, he admonished them to "be of one mind" (2 Corinthians 13:11). Peter's words provide the same counsel:

1 Peter 3:8	Finally, be ye all of one mind.

John bore further testimony that the Godhead is composed of three separate individuals who are one in purpose:

1 John 5:7	For there are three that bear witness in heaven, the Father, the Word, and the Holy Ghost: and these three are one.

Book of Mormon

Again, the Book of Mormon and the Doctrine and Covenants echo the same teachings: God the Father, Jesus Christ, and the Holy Ghost are one in purpose. The following scriptures do not negate the separate nature of the members of the Godhead; they are one—but one in purpose, not in the sense of being a single physical unit.

2 Nephi 31:21	And now, behold, this is the doctrine of Christ, and the only and true doctrine of the Father, and of the Son, and of the Holy Ghost, which is one God, without end.
Mosiah 15:4	And they are one God, yea, the very Eternal Father of heaven and of earth.

Alma 11:44	But every thing shall be restored to its perfect frame, as it is now, or in the body, and shall be brought and be arraigned before the bar of Christ the Son, and God the Father, and the Holy Spirit, which is one Eternal God.
3 Nephi 11:27	And after this manner shall ye baptize in my name; for behold, verily I say unto you, that the Father, and the Son, and the Holy Ghost are one; and I am in the Father, and the Father in me, and the Father and I are one.

Doctrine and Covenants

In latter-day revelations, the word *one* is used in the same sense that it was used in the Bible by prophets of the Old and New Testaments.

D&C 35:2	I am Jesus Christ, the Son of God, who was crucified for the sins of the world, even as many as will believe on my name, that they may become the sons of God, even one in me as I am one in the Father, as the Father is one in me, that we may be one.
D&C 50:43	And the Father and I are one. I am in the Father and the Father in me; and inasmuch as ye have received me, ye are in me and I in you.
D&C 51:9	And let every man deal honestly, and be alike among this people, and receive alike, that ye may be one, even as I have commanded you.
D&C 93: 1, 3	Know that I am. . . . And that I am in the Father, and the Father in me, and the Father and I are one.

Pearl of Great Price

Moses 6:68	Behold, thou art one in me, a son of God.
Moses 7:18	And the Lord called his people ZION, because they were of one heart and one mind.
Abraham 5:17–18	And Adam said: This was bone of my bones, and flesh of my flesh; now she shall be called Woman,

> because she was taken out of man.
>
> Therefore, shall a man leave his father and his mother, and shall cleave unto his wife, and they shall be one flesh.

(C) God the Father and Jesus Christ have tangible, albeit immortal, bodies.

The Holy Ghost is a personage of spirit.

Even though the Godhead is united and is one in purpose, the various members of the Godhead serve in different roles. God the Father is the literal father of our spirits. We are created in his likeness. He delegated the responsibility of creating the earth to his son, Jesus Christ, known also as Jehovah, and taught him all that he should do.

Christ is the Creator of the earth and is our Savior and Redeemer. He atoned for our sins, died upon the cross, and was resurrected. He has an immortal body of flesh and bones, as does the Father. He is our intercessor with the Father.

The Holy Ghost, on the other hand, has a body of spirit in order for him to fulfill his responsibilities of being a testifier and comforter.

1. God the Father

a. He is the father of our spirits

The scriptures indicate that prior to this earth life, we lived in a premortal state as spirit children of our Heavenly Father.

Old Testament

Moses and Aaron acknowledged that God is:

Numbers 16:22 The God of the spirits of all flesh.

God, referring to the premortal life, inquired of Job where he was "When the morning stars sang together, and all the sons of God shouted for joy?" (Job 38:7).

In Ecclesiastes, the reality of our being premortal spirit children of our Heavenly Father is reaffirmed.

Ecclesiastes 12:7 Then shall the dust return to the earth as it was: and the spirit shall return unto God who gave it.

The scripture says that "the spirit will return unto God"—it is impossible to return to a place one has never been.

The Prophet Jeremiah was told by the Lord:

Jeremiah 1:5	Before I formed thee in the belly I knew thee; and before thou camest forth out of the womb I sanctified thee, and I ordained thee a prophet unto the nations.

New Testament

New Testament prophets also understood that we are spirit children of God. Paul, while standing in the midst of Mars' hill, reminded the men what happened in Athens.

Acts 17:28–29	For in him [God] we live, and move, and have our being; as certain also of your own poets have said, For we are also his offspring. Forasmuch then as we are the offspring of God, we ought not to think that the Godhead is like unto gold, or silver, or stone, graven by art and man's device.

Paul also reminded the Romans that God knew us before this mortal state.

Romans 8:29	For whom he did foreknow, he also did predestinate to be conformed to the image of his Son, that he might be the firstborn among many brethren.

This same doctrine was preached to the Ephesians.

Ephesians 1:3–4	Blessed be the God and Father of our Lord Jesus Christ, who hath blessed us with all spiritual blessings in heavenly places in Christ: According as he hath chosen us in him before the foundation of the world.

Again, Paul reminded the people that God knew us before the earth was even created—in our premortal life.

As Paul reminded the Hebrews that our earthly fathers reprimand us because they love us, he pointed out that our Heavenly Father is literally the father of our spirits, and, as the Father of our spirits, he chastens us whom he loves.

Hebrews 12:9 Furthermore we have had fathers of our flesh which corrected us, and we gave them reverence: shall we not much rather be in subjection unto the Father of spirits, and live?

In the Revelation of John, we read:

Revelation 12:7–10 And there was war in heaven: Michael and his angels fought against the dragon; and the dragon fought and his angels,

And prevailed not; neither was their place found any more in heaven.

And the great dragon was cast out, that old serpent, called the Devil, and Satan, which deceiveth the whole world: he was cast out into the earth, and his angels were cast out with him,

And I heard a loud voice saying in heaven, Now is come salvation, and strength, and the kingdom of our God, and the power of his Christ: for the accuser of our brethren is cast down, which accused them before our God day and night.

This revelation points out that we existed in a premortal state. Specifically mentioned are Michael and his angels, Satan and his followers (his angels), Christ, and "our brethren." A war ensued resulting in Satan and his angels being cast out of heaven.

Book of Mormon

Just as biblical prophets knew and understood that we are the spiritual offspring of an eternal God and that we lived with him in a premortal state, Book of Mormon prophets also understood this same truth.

Alma 13:3 And this is the manner after which they were ordained —being called and prepared from the foundation of the world according to the foreknowledge of God, on account of their exceeding faith and good works.

Alma's son, Helaman, speaking of the resurrection of Christ and his redemption of all mankind, taught:

Helaman 14:17 But behold, the resurrection of Christ redeemeth mankind, yea, even all mankind, and bringeth them back into the presence of the Lord.

As mentioned previously, one cannot be brought back to a place that one has never been to before. In order to be brought back into the presence of the Lord, one must have been there before.

Doctrine and Covenants

Because God is the same yesterday, today, and tomorrow, he teaches the same truths to all generations of his children. In a revelation given to the Prophet Joseph Smith, the Lord confirmed that we did, indeed, live in a premortal state prior to this earthly existence.

D&C 93:29, 33 — Man was also in the beginning with God. Intelligence, or the light of truth, was not created or made, neither indeed can be.

For man is spirit. The elements are eternal, and spirit and element inseparably connected, receive a fulness of joy.

Years later, on October 3, 1918, the Prophet Joseph F. Smith received a revelation which confirmed our spiritual beginnings:

D&C 138:56 — Even before they were born, they, with many others, received their first lessons in the world of spirits and were prepared to come forth in the due time of the Lord to labor in his vineyard for the salvation of the souls of men.

Pearl of Great Price

In ancient times, the Lord told Enoch:

Moses 6:35–36 — Anoint thine eyes with clay, and wash them, and thou shalt see. And he did so.

And he beheld the spirits that God had created.

Abraham was provided the same knowledge:

Abraham 3:22–23 — Now the Lord had shown unto me, Abraham, the intelligences that were organized before the world was; and among all these there were many of the noble and great ones;

And God saw these souls that they were good, and he stood in the midst of them, and he said: These I will make my rulers; for he stood among those that were spirits, and he saw that they were good; and he said unto me: Abraham, thou art one of them; thou wast chosen before thou wast born.

b. We are created in the image of God

God has a body of parts and passions and we are created in his image and likeness.

OLD TESTAMENT

The scriptures record that God created man in his own image.

Genesis 1:26–27 And God said, Let us make man in our image, after our likeness. . . .

So God created man in his own image, in the image of God created he him; male and female created he them.

Noah also testified that God created man in his own image:

Genesis 9:6 For in the image of God made he man.

Webster's New World Dictionary defines *image* as "a person or thing very much like another" and as a "likeness."[4] *Image* is also defined as "a person who is strikingly like another person in appearance, manner, or thought."[5] Words used to define *likeness* include "resemblance, similarity."[6]

If man is in the image and likeness of God, then God has a body with parts and passions.

God has hands, as shown in Exodus:

Exodus 33:21–23 And the Lord said, Behold, there is a place by me, and thou shalt stand upon a rock:

And it shall come to pass, while my glory passeth by, that I will put thee in a clift of the rock, and will cover thee with my hand while I pass by:

And I will take away mine hand, and thou shalt see my back parts: but my face shall not be seen.

New Testament

We know God has a voice. When Jesus was baptized, God declared:

Matthew 3:17	This is my beloved Son, in whom I am well pleased.

On the Mount of Transfiguration the disciples heard the voice of God saying:

Matthew 17:5	This is my beloved Son, in whom I am well pleased; hear ye him.

God has a mouth:

Matthew 4:4	Man shall not live by bread alone, but by every word that proceedeth out of the mouth of God.

Steven's vision of Christ reaffirms what is stated in Exodus, that God has hands. Stephen said:

Acts 7:56	Behold, I see the heavens opened, and the Son of man standing on the right hand of God.

Christ declared that he looks like the Father:

John 14:9	He that hath seen me hath seen the Father.

James also points out that we are in the similitude of God.

James 3:8–9	But the tongue can no man tame; it is an unruly evil, full of deadly poison. Therewith bless we God, even the Father; and therewith curse we men, which are made after the similitude of God.

Book of Mormon

Christ showed himself to the brother of Jared, sustaining the truth that we are created in his image.

Ether 3:6, 9, 15–16	And it came to pass that when the brother of Jared had said these words, behold, the Lord stretched forth his hand and touched the stones one by one with his finger. And the veil was taken from off the eyes of the brother of Jared, and he saw the finger of the Lord; and it was as the finger of a man, like unto flesh and blood. . . .

> And the Lord said unto him: Because of thy faith thou hast seen that I shall take upon me flesh and blood; and never has man come before me with such exceeding faith as thou hast for were it not so ye could not have seen my finger. . . .
>
> Seest thou that ye are created after mine own image? Yea, even all men were created in the beginning after mine own image.
>
> Behold, this body, which ye now behold, is the body of my spirit; and man have I created after the body of my spirit; and even as I appear unto thee to be in the spirit will I appear unto my people in the flesh.

DOCTRINE AND COVENANTS
Modern-day revelation declares the same doctrine.

D&C 20:17–18 By these things we know that there is a God in heaven, who is infinite and eternal, from everlasting to everlasting the same unchangeable God, the framer of heaven and earth, and all things which are in them;

And that he created man, male and female, after his own image and in his own likeness, created he them.

D&C 130:22 The Father has a body of flesh and bones as tangible as man's; the Son also; but the Holy Ghost has not a body of flesh and bones, but is a personage of Spirit. Were it not so, the Holy Ghost could not dwell in us.

PEARL OF GREAT PRICE
Moses testified that God declared unto him:

Moses 1:16 Thou art after the similitude of mine Only Begotten.

c. The Son remains subject unto the Father

God the Father delegated the responsibility for the creation to his son, Jesus Christ, and taught him all that he should do; nevertheless, the Son remains subject unto the Father.

NEW TESTAMENT
During Christ's sojourn here upon the earth, he was even more explicit in

explaining that he did nothing but what the Father showed or told him to do.

John 5:19, 30 Then answered Jesus and said unto them, Verily, verily, I say unto you, The Son can do nothing of himself, but what he seeth the Father do; for what things soever he doeth, these also doeth the Son likewise. . . .

I can of mine own self do nothing: as I hear, I judge: and my judgment is just; because I seek not mine own will, but the will of the Father which hath sent me.

1 Corinthians 11:3 But I would have you know, that the head of every man is Christ; and the head of the woman is the man; and the head of Christ is God.

1 Corinthians 15:27–28

For he hath put all things under his feet. But when he saith all things are put under him, it is manifest that he is excepted, which did put all things under him.

And when all things shall be subdued unto him, then shall the Son also himself be subject unto him that put all things under him, that God may be all in all.

The Apostle Paul reminded the Ephesians that God the Father delegated the task of the creation to his Son, Jesus Christ.

Ephesians 3:9 And to make all men see what is the fellowship of mystery, which from the beginning of the world hath been hid in God, who created all things by Jesus Christ.

The Hebrews were also taught this doctrine:

Hebrews 1:1–2 God, who at sundry times and in divers manners spake in time past unto the fathers by the prophets,

Hath in these last days spoken unto us by his Son, whom he hath appointed heir of all things, by whom also he made the worlds.

Book of Mormon

When Jesus appeared to his people on the American continent following his resurrection, as recorded in the Book of Mormon, he pointed out that he was acting under the direction of his Father.

3 Nephi 18:27	Behold verily, verily, I say unto you, I give unto you another commandment, and then I must go unto my Father that I may fulfill other commandments which he hath given me.

Doctrine and Covenants

The Doctrine and Covenants also records that Christ works under the direction of the Father and that the day will come when he will deliver up the kingdom to his Father.

D&C 76:107	When he [Jesus Christ] shall deliver up the kingdom, and present it unto the Father, spotless, saying: I have overcome and have trodden the wine-press alone, even the wine-press of the fierceness of the wrath of Almighty God.

Pearl of Great Price

Moses 2:1	And it came to pass that the Lord spake unto Moses, saying: Behold, I reveal unto you concerning this heaven, and this earth; write the words which I speak. I am the Beginning and the End, the Almighty God; by mine Only Begotten I created these things; yea, in the beginning I created the heaven, and the earth upon which thou standest.
Moses 1:32–33	And by the word of my power, have I created them, which is mine Only Begotten Son, who is full of grace and truth. And worlds without number have I created; and I also created them for mine own purpose; and by the Son I created them, which is mine Only Begotten.

Thus, we see that Heavenly Father presides over all, but he delegated certain responsibilities to his Son, another, but separate, member of the Godhead.

2. Jesus Christ: The Only Begotten of the Father

Jesus Christ is (a) the creator of all things; (b) our Savior; and (c) our Redeemer; (d) he died upon the cross and was resurrected; (e) he has an immortal body of flesh and bones, as does the Father; (f) he is our intercessor with the Father.

a. Creator of all things

The Son was with the Father in the beginning and was one of the Gods referred to in the biblical account of the creation. The scriptures are replete with passages declaring the Savior to be the creator of the world.

Old Testament

Genesis 1:26	And God said, Let us make man in our image, after our likeness.
Genesis 2:4–5	These are the generations of the heavens and of the earth when they were created, in the day that the Lord God made the earth and the heavens, And every plant of the field before it was in the earth [spiritually], and every herb of the field before it grew: for the Lord God had not caused it to rain upon the earth, and there was not a man to till the ground.
Psalm 33: 6, 8–9	By the word of the Lord were the heavens made; and all the host of them by the breath of his mouth. . . . Let all the earth fear the Lord: let all the inhabitants of the world stand in awe of him. For he spake, and it was done; he commanded, and it stood fast.

The Prophet Isaiah wrote:

Isaiah 40:28	Hast thou not known? hast thou not heard, that the everlasting God, the Lord, the Creator of the ends of the earth, fainteth not, neither is weary?

New Testament

John 1:1–3	In the beginning was the Word, and the Word was with God, and the Word was God.

The same was in the beginning with God.

All things were made by him; and without him was not any thing made that was made.

Prior to his martyrdom, Stephen quoted the Savior.

Acts 7:49–50 Heaven is my throne, and earth is my footstool: what house will ye build me? saith the Lord: or what is the place of my rest?

Hath not my hand made all these things?

Book of Mormon

In the Book of Mormon, Nephi also taught the people that Christ was the Creator.

2 Nephi 9:5 Yea, I know that ye know that in the body he shall show himself unto those at Jerusalem, from whence we came; for it is expedient that it should be among them; for it behooveth the great Creator that he suffereth himself to become subject unto man in the flesh, and die for all men, that all men might become subject unto him.

Prior to the birth of Christ, King Benjamin, the ancient Nephite prophet, taught his people about the birth and mission of Christ.

Mosiah 3:8 And he shall be called Jesus Christ, the Son of God, the Father of heaven and earth, the Creator of all things from the beginning; and his mother shall be called Mary.

Doctrine and Covenants

In revelations given to the Prophet Joseph Smith, the Lord declared that he was the Creator.

D&C 29:31–32 For by the power of my Spirit created I them; yea, all things both spiritual and temporal—

First spiritual, secondly temporal, which is the beginning of my work; and again, first temporal, and secondly spiritual, which is the last of my work [September 1830].

D&C 38:1–3 — Thus saith the Lord your God, even Jesus Christ, the Great I Am, Alpha and Omega, the beginning and the end, the same which looked upon the wide expanse of eternity, and all the seraphic hosts of heaven, before the world was made;

The same which knoweth all things, for all things are present before mine eyes;

I am the same which spake, and the world was made, and all things came by me [January 2, 1831].

b. Christ is our Savior

From the earliest of time, man knew that there would be a Savior, and that that Savior would be the Lord. The children of Israel proclaimed this truth as they sang the song of Moses.

Exodus 15:2 — The Lord is my strength and song, and he is become my salvation.

David declared this same truth.

Psalm 27:1 — The Lord is my light and my salvation.

The Prophet Isaiah makes multiple references to a Savior.

Isaiah 19:20 — And it shall be for a sign and for a witness unto the Lord of hosts in the land of Egypt: for they shall cry unto the Lord because of the oppressors, and he shall send them a saviour, and a great one, and he shall deliver them.

Isaiah 43:3 — For I am the Lord thy God, the Holy One of Israel, thy Saviour.

Isaiah 43:11 — I, even I, am the Lord; and beside me there is no saviour.

New Testament

In Matthew, in the New Testament, we read of the angel telling Joseph:

Matthew 1:21 — And she shall bring forth a son, and thou shalt call his name JESUS: for he shall save his people from their sins.

John taught:

John 3:16–17	For God so loved the world, that he gave his only begotten Son, that whosoever believeth in him should not perish, but have everlasting life. For God sent not his Son into the world to condemn the world; but that the world through him might be saved.

The Apostle Paul preached that Jesus was indeed the Savior.

Acts 13:23	Of this man's seed hath God according to his promise raised unto Israel a Saviour, Jesus.

Book of Mormon

The same doctrine was revealed to Book of Mormon prophets.

1 Nephi 13:40	And the angel spake unto me, saying: These last records, which thou hast seen among the Gentiles, shall establish the truth of the first, which are of the twelve apostles of the Lamb, and shall make known the plain and precious things which have been taken away from them; and shall make known to all kindreds, tongues, and people, that the Lamb of God is the Son of the Eternal Father, and the Savior of the world; and that all men must come unto him, or they cannot be saved.
Mosiah 3:20	And moreover, I say unto you, that the time shall come when the knowledge of a Savior shall spread throughout every nation, kindred, tongue, and people.

Doctrine and Covenants

In 1831, the Lord declared in a revelation given to Joseph Smith:

D&C 43:34	Hearken ye to these words. Behold, I am Jesus Christ, the Savior of the world.

Pearl of Great Price

In the Pearl of Great Price, we also read that God spoke to Moses and declared:

Moses 1:6 And I have a work for thee, Moses, my son; and thou art in the similitude of mine Only Begotten; and mine Only Begotten is and shall be the Savior, for he is full of grace and truth.

Thus we can see that people throughout the ages, and in divers places, were given to know that there would be a savior and that that savior would be, and is, Jesus Christ.

c. Christ is our Redeemer

The dictionary defines *redeem* (in part) as "(1) to buy back; (2) to get or win back; (3) to liberate (as from slavery or captivity) by paying a price: ransom; (4) to extricate from or help to surmount (a detrimental influence or circumstance); (5) to release from blame or debt: clear, justify; (6) to absolve from the bondage of sin; to put back into proper condition: Repair, restore; (7) to atone for or cleanse; (8) to cancel out the detrimental effect of: make up for: compensate, offset."[7] The synonym is *rescue*. These definitions all apply to Jesus Christ as our Redeemer.

To "buy back" or "win back" indicates that a person or thing had to belong to or be owned by someone before, and that it was now in the possession of another. In the case of mankind, we were originally in the presence of our Heavenly Father. When we became mortal, we were shut off from his presence and became subject to sin and the devil. Since no unclean thing can enter the kingdom of heaven, we are forever cut off from our Heavenly home unless we can somehow become clean. This is something we cannot do on our own. Thus, a Savior was required who could and would atone for our sins, pay our debt, and "rescue" us from our fallen state.

Prophets have known since the beginning of time that the Lord was to be our Redeemer.

Old Testament

Isaiah 60:16 Thou shalt also suck the milk of the Gentiles, and shalt suck the breast of kings: and thou shalt know that I the Lord am thy Saviour and thy Redeemer, the mighty One of Jacob.

New Testament

When the angel spoke to Joseph and told him to fear not to take Mary unto himself, he told him that the child's name should be Jesus.

Matthew 1:21	For he shall save his people from their sins.

We also read in Matthew that Jesus came to "give his life a ransom for many" (Matthew 20:28).

John, Christ's beloved apostle, recognized Jesus' role as Redeemer.

John 1:29	The next day John seeth Jesus coming unto him, and saith, Behold the Lamb of God, which taketh away the sin of the world.

Paul reminded the followers of Christ that Christ had purchased them with his own blood.

Acts 20:28	Take heed therefore unto yourselves, and to all the flock, over the which the Holy Ghost hath made you overseers, to feed the church of God, which he hath purchased with his own blood.

He reminded the Corinthians to be clean and flee fornication, that their body is a temple, and that they had been "bought with a price" (1 Corinthians 6:18–20).

In his epistle to the Romans, Paul explained the need for a Redeemer. When one man [Adam] partook of the forbidden fruit, mortality was ushered in, and with mortality came the ability to sin and both spiritual and physical death. We were cut off from the presence of our Heavenly Father and the only way we could return to his presence is through the atonement of a Redeemer. Just as mortality and the ability to sin were the result of one man's transgression, the gift of redemption was to be through one person, one perfect person, Jesus Christ. Thus, Christ paid the price for our sins so that we might be reconciled to our Heavenly Father.

Romans 5:8–21	But God commendeth his love toward us, in that, while we were yet sinners, Christ died for us. Much more then, being now justified by his blood, we shall be saved from wrath through him. For if, when we were enemies, we were reconciled to God by the death of his Son, much more,

being reconciled, we shall be saved by his life.

And not only so, but we also joy in God through our Lord Jesus Christ, by whom we have now received the atonement.

Wherefore, as by one man sin entered into the world, and death by sin; and so death passed upon all men, for that all have sinned:

(For until the law sin was in the world: but sin is not imputed when there is no law.

Nevertheless death reigned from Adam to Moses, even over them that had not sinned after the similitude of Adam's transgression, who is the figure of him that was to come.

But not as the offence, so also is the free gift. For if through the offence of one many be dead, much more the grace of God, and the gift by grace, which is by one man, Jesus Christ, hath abounded unto many.

And not as it was by one that sinned, so is the gift: for the judgment was by one to condemnation, but the free gift is of many offences unto justification.

For if by one man's offence death reigned by one; much more they which receive abundance of grace and of the gift of righteousness shall reign in life by one, Jesus Christ.)

Therefore as by the offence of one judgment came upon all men to condemnation; even so by the righteousness of one the free gift came upon all men unto justification of life.

For as by one man's disobedience many were made sinners, so by the obedience of one shall many be made righteous.

Moreover the law entered, that the offence might abound. But where sin abounded, grace did much more abound:

That as sin hath reigned unto death, even so might grace reign through righteousness unto eternal life by Jesus Christ our Lord.

Book of Mormon

Ancient prophets in America had the same truths revealed unto them.

Alma 5:48 I say unto you, that I know of myself that whatsoever I shall say unto you, concerning that which is to come, is true; and I say unto you, that I know that Jesus Christ shall come, yea, the Son, the Only Begotten of the Father, full of grace, and mercy, and truth. And behold, it is he that cometh to take away the sins of the world, yea, the sins of every man who steadfastly believeth on his name.

The Prophet Alma explained the doctrine to his son Corianton.

Alma 42:2, 7, 10–11, 14–15

Now behold, my son, I will explain this thing unto thee. For behold, after the Lord God sent our first parents forth from the garden of Eden, to till the ground, from whence they were taken—yea, he drew out the man, and he placed at the east end of the garden of Eden, cherubim, and a flaming sword which turned every way, to keep the tree of life. . . .

And now, ye see by this that our first parents were cut off both temporally and spiritually from the presence of the Lord; and thus we see they became subjects to follow after their own will. . . .

Therefore, as they had become carnal, sensual, and devilish, by nature, this probationary state became a state for them to prepare; it became a preparatory state.

And now remember, my son, if it were not for the plan of redemption, (laying it aside) as soon as they were dead their souls were miserable, being cut off from the presence of the Lord.

And thus we see that all mankind were fallen, and they were in the grasp of justice; yea, the justice of God, which consigned them forever to be cut off from his presence.

And now, the plan of mercy could not be

brought about except an atonement should be made; therefore God himself atoneth for the sins of the world, to bring about the plan of mercy, to appease the demands of justice, that God might be a perfect, just God, and a merciful God also.

Amulek, Alma's friend and colleague, explained that Christ would come into the world to redeem it.

Alma 11:40 — And he shall come into the world to redeem his people; and he shall take upon him the transgressions of those who believe on his name.

Samuel, the Lamanite prophet, taught the Nephites, saying:

Helaman 14:16–17 — Yea, behold this death [Christ's death] bringeth to pass the resurrection, and redeemeth all mankind from the first death—that spiritual death; for all mankind, by the fall of Adam being cut off from the presence of the Lord, are considered as dead, both as to things temporal and to things spiritual.

But behold, the resurrection of Christ redeemeth mankind, yea, even all mankind, and bringeth them back into the presence of the Lord.

King Benjamin, speaking of the Savior, taught:

Mosiah 3:7, 11 — And lo, he shall suffer temptations, and pain of body, hunger, thirst, and fatigue, even more than man can suffer, except it be unto death; for behold, blood cometh from every pore, so great shall be his anguish for the wickedness and the abominations of his people. . . .

For behold, and also his blood atoneth for the sins of those who have fallen by the transgression of Adam, who have died not knowing the will of God concerning them, or who have ignorantly sinned.

Doctrine and Covenants

In June of 1829, the Lord revealed to Joseph Smith that he [the Lord] was indeed the Redeemer.

D&C 18:11 — For, behold, the Lord your Redeemer suffered death in the flesh; wherefore he suffered the pain of all men, that all men might repent and come unto him.

d. Christ died upon the cross and was resurrected the third day

Mark 16:6 He is risen; he is not here.

Those simple statements marked one of the most exciting and significant events to ever occur in all of history. Jesus Christ, who had been crucified just three days before, had been resurrected, just as he had foretold. Never before had anyone been resurrected! And with Christ's resurrection came the promise that every person who ever lived upon the earth would also eventually be resurrected. The Bible Dictionary states the following about the resurrection: "The resurrection consists in the uniting of a spirit body with a body of flesh and bones, never again to be divided. . . . Others had been brought back from death, but were restored to mortality . . . whereas a resurrection means to become immortal, without blood, yet with a body of flesh and bone."[8]

Writings of both Old and New Testament prophets show they knew of Christ's eventual crucifixion.

Old Testament

Speaking messianically, David wrote:

Psalm 22:1, 16 My God, my God, why hast thou forsaken me? . . .
They pierced my hands and my feet.

Isaiah wrote:

Isaiah 25:8 He will swallow up death in victory; and the Lord God will wipe away tears from off all faces; and the rebuke of his people shall he take away from off all the earth: for the Lord hath spoken it.

Also speaking messianically, Isaiah said:

Isaiah 53:10–12 Yet it pleased the Lord to bruise him; he hath put him to grief: when thou shalt make his soul an offering for sin, he shall see his seed, he shall prolong his days, and the pleasure of the Lord shall prosper in his hand.

He shall see of the travail of his soul, and shall

be satisfied: by his knowledge shall my righteous servant justify many; for he shall bear their iniquities.

Therefore will I divide him a portion with the great, and he shall divide the spoil with the strong; because he hath poured out his soul unto death: and he was numbered with the transgressors; and he bare the sin of many, and made intercession for the transgressors.

The Prophet Zechariah, speaking messianically, referred to the thirty pieces of silver which Judas would receive for betraying the Savior:

Zechariah 11:12–13 And I said unto them, If ye think good, give me my price; and if not, forbear. So they weighed for my price thirty pieces of silver.

And the Lord said unto me, Cast it unto the potter: a goodly price that I was prised at of them. And I took the thirty pieces of silver, and cast them to the potter in the house of the Lord.

He also spoke of Christ's wounds:

Zechariah 13:6 And one shall say unto him, What are these wounds in thine hands? Then he shall answer, Those with which I was wounded in the house of my friends.

New Testament

Christ explained to his disciples that he would be betrayed, condemned, and crucified, and that he would rise on the third day.

Matthew 16:21 From that time forth began Jesus to shew unto his disciples, how that he must go unto Jerusalem, and suffer many things of the elders and chief priests and scribes, and be killed, and be raised again the third day.

Matthew 20:17–19 And Jesus going up to Jerusalem took the twelve disciples apart in the way, and said unto them,

Behold, we go up to Jerusalem; and the Son of man shall be betrayed unto the chief priests and unto the scribes, and they shall condemn him to death,

And shall deliver him to the Gentiles to mock, and to scourge, and to crucify him: and the third day he shall rise again.

Luke 18:33 — And they shall scourge him, and put him to death: and the third day he shall rise again.

Just as Isaiah had prophesied that the Savior would be "numbered with the transgressors," Luke recounted:

Luke 23:32–33 — And there were also two other, malefactors, led with him to be put to death.

And when they were come to the place, which is called Calvary, there they crucified him, and the malefactors, one on the right hand, and the other on the left.

Paul taught the Corinthians:

1 Corinthians 15:3–4

For I delivered unto you first of all that which I also received, how that Christ died for our sins according to the scriptures;

And that he was buried, and that he rose again the third day according to the scriptures.

BOOK OF MORMON

As early as 600 to 592 years B.C., Lehi taught his family that Christ would come, be crucified, and rise again.

1 Nephi 10:11 — And it came to pass after my father had spoken these words he spake unto my brethren concerning the gospel which should be preached among the Jews, and also concerning the dwindling of the Jews in unbelief. And after they had slain the Messiah, who should come, and after he had been slain he should rise from the dead.

Many years later, about 124 B.C., King Benjamin taught these same truths.

Mosiah 3:8–10 — And he shall be called Jesus Christ, the Son of God, the Father of heaven and earth, the Creator of all things from the beginning; and his mother shall be called Mary.

And lo, he cometh unto his own, that salvation might come unto the children of men even through faith on his name; and even after all this they shall consider him a man, and say that he hath a devil, and shall scourge him, and shall crucify him.

And he shall rise the third day from the dead.

Doctrine and Covenants

In more recent times, the Lord revealed to Joseph Smith the following:

D&C 45:51–52 And then shall the Jews look upon me and say: What are these wounds in thine hands and in thy feet?

Then shall they know that I am the Lord; for I will say unto them: These wounds are the wounds with which I was wounded in the house of my friends. I am he who was lifted up. I am Jesus that was crucified. I am the Son of God [March 7, 1831].

e. Christ has an immortal body of flesh and bones, as does the Father

After Christ's resurrection, he appeared to many people. He showed them the wounds in his hands and feet and assured them that he was not a spirit, but that he had his physical body and could eat and drink.

New Testament

Luke 24:36–43 And as they [Christ's disciples] thus spake, Jesus himself stood in the midst of them, and saith unto them, Peace be unto you.

But they were terrified and affrighted, and supposed that they had seen a spirit.

And he said unto them, Why are ye troubled? and why do thoughts arise in your hearts?

Behold my hands and my feet, that it is I myself: handle me, and see; for a spirit hath not flesh and bones, as ye see me have.

And when he had thus spoken, he shewed them his hands and his feet.

And while they yet believed not for joy, and wondered, he said unto them, Have ye here any meat?

And they gave him a piece of a broiled fish, and of an honeycomb.

And he took it, and did eat before them.

Thomas was not with the other disciples when the Savior appeared to them, and he refused to believe what they told him.

John 20:25 — Except I shall see in his hands the print of the nails, and put my finger into the print of the nails, and thrust my hand into his side, I will not believe.

Eight days later, the disciples, including Thomas, were gathered together when the Lord appeared in their midst, even though the doors were shut, and told Thomas:

John 20:27 — Reach hither thy finger, and behold my hands; and reach hither thy hand, and thrust it into my side: and be not faithless, but believing.

Thomas then believed, but the Lord gently chided him, saying:

John 20:29 — Because thou hast seen me, thou hast believed: blessed are they that have not seen, and yet have believed.

Peter testified:

Acts 10:39–41 — And we are witnesses of all things which he did both in the land of the Jews and in Jerusalem; whom they slew and hanged on a tree:

Him God raised up the third day, and shewed him openly;

Not to all the people, but unto witnesses chosen before of God, even to us, who did eat and drink with him after he rose from the dead.

Book of Mormon

Consistent with that teaching, Christ appeared, as prophesied, to the Nephites on the American continent following his resurrection.

3 Nephi 11:8–15

And it came to pass, as they understood they cast their eyes up again towards heaven; and behold, they saw a Man descending out of heaven; and he was clothed in a white robe; and he came down and stood in the midst of them; and the eyes of the whole multitude were turned upon him, and they durst not open their mouths, even one to another, and wist not what it meant, for they thought it was an angel that had appeared unto them.

And it came to pass that he stretched forth his hand and spake unto the people, saying:

Behold, I am Jesus Christ, whom the prophets testified shall come into the world.

And behold, I am the light and the life of the world; and I have drunk out of that bitter cup which the Father hath given me, and have glorified the Father in taking upon me the sins of the world, in the which I have suffered the will of the Father in all things from the beginning.

And it came to pass that when Jesus had spoken these words the whole multitude fell to the earth; for they remembered that it had been prophesied among them that Christ should show himself unto them after his ascension into heaven.

And it came to pass that the Lord spake unto them saying:

Arise and come forth unto me, that ye may thrust your hands into my side, and also that ye may feel the prints of the nails in my hands and in my feet, that ye may know that I am the God of Israel, and the God of the whole earth, and have been slain for the sins of the world.

And it came to pass that the multitude went forth, and thrust their hands into his side, and did feel the prints of the nails in his hands and in his feet; and this they did do, going forth one by one until they had all gone forth, and did see with their eyes and did feel with their hands, and did know of a surety and did bear record, that it was he, of whom it was written by the prophets, that should come.

DOCTRINE AND COVENANTS

The resurrected Lord appeared to Joseph and Oliver Cowdery in the Kirtland temple.

D&C 110: 1–4 The veil was taken from our minds, and the eyes of our understanding were opened.

We saw the Lord standing upon the breastwork of the pulpit before us; and under his feet was a paved work of pure gold, in color like amber.

His eyes were as a flame of fire; the hair of his head was white like the pure snow; his countenance shone above the brightness of the sun; and his voice was as the sound of the rushing of great waters, even the voice of Jehovah, saying:

I am the first and the last; I am he who liveth, I am he who was slain; I am your advocate with the Father [April 3, 1836].

PEARL OF GREAT PRICE

Christ had revealed himself earlier in these latter days in 1820 when he and the Father appeared to Joseph Smith as Joseph prayed to know which church he should join. Joseph recounts:

JS—H 1:16–17 I saw a pillar of light exactly over my head, above the brightness of the sun, which descended gradually until it fell upon me. . . .

When the light rested upon me I saw two Personages, whose brightness and glory defy all description, standing above me in the air. One of them spake unto me, calling me by name and said, pointing to the other—This is my Beloved Son. Hear Him!

f. He is our intercessor with the Father

Advocate, intercessor, mediator, propitiator, conciliator: these words all describe one of the Savior's roles toward each person on earth. The dictionary defines (a) *advocate* as "a person who pleads another's cause"[9];

(b) *intercessor* as "a person who intercedes"[10]; (c) *mediator* as "one that mediates between parties at variance to reconcile them"[11]; (d) *propitiator* as one that "appeases or conciliates a diety: atonement," and more specifically: "the self-sacrifice and death of Jesus Christ to appease divine justice and to effect reconciliation between God and man"[12]; and (e) *conciliator* as "peacemaker," and *conciliate* as "to make compatible: cause to be in accord."[13]

Why do we need an advocate? With the fall of Adam, all mankind was born into mortality, and as such are subject to sin. Every person, except Christ, sins and is subject to the laws of justice which require that a penalty be paid for every violation of the Lord's laws. However, the law of mercy allows for that penalty to be paid by a proxy. Christ, in the premortal life, agreed to be our proxy and to atone for our sins. Nevertheless, mercy is conditional upon our repentance.

New Testament

John 14:6	Jesus saith unto him, I am the way, the truth, and the life: no man cometh unto the Father, but by me.
Romans 3:20–26	Therefore by the deeds of the law there shall no flesh be justified in his sight: for by the law is the knowledge of sin. But now the righteousness of God without the law is manifested, being witnessed by the law and the prophets; Even the righteousness of God which is by faith of Jesus Christ unto all and upon all them that believe: for there is no difference: For all have sinned, and come short of the glory of God; Being justified freely by his grace through the redemption that is in Christ Jesus: Whom God hath set forth to be a propitiation through faith in his blood, to declare his righteousness for the remission of sins that are past, through the forbearance of God; To declare, I say, at this time his righteousness:

that he might be just, and the justifier of him which believeth in Jesus.

In Paul's epistle to the Galatians, he explained that man could not be saved by temporal laws such as the law of Moses. There was a plan "ordained by angels," and a mediator had been appointed that through faith we could be justified. That is, mercy could replace justice if we were faithful, or in other words, mercy could replace justice if we repented of our sins and followed Christ.

Galatians 3:17–24 And this I say, that the covenant, that was confirmed before of God in Christ, the law, which was four hundred and thirty years after, cannot disannul, that it should make the promise of none effect.

For if the inheritance be of the law, it is no more of promise: but God gave it to Abraham by promise.

Wherefore then serveth the law? It was added because of transgressions, till the seed should come to whom the promise was made; and it was ordained by angels in the hand of a mediator.

Now a mediator is not a mediator of one, but God is one.

Is the law then against the promises of God? God forbid: for if there had been a law given which could have given life, verily righteousness should have been by the law.

But the scripture hath concluded all under sin, that the promise by faith of Jesus Christ might be given to them that believe.

But before faith came, we were kept under the law, shut up unto the faith which should afterwards be revealed.

Wherefore the law was our schoolmaster to bring us unto Christ, that we might be justified by faith.

1 Timothy 2:5–6 For there is one God, and one mediator between God and men, the man Christ Jesus;

Who gave himself a ransom for all, to be testified in due time.

JST, Hebrews 9:14–15

How much more shall the blood of Christ, who through the eternal Spirit offered himself without spot to God, purge your conscience from dead works to serve the living God?

And for this cause he is the mediator of the new covenant, that by means of death, for the redemption of the transgressions that were under the first covenant, they which are called might receive the promise of eternal inheritance.

1 John 2:1–2

My little children, these things write I unto you, that ye sin not. And if any man sin, we have an advocate with the Father, Jesus Christ the righteous:

And he is the propitiation for our sins: and not for ours only, but also for the sins of the whole world.

1 John 4:10

Herein is love, not that we loved God, but that he loved us, and sent his Son to be the propitiation for our sins.

Book of Mormon

Alma explained the concepts of justice, mercy, and the law.

Alma 42:2–26

Now behold, my son, I will explain this thing unto thee. For behold, after the Lord God sent our first parents forth from the garden of Eden, to till the ground, from whence they were taken—yea, he drew out the man, and he placed at the east end of the garden of Eden, cherubim, and a flaming sword which turned every way, to keep the tree of life—

Now, we see that the man had become as God, knowing good and evil; and lest he should put forth his hand, and take also of the tree of life, and eat and live forever, the Lord God placed cherubim and the flaming sword, that he should not partake of the fruit—

And thus we see, that there was a time granted unto man to repent, yea, a probationary time, a time to repent and serve God.

For behold, if Adam had put forth his hand immediately, and partaken of the tree of life, he would have lived forever, according to the word of God, having no space for repentance; yea, and also the word of God would have been void, and the great plan of salvation would have been frustrated.

But behold, it was appointed unto man to die—therefore, as they were cut off from the tree of life they should be cut off from the face of the earth—and man became lost forever, yea, they became fallen man.

And now, ye see by this that our first parents were cut off both temporally and spiritually from the presence of the Lord; and thus we see they became subjects to follow after their own will.

Now behold, it was not expedient that man should be reclaimed from this temporal death, for that would destroy the great plan of happiness.

Therefore, as the soul could never die, and the fall had brought upon all mankind a spiritual death as well as a temporal, that is, they were cut off from the presence of the Lord, it was expedient that mankind should be reclaimed from this spiritual death.

Therefore, as they had become carnal, sensual, and devilish, by nature, this probationary state became a state for them to prepare; it became a preparatory state.

And now remember, my son, if it were not for the plan of redemption, (laying it aside) as soon as they were dead their souls were miserable, being cut off from the presence of the Lord.

And now, there was no means to reclaim men from this fallen state, which man had brought upon himself because of his own disobedience;

Therefore, according to justice, the plan of redemption could not be brought about, only on conditions of repentance of men in this probationary state, yea, this preparatory state; for except it were for these conditions, mercy could not take effect except it should destroy the work of justice. Now the work of justice could not be destroyed; if so, God would cease to be God.

And thus we see that all mankind were fallen, and they were in the grasp of justice; yea, the justice of God, which consigned them forever to be cut off from his presence.

And now, the plan of mercy could not be brought about except an atonement should be made; therefore God himself atoneth for the sins of the world, to bring about the plan of mercy, to appease the demands of justice, that God might be a perfect, just God, and a merciful God also.

Now, repentance could not come unto men except there were a punishment, which also was eternal as the life of the soul should be, affixed opposite to the plan of happiness, which was as eternal also as the life of the soul.

Now, how could a man repent except he should sin? How could he sin if there was no law? How could there be a law save there was a punishment?

Now, there was a punishment affixed, and a just law given, which brought remorse of conscience unto man.

Now, if there was no law given—if a man murdered he should die—would he be afraid he would die if he should murder?

And also, if there was no law given against sin men would not be afraid to sin.

And if there was no law given, if men sinned what could justice do, or mercy either, for they would have no claim upon the creature?

But there is a law given, and a punishment affixed, and a repentance granted; which repentance, mercy claimeth; otherwise, justice claimeth the creature and executeth the law, and the law inflicteth the punishment; if not so, the works of justice would be destroyed, and God would cease to be God.

But God ceaseth not to be God, and mercy claimeth the penitent, and mercy cometh because of the atonement; and the atonement bringeth to pass the resurrection of the dead; and the resurrection of the dead bringeth back men into the presence of God; and thus they are restored into his presence, to be judged according to their works, according to the law and justice.

For behold, justice exerciseth all his demands, and also mercy claimeth all which is her own; and thus, none but the truly penitent are saved.

What, do ye suppose that mercy can rob justice? I say unto you, Nay; not one whit. If so God would cease to be God.

And thus God bringeth about his great and eternal purposes, which were prepared from the foundation of the world. And thus cometh about the salvation and the redemption of men, and also their destruction and misery.

DOCTRINE AND COVENANTS

On September 26, 1830, the Lord, in this modern dispensation of time, once again declared that he is our advocate with the Father (D&C 29:5). He repeated and expanded that statement on March 7, 1831.

D&C 45:3–5 Listen to him who is the advocate with the Father, who is pleading your cause before him—

Saying: Father, behold the sufferings and death of him who did no sin, in whom thou wast well pleased; behold the blood of thy Son which was shed, the blood of him whom thou gavest that thyself might be glorified;

Wherefore, Father, spare these my brethren that believe on my name, that they may come unto me and have everlasting life.

In a revelation received by Joseph Smith on March 28, 1835, regarding the priesthood, Christ's role as mediator is reaffirmed.

D&C 107:19 — Enjoy the communion and presence of God the Father, and Jesus the mediator of the new covenant.

3. The Holy Ghost

The scriptures attest that the mission of the third member of the Godhead differs from that of the Father and the Son. The Holy Ghost is a comforter, a witness, a teacher, a testifier of truth, a testifier of the divinity of Jesus Christ, a reprover of our sins, a guide, and an intercessor. His presence is given as a gift to the faithful. Unlike the Father and the Son, the Holy Ghost has a body of spirit.

D&C 130:22 — The Father has a body of flesh and bones as tangible as man's; the Son also; but the Holy Ghost has not a body of flesh and bones, but is a personage of Spirit. Were it not so, the Holy Ghost could not dwell in us.

Old Testament

In the Old Testament, we read:

Nehemiah 9:20 — Thou gavest also thy good spirit to instruct them.

Nehemiah also wrote:

Nehemiah 9:30 — Yet many years didst thou forbear them, and testifiedst against them by thy spirit [the Holy Ghost] in thy prophets.

The Prophet Ezekiel was told by the Lord:

Ezekiel 36:27 — And I will put my spirit within you, and cause you to walk in my statutes, and ye shall keep my judgments, and do them.

The Prophet Micah testified that he was:

Micah 3:8 — Full of power by the spirit of the Lord, and of judgment, and of might, to declare unto Jacob his transgression, and to Israel his sin.

New Testament

Christ taught his disciples:

Mark 13:11 — But when they shall lead you, and deliver you up, take no thought beforehand what ye shall speak, neither do ye premeditate: but whatsoever shall be given you in that hour, that speak ye: for it is not ye that speak, but the Holy Ghost.

This same counsel is given in Luke:

Luke 12:12 — For the Holy Ghost shall teach you in the same hour what ye ought to say.

We also read the words of the Savior in the book of John:

John 14:26 — But the Comforter, which is the Holy Ghost, whom the Father will send in my name, he shall teach you all things, and bring all things to your remembrance, whatsoever I have said unto you.

Jesus also said:

John 15:26–27 — But when the Comforter is come, whom I will send unto you from the Father, even the Spirit of truth, which proceedeth from the Father, he shall testify of me:

And ye also shall bear witness, because ye have been with me from the beginning.

As long as the Savior was on the earth, the apostles could not receive the gift of the Holy Ghost and have him as a constant companion. The Savior taught:

John 16:7–8 — Nevertheless I tell you the truth; It is expedient for you that I go away: for if I go not away, the Comforter will not come unto you; but if I depart, I will send him unto you.

And when he is come, he will reprove the world of sin, and of righteousness, and of judgment.

Paul taught the Corinthian saints:

1 Corinthians 2:10–11

But God hath revealed them unto us by his Spirit: for the Spirit searcheth all things, yea, the deep things of God.

For what man knoweth the things of a man, save the spirit of man which is in him? even so the things of God knoweth no man, but the Spirit of God.

In his epistle to the Hebrews, Paul reminded the people of one of the roles of the Holy Ghost:

Hebrews 10:15 — Whereof the Holy Ghost also is a witness to us.

The apostle Peter reminded the saints that the Holy Ghost tells prophets what to say:

2 Peter 1:21 — For the prophecy came not in old time by the will of man: but holy men of God spake as they were moved by the Holy Ghost.

Book of Mormon

These same truths have been revealed in other scriptures. The Book of Mormon teaches that the Holy Ghost is to be a witness of the Father and the Son.

2 Nephi 31:17–18 — For the gate by which ye should enter is repentance and baptism by water; and then cometh a remission of your sins by fire and by the Holy Ghost.

And then are ye in this strait and narrow path which leads to eternal life; yea, ye have entered in by the gate; ye have done according to the commandments of the Father and the Son; and ye have received the Holy Ghost, which witnesses of the Father and the Son, unto the fulfilling of the promise which he hath made, that if ye entered in by the way ye should receive.

Nephi also taught:

2 Nephi 32:5 — For behold, again I say unto you that if ye will enter in by the way, and receive the Holy Ghost, it will show unto you all things what ye should do.

Again, speaking of the Holy Ghost, Nephi taught:

2 Nephi 33:1 — For when a man speaketh by the power of the Holy Ghost the power of the Holy Ghost carrieth it unto the hearts of the children of men.

Jacob, a younger brother of Nephi, reaffirmed the mission and power of the Holy Ghost.

Jacob 4:13 Behold, my brethren, he that prophesieth, let him prophesy to the understanding of men; for the Spirit speaketh the truth and lieth not. Wherefore, it speaketh of things as they really are, and of things as they really will be; wherefore, these things are manifested unto us plainly, for the salvation of our souls. But behold, we are not witnesses alone in these things; for God also spake them unto prophets of old.

Moroni, the final prophet of the Book of Mormon, testified as to the power of the Holy Ghost.

Moroni 10:4–5 And when ye shall receive these things, I would exhort you that ye would ask God, the Eternal Father, in the name of Christ, if these things are not true; and if ye shall ask with a sincere heart, with real intent, having faith in Christ, he will manifest the truth of it unto you, by the power of the Holy Ghost.

And by the power of the Holy Ghost ye may know the truth of all things.

Doctrine and Covenants

Revelations received in these latter days as recorded in the Doctrine and Covenants are consistent with those received in ancient times. As Joseph Smith was engaged in the work of translation and Oliver Cowdery was acting as scribe, the Lord told them:

D&C 6:15 Behold, thou knowest that thou hast inquired of me and I did enlighten thy mind; and now I tell thee these things that thou mayest know that thou hast been enlightened by the Spirit of truth.

In that same month and year (April 1829), the Lord gave further instruction regarding the Holy Ghost:

D&C 8:2–3 Yea, behold, I will tell you in your mind and in your heart, by the Holy Ghost, which shall come upon you and which shall dwell in your heart.

Now, behold, this is the spirit of revelation; behold, this is the spirit by which Moses brought the children of Israel through the Red Sea on dry ground.

A month later, the Lord again revealed information regarding the Holy Ghost:

D&C 11:12 — And now, verily, verily, I say unto thee, put your trust in that Spirit which leadeth to do good—yea, to do justly, to walk humbly, to judge righteously; and this is my Spirit.

The Doctrine and Covenants reaffirms that two of the roles of the Holy Ghost are that of comforter and of teacher.

D&C 39:6 — And this is my gospel—repentance and baptism by water, and then cometh the baptism of fire and the Holy Ghost, even the Comforter, which showeth all things and teacheth the peaceable things of the kingdom.

As mentioned previously, one of the roles of the Holy Ghost is that of being a guide. The Savior revealed:

D&C 45:57 — For they that are wise and have received the truth, and have taken the Holy Spirit for their guide, and have not been deceived—verily I say unto you, they shall not be hewn down and cast into the fire, but shall abide the day.

Pearl of Great Price

Consistent with the teachings of the Old Testament, New Testament, Book of Mormon, and Doctrine and Covenants regarding the role of the Holy Ghost, the Pearl of Great Price reveals:

Moses 1:27–28 — And it came to pass, as the voice was still speaking, Moses cast his eyes and beheld the earth, yea, even all of it; and there was not a particle of it which he did not behold, discerning it by the spirit of God.

And he beheld also the inhabitants thereof, and there was not a soul which he beheld not; and he discerned them by the Spirit of God; and their numbers were great, even numberless as the sand upon the sea shore.

Notes

1. *Webster's New World Dictionary,* 2nd College ed. (Cleveland, OH: World Publishing, 1976), 994.
2. Ibid., 993.
3. *Webster's Third New International Dictionary*, Unabridged (Springfield, MA: G. & C. Merriam, 1976), 1575.
4. *Webster's New World Dictionary,* 700.
5. *Webster's Third New International Dictionary*, 1128.
6. Ibid., 1310.
7. Ibid., 1902.
8. Bible Dictionary, "Resurrection," 761.
9. *Webster's New World Dictionary,* 20.
10. Ibid., 733.
11. *Webster's Third New International Dictionary*, 1402
12. Ibid., 1818.
13. Ibid., 471.

Chapter 5

The Need for a Redeemer: The Birth, Death, and Second Coming of Christ Foretold

TENET: Because of the fall of Adam, man was separated from our Father in Heaven both physically and spiritually. A Redeemer was required in order for us to overcome these separations. Christ was chosen to be that Redeemer. His birth was foretold by prophets in all the scriptures. His death was also foretold, as is his Second Coming.

(A) The Fall of Adam

Old Testament

Adam and Eve were warned that if they partook of the fruit of the tree of knowledge of good and evil it would cause them to be subject to death. They partook of the forbidden fruit which ushered in mortality with its physical and spiritual death.

Genesis 2:17	But of the tree of the knowledge of good and evil, thou shalt not eat of it: for in the day that thou eatest thereof thou shalt surely die.
Genesis 3:6	And when the woman saw that the tree was good for food, and that it was pleasant to the eyes, and a tree to be desired to make one wise, she took of the fruit thereof, and did cat, and gave also unto her husband with her; and he did eat.
Genesis 3:19	In the sweat of thy face shalt thou eat bread, till thou return unto the ground; for out of it wast thou

taken: for dust thou art, and unto dust shalt thou return.

New Testament

The Apostle Paul wrote to the Romans:

Romans 5:12 — Wherefore, as by one man sin entered into the world, and death by sin; and so death passed upon all men, for that all have sinned.

He also wrote to Timothy regarding the fall of Adam and Eve:

1 Timothy 2:14 — And Adam was not deceived, but the woman being deceived was in the transgression.

However, Adam also partook of the forbidden fruit. This transgression resulted in the fall from grace of both Adam and Eve, and, thus, a Redeemer was necessary in order that we might not remain in the grave and that we might become as our Father in Heaven and live with him again.

Book of Mormon

The prophets of the Book of Mormon understood the Fall of Adam and they taught the people accordingly. The explanation they give is a little more extensive than in the Old and New Testaments.

2 Nephi 2:4–5 — And the way is prepared from the fall of man, and salvation is free. . . .

Yea, by the temporal law they were cut off; and also by the spiritual law they perish from that which is good, and become miserable forever.

2 Nephi 2:25 — Adam fell that men might be; and men are, that they might have joy.

Mosiah 16:4 — Thus all mankind were lost; and behold, they would have been endlessly lost were it not that God redeemed his people from their lost and fallen state.

Alma 12:22–25 — Now Alma said unto him: This is the thing which I was about to explain. Now we see that Adam did fall by the partaking of the forbidden fruit, according to the word of God; and thus we see, that by his fall, all mankind became a lost and fallen people.

And now behold, I say unto you that if it had been possible for Adam to have partaken of the fruit of the tree of life at that time, there would have been no death, and the word would have been void, making God a liar, for he said: If thou eat thou shalt surely die.

And we see that death comes upon mankind, yea, the death which has been spoken of by Amulek, which is the temporal death; nevertheless there was a space granted unto man in which he might repent; therefore this life became a probationary state; a time to prepare to meet God; a time to prepare for that endless state which has been spoken of by us, which is after the resurrection of the dead.

Now, if it had not been for the plan of redemption, which was laid from the foundation of the world, there could have been no resurrection of the dead; but there was a plan of redemption laid, which shall bring to pass the resurrection of the dead, of which has been spoken.

Alma 42: 4–9

And thus we see, that there was a time granted unto man to repent, yea, a probationary time, a time to repent and serve God.

For behold, if Adam had put forth his hand immediately, and partaken of the tree of life, he would have lived forever, according to the word of God, having no space for repentance; yea, and also the word of God would have been void, and the great plan of salvation would have been frustrated.

But behold, it was appointed unto man to die—therefore, as they were cut off from the tree of life they should be cut off from the face of the earth—and man became lost forever, yea, they became fallen man.

And now, ye see by this that our first parents were cut off both temporally and spiritually from the presence of the Lord; and thus we see they became subjects to follow after their own will.

Now behold, it was not expedient that man should be reclaimed from this temporal death, for that would destroy the great plan of happiness.

Therefore, as the soul could never die; and the fall had brought upon all mankind a spiritual death as well as a temporal, that is, they were cut off from the presence of the Lord, it was expedient that mankind should be reclaimed from this spiritual death.

Mormon 9:12 — Behold, he created Adam, and by Adam came the fall of man.

Doctrine and Covenants

Widely diverse peoples, separated by centuries of time and distant continents, have all received revelation regarding the Fall of Adam. In April 1830, the following was revealed to Joseph Smith:

D&C 20:18–20 — He created man, male and female, after his own image and in his own likeness, created he them;

And gave unto them commandments. . . .

But by the transgression of these holy laws man became sensual and devilish, and became fallen man.

Five months later, the Lord gave Joseph Smith another revelation regarding the Fall of Adam.

D&C 29:40–41 — Wherefore, it came to pass that the devil tempted Adam, and he partook of the forbidden fruit and transgressed the commandment, wherein he became subject to the will of the devil, because he yielded unto temptation.

Wherefore, I, the Lord God, caused that he should be cast out from the Garden of Eden, from my presence, because of his transgression, wherein he became spiritually dead.

Pearl of Great Price

Centuries earlier, the Lord told Moses:

Moses 3:15–17 — And I, the Lord God, took the man, and put him into the Garden of Eden, to dress it, and to keep it.

And I, the Lord God, commanded the man, saying: Of every tree of the garden thou mayest freely eat,

But of the tree of the knowledge of good and evil, thou shalt not eat of it, nevertheless, thou mayest choose for thyself, for it is given unto thee; but, remember that I forbid it, for in the day thou eatest thereof thou shalt surely die.

Moses 4:12

And when the woman saw that the tree was good for food, and that it became pleasant to the eyes, and a tree to be desired to make her wise, she took of the fruit thereof, and did eat, and also gave unto her husband with her, and he did eat.

Moses 5:4, 9

And Adam and Eve, his wife, called upon the name of the Lord, and they heard the voice of the Lord from the way toward the Garden of Eden, speaking unto them, and they saw him not; for they were shut out from his presence. . . .

And in that day the Holy Ghost fell upon Adam, which beareth record of the Father and the Son, saying: I am the Only Begotten of the Father from the beginning, henceforth and forever, that as thou hast fallen thou mayest be redeemed, and all mankind, even as many as will.

Prior to Moses, the Lord spoke to Enoch and Enoch taught his people accordingly.

Moses 6:48

And he [Enoch] said unto them: Because that Adam fell, we are; and by his fall came death; and we are made partakers of misery and woe.

Abraham 5:11–13

And the Gods took the man and put him in the Garden of Eden, to dress it and to keep it.

And the Gods commanded the man, saying: Of every tree of the garden thou mayest freely eat,

But of the tree of knowledge of good and evil, thou shalt not eat of it; for in the time that thou eatest thereof, thou shalt surely die.

Because of the fall of Adam, every man, woman, and child who has ever lived, lives now, or will yet live will experience both physical and spiritual death. However, that is not the end plan of our heavenly Father for his children. The Plan of Salvation provided for a Redeemer who would overcome the grave with the result that all mankind would also be resurrected and that if we accept his atoning sacrifice for our sins we could also become like our Father in Heaven and live with him again in the Celestial Kingdom. Christ was chosen from before the foundation of the earth to be that Redeemer.

(B) Christ was chosen to be the Redeemer of mankind

Old Testament

Prophets of the Old Testament understood that there would be a Redeemer: the grave was not to be our final destiny.

Job 19:25–26	For I know that my redeemer liveth, and that he shall stand at the latter day upon the earth: And though after my skin worms destroy this body, yet in my flesh shall I see God.
Psalm 49:15	But God will redeem my soul from the power of the grave: for he shall receive me. Selah.
Isaiah 25:8	He will swallow up death in victory; and the Lord God will wipe away tears from off all faces; and the rebuke of his people shall he take away from off all the earth: for the Lord hath spoken it.
Isaiah 41:14	Fear not, thou worm Jacob, and ye men of Israel; I will help thee, saith the Lord, and thy redeemer, the Holy One of Israel.
Isaiah 49:26	I the Lord am thy Saviour and thy Redeemer, the mighty One of Jacob.
Isaiah 54:5	For thy Maker is thine husband; the Lord of hosts is his name; and thy Redeemer the Holy One of Israel; The God of the whole earth shall he be called.
Isaiah 63:16	Thou, O Lord, art our father, our redeemer; thy name is from everlasting.

New Testament

Prior to the birth of the Savior, an angel informed Joseph that Mary would give birth to a child and that this child would be the Redeemer.

Matthew 1:21 — And she shall bring forth a son, and thou shalt call his name Jesus: for he shall save his people from their sins.

Christ himself told the people that he was the Redeemer.

Matthew 20:28 — Even as the Son of man came not to be ministered unto, but to minister, and to give his life a ransom for many.

Elisabeth, the expectant mother of John the Baptist and cousin to Mary, recognized that the baby Mary was carrying in her womb was the chosen savior of the world:

Luke 1:41–44 — And it came to pass, that, when Elisabeth heard the salutation of Mary, the babe leaped in her womb; and Elisabeth was filled with the Holy Ghost:

And she spake out with a loud voice, and said, Blessed art thou among women, and blessed is the fruit of thy womb.

And whence is this to me, that the mother of my Lord should come to me?

For, lo, as soon as the voice of thy salutation sounded in mine ears, the babe leaped in my womb for joy.

John the Baptist recognized Jesus as the Redeemer, not only when John was still in Elisabeth's womb but also as an adult.

John 1:29 — The next day John seeth Jesus coming unto him, and saith, Behold the Lamb of God, which taketh away the sin of the world.

Paul taught the Romans that just as death was ushered in by one man [Adam], life was also by the gift of one man [Jesus Christ].

Romans 5:13–15, 17 — For until the law sin was in the world: but it is not imputed when there is no law.

Nevertheless death reigned from Adam to

> Moses, even over them that had not sinned after the similitude of Adam's transgression, who is the figure of him that was to come.
>
> But not as the offence, so also is the free gift. For if through the offence of one many be dead, much more the grace of God, and the gift by grace, which is by one man, Jesus Christ, hath abounded unto many. . . .
>
> For if by one man's offence death reigned by one; much more they which receive abundance of grace and of the gift of righteousness shall reign in life by one, Jesus Christ.

He taught the Corinthian saints:

1 Corinthians 15:22 For as in Adam all die, even so in Christ shall all be made alive.

Peter also taught that Christ was foreordained before the foundation of the world to be the Redeemer.

1 Peter 1:13, 18–20 Wherefore gird up the loins of your mind, be sober, and hope to the end for the grace that is to be brought unto you at the revelation of Jesus Christ. . . .

> Forasmuch as ye know that ye were not redeemed with corruptible things, as silver and gold, from your vain conversation, received by tradition from your fathers;
>
> But with the precious blood of Christ, as a lamb without blemish and without spot:
>
> Who verily was foreordained before the foundation of the world.

Book of Mormon

Six hundred years before the birth of Jesus Christ, Lehi taught his family about Jesus Christ and his [the Lord's] role as our Redeemer.

1 Nephi 10:5–6 And he also spake concerning the prophets, how great a number had testified of these things, concerning this Messiah, of whom he had spoken, or the Redeemer of the world.

Wherefore, all mankind were in a lost and in a fallen state, and ever would be save they should rely on this Redeemer.

2 Nephi 2:6–8 Wherefore, redemption cometh in and through the Holy Messiah; for he is full of grace and truth.

Behold he offereth himself a sacrifice for sin, to answer the ends of the law, unto all those who have a broken heart and a contrite spirit; and unto none else can the ends of the law be answered.

Wherefore, how great the importance to make these things known unto the inhabitants of the earth, that they may know that there is no flesh that can dwell in the presence of God, save it be through the merits, and mercy, and grace of the Holy Messiah, who layeth down his life according to the flesh, and taketh it again by the power of the Spirit, that he may bring to pass the resurrection of the dead, being the first that should rise.

2 Nephi 2:26 And the Messiah cometh in the fulness of time, that he may redeem the children of men from the fall.

Centuries later (about 124 B.C.), King Benjamin taught the Nephites:

Mosiah 3:17, 19 And moreover, I say unto you, that there shall be no other name given nor any other way nor means whereby salvation can come unto the children of men, only in and through the name of Christ, the Lord Omnipotent. . . .

For the natural man is an enemy to God, and has been from the fall of Adam and will be, forever and ever, unless he yields to the enticings of the Holy Spirit, and putteth off the natural man and becometh a saint through the atonement of Christ the Lord.

King Benjamin reiterated the fact that Christ was chosen to be our Redeemer in the premortal life.

Mosiah 4:7 I say, that this is the man who receiveth salvation, through the atonement which was prepared from the foundation of the world for all mankind, which ever were since the fall of Adam, or who are, or who ever shall be, even unto the end of the world.

When Christ appeared to the Nephites following his resurrection, he declared to them:

3 Nephi 9:15–17 Behold, I am Jesus Christ the Son of God. I created the heavens and the earth, and all things that in them are. . . .

I came unto my own, and my own received me not. . . .

And as many as have received me, to them have I given to become the sons of God; and even so will I to as many as shall believe on my name, for behold, by me redemption cometh.

Moroni, the last prophet of the Book of Mormon, wrote for future generations to read that:

Mormon 9:12–13 Because of the fall of man came Jesus Christ, even the Father and the Son; and because of Jesus Christ came the redemption of man.

And because of the redemption of man, which came by Jesus Christ, they are brought back into the presence of the Lord; yea, this is wherein all men are redeemed, because the death of Christ bringeth to pass the resurrection which bringeth to pass a redemption from an endless sleep.

Records of an earlier people, the Jaredites, who were separated from the rest of the world and brought to America when the languages were confounded at the tower of Babel, show that they also knew that Christ would be the Savior and Redeemer of the world. Christ showed himself to the brother of Jared and told him:

Ether 3:14 Behold, I am he who was prepared from the foundation of the world to redeem my people. Behold, I am Jesus Christ. I am the Father and the Son.

Doctrine and Covenants

There are multiple references in the Doctrine and Covenants reflecting the teaching that Christ is the Savior and Redeemer of the world. Just a few are quoted to show that these teachings mirror those of the Bible and the Book of Mormon.

D&C 15:1	Hearken, my servant John, and listen to the words of Jesus Christ, your Lord and your Redeemer.
D&C 18:11, 47	For, behold, the Lord your Redeemer suffered death in the flesh; wherefore he suffered the pain of all men, that all men might repent and come unto him. . . . Behold, I, Jesus Christ, your Lord and your God, and your Redeemer, by the power of my Spirit have spoken it. Amen.
D&C 49:5	Thus saith the Lord; for I am God, and have sent mine Only Begotten Son into the world for the redemption of the world, and have decreed that he that receiveth him shall be saved, and he that receiveth him not shall be damned.

Joseph F. Smith recorded in October 1918 the following, which echoes the testimony recorded in other scriptures that Jesus Christ is our Savior and Redeemer.

D&C 138:1–4	On the third of October, in the year nineteen hundred and eighteen, I sat in my room pondering over the scriptures; And reflecting upon the great atoning sacrifice that was made by the Son of God, for the redemption of the world; And the great and wonderful love made manifest by the Father and the Son in the coming of the Redeemer into the world; That through his atonement, and by obedience to the principles of the gospel, mankind might be saved.

He then quoted from the first epistle of Peter where Peter wrote:

D&C 138:7 — "For Christ also hath once suffered for sins, the just for the unjust, that he might bring us to God, being put to death in the flesh, but quickened by the Spirit."

Pearl of Great Price

Other ancient records that were translated and recorded in the Pearl of Great Price state:

Moses 4:1–2 — And I, the Lord God, spake unto Moses, saying: That Satan, whom thou hast commanded in the name of mine Only Begotten, is the same which was from the beginning, and he came before me, saying—Behold, here am I, send me, I will be thy son, and I will redeem all mankind, that one soul shall not be lost, and surely I will do it; wherefore give me thine honor.

But behold, my Beloved Son, which was my Beloved and Chosen from the beginning, said unto me—Father, thy will be done, and the glory be thine forever.

Abraham 3:27 — And the Lord said: Whom shall I send? And one answered like unto the Son of Man: Here am I, send me. And another answered and said: Here am I, send me. And the Lord said: I will send the first.

(C) The birth of the Savior foretold—the prophecy fulfilled

Old Testament

Prophets not only knew there was a need for a Redeemer and that Jesus Christ was foreordained before the foundation of the world to be that Redeemer, but they were given signs foretelling his birth.

Isaiah 7:14 — Therefore the Lord himself shall give you a sign; Behold, a virgin shall conceive, and bear a son, and shall call his name Immanuel.

Referring to the eventual birth of Jesus Christ, Isaiah recorded:

Isaiah 9:6–7 — For unto us a child is born, unto us a son is given: and the government shall be upon his shoulder: and his name shall be called Wonderful, Counsellor, The mighty God, The everlasting Father, The Prince of Peace.

Of the increase of his government and peace there shall be no end, upon the throne of David, and upon his kingdom, to order it, and to establish it with judgment and with justice from henceforth even for ever.

Another Old Testament prophet recorded:

Micah 5:2 — But thou, Beth-lehem Ephratah, though thou be little among the thousands of Judah, yet out of thee shall he come forth unto me that is to be ruler in Israel; whose going forth have been from of old, from everlasting.

NEW TESTAMENT

People of the New Testament were also given signs and wonders foretelling the birth of the Savior.

Matthew 1:23 — Behold, a virgin shall be with child, and shall bring forth a son, and they shall call his name Emmanuel, which being interpreted is, God with us.

Matthew 2:1 — Now when Jesus was born in Bethlehem of Judæa in the days of Herod the king, behold, there came wise men from the east to Jerusalem,

Saying, Where is he that is born King of the Jews? for we have seen his star in the east, and are come to worship him.

Luke 1:30–33 — And the angel said unto her, Fear not, Mary: for thou hast found favour with God.

And, behold, thou shalt conceive in thy womb, and bring forth a son, and shalt call his name JESUS.

He shall be great, and shall be called the Son of the Highest: and the Lord God shall give unto him the throne of his father David:

And he shall reign over the house of Jacob for

ever; and of his kingdom there shall be no end.

Luke 2:11–12 For unto you is born this day in the city of David a Saviour, which is Christ the Lord.

And this shall be a sign unto you; Ye shall find the babe wrapped in swaddling clothes, lying in a manger.

John 1:1, 14 In the beginning was the Word, and the Word was with God, and the Word was God. . . .

And the Word was made flesh, and dwelt among us, (and we beheld his glory, the glory as of the only begotten of the Father,) full of grace and truth.

Book of Mormon

The Lord is no respecter of persons—he provided the same information to Lehi and his descendants.

1 Nephi 10:4 Yea, even six hundred years from the time that my father left Jerusalem, a prophet would the Lord God raise up among the Jews—even a Messiah, or, in other words, a Savior of the world.

1 Nephi 11:14–15, 18–21

And it came to pass that I saw the heavens open; and an angel came down and stood before me; and he said unto me: Nephi, what beholdest thou?

And I said unto him: A virgin, most beautiful and fair above all other virgins.

And he said unto me: Behold, the virgin whom thou seest is the mother of the Son of God, after the manner of the flesh.

And it came to pass that I beheld that she was carried away in the Spirit; and after she had been carried away in the Spirit for the space of a time the angel spake unto me, saying: Look!

And I looked and beheld the virgin again, bearing a child in her arms.

And the angel said unto me: Behold the Lamb of God, yea, even the Son of the Eternal Father!

2 Nephi 17:14	Therefore, the Lord himself shall give you a sign—Behold, a virgin shall conceive, and shall bear a son, and shall call his name Immanuel.
2 Nephi 19:6–7	For unto us a child is born, unto us a son is given; and the government shall be upon his shoulder; and his name shall be called, Wonderful, Counselor, The Mighty God, The Everlasting Father, The Prince of Peace. Of the increase of government and peace there is no end, upon the throne of David, and upon his kingdom to order it, and to establish it with judgment and with justice from henceforth, even forever.
2 Nephi 25:19	For according to the words of the prophets, the Messiah cometh in six hundred years from the time that my father left Jerusalem; and according to the words of the prophets, and also the word of the angel of God, his name shall be Jesus Christ, the Son of God.
2 Nephi 26:3	And after the Messiah shall come there shall be signs given unto my people of his birth.
Alma 7:9–10	But behold, the Spirit hath said this much unto me, saying: Cry unto this people, saying—Repent ye, and prepare the way of the Lord, and walk in his paths, which are straight; for behold, the kingdom of heaven is at hand, and the Son of God cometh upon the face of the earth. And behold, he shall be born of Mary, at Jerusalem which is the land of our forefathers, she being a virgin, a precious and chosen vessel, who shall be overshadowed and conceive by the power of the Holy Ghost, and bring forth a son, yea, even the Son of God.
Helaman 14:2–5	And behold, he [Samuel the Lamanite] said unto them: Behold, I give unto you a sign; for five years more cometh, and behold, then cometh the Son of God to

redeem all those who shall believe on his name.

And behold, this will I give unto you for a sign at the time of his coming; for behold, there shall be great lights in heaven, insomuch that in the night before he cometh there shall be no darkness, insomuch that it shall appear unto man as if it was day.

Therefore, there shall be one day and a night and a day, as if it were one day and there were no night; and this shall be unto you for a sign; for ye shall know of a surety that there shall be two days and a night; nevertheless the night shall not be darkened; and it shall be the night before he is born.

And behold, there shall a new star arise, such an one as ye never have beheld; and this also shall be a sign unto you.

3 Nephi 1:12–13, 19 And it came to pass that he [Nephi the son of Nephi the son of Helaman] cried mightily unto the Lord all that day; and behold, the voice of the Lord came unto him, saying:

Lift up your head and be of good cheer; for behold, the time is at hand, and on this night shall the sign be given, and on the morrow come I into the world, to show unto the world that I will fulfil all that which I have caused to be spoken by the mouth of my holy prophets.

And it came to pass that there was no darkness in all that night, but it was as light as though it was mid-day. And it came to pass that the sun did rise in the morning again according to its proper order; and they knew that it was the day that the Lord should be born, because of the sign which he had been given.

Doctrine and Covenants

Modern-day prophets have also acknowledged and recorded the birth of the Savior.

D&C 20:1 The rise of the Church of Christ in these last days, being one thousand eight hundred and thirty years since the coming of our Lord and Savior Jesus Christ in the flesh.

D&C 76:40–41 And this is the gospel, the glad tidings, which the voice out of the heavens bore record unto us—

That he came into the world, even Jesus.

D&C 93:3–4 And that I am in the Father, and the Father in me, and the Father and I are one—

The Father because he gave me of his fulness, and the Son because I was in the world and made flesh my tabernacle, and dwelt among the sons of men.

Pearl of Great Price

Moses 5:56–57, 59 And God cursed the earth with a sore curse, and was angry with the wicked, with all the sons of men whom he had made;

For they would not hearken unto his voice, nor believe on his Only Begotten Son, even him whom he declared should come in the meridian of time, who was prepared from before the foundation of the world. . . .

And thus all things were confirmed unto Adam, by an holy ordinance, and the Gospel preached, and a decree sent forth, that it should be in the world, until the end thereof; and thus it was. Amen.

Moses 6:57 Wherefore teach it unto our children, that all men, everywhere, must repent, or they can in nowise inherit the kingdom of God, for no unclean thing can dwell there, or dwell in his presence; for, in the language of Adam, Man of Holiness is his name, and the name of his Only Begotten is the Son of Man, even Jesus Christ, a righteous Judge, who shall come in the meridian of time.

(D) Christ's death was prophesied and foreshadowed

Just as Christ's birth was prophesied, so was his death. Prophets of the Old Testament sometimes spoke Messianically. Compare the words they wrote with events and words recorded in the New Testament (see New Testament entries).

Old Testament

Psalm 22:1	My God, my God, why hast thou forsaken me?
Psalm 22:16–18	For dogs have compassed me: the assembly of the wicked have inclosed me: they pierced my hands and my feet. I may tell all my bones: they look and stare upon me. They part my garments among them, and cast lots upon my vesture.
Psalm 69:21	They gave me also gall for my meat; and in my thirst they gave me vinegar to drink.
Proverbs 14:31–32	He that oppresseth the poor reproacheth his Maker: but he that honoureth him hath mercy on the poor. The wicked is driven away in his wickedness: but the righteous hath hope in his death.
Isaiah 25:8	He will swallow up death in victory; and the Lord God will wipe away tears from off all faces; and the rebuke of his people shall he take away from off all the earth: for the Lord hath spoken it.
Isaiah 53:3–12	He is despised and rejected of men; a man of sorrows, and acquainted with grief: and we hid as it were our faces from him; he was despised, and we esteemed him not. Surely he hath borne our griefs, and carried our sorrows: yet we did esteem him stricken, smitten of God, and afflicted. But he was wounded for our transgressions, he was bruised for our iniquities: the chastisement of our peace was upon him; and with his stripes we are healed. . . . And the Lord hath laid on him the iniquity of us all. He was oppressed, and he was afflicted, yet he

opened not his mouth: he is brought as a lamb to the slaughter, and as a sheep before her shearers is dumb, so he openeth not his mouth.

He was taken from prison and from judgment: and who shall declare his generation? for he was cut off out of the land of the living: for the transgression of my people was he stricken.

And he made his grave with the wicked, and with the rich in his death; because he had done no violence, neither was any deceit in his mouth.

Yet it pleased the Lord to bruise him; he hath put him to grief: when thou shalt make his soul an offering for sin, he shall see his seed, he shall prolong his days, and the pleasure of the Lord shall prosper in his hand.

He shall see of the travail of his soul, and shall be satisfied: by his knowledge shall my righteous servant justify many; for he shall bear their iniquities.

Therefore will I divide him a portion with the great, and he shall divide the spoil with the strong; because he hath poured out his soul unto death: and he was numbered with the transgressors; and he bare the sin of many, and made intercession for the transgressors.

Hosea 13:14 — I will ransom them from the power of the grave; I will redeem them from death: O death, I will be thy plagues; O grave, I will be thy destruction.

Zechariah 12:10 — And I will pour upon the house of David, and upon the inhabitants of Jerusalem, the spirit of grace and of supplications: and they shall look upon me whom they have pierced, and they shall mourn for him, as one mourneth for his only son, and shall be in bitterness for him, as one that is in bitterness for his firstborn.

Zechariah 13:6 — And one shall say unto him, What are these wounds in thine hands? Then he shall answer, Those with which I was wounded in the house of my friends.

New Testament

Christ testified of his own crucifixion.

Matthew 20:17–19 And Jesus going up to Jerusalem took the twelve disciples apart in the way, and said unto them,

Behold, we go up to Jerusalem; and the Son of man shall be betrayed unto the chief priests and unto the scribes, and they shall condemn him to death,

And shall deliver him to the Gentiles to mock, and to scourge, and to crucify him.

Matthew 26:2 Ye know that after two days is the feast of the passover, and the Son of man is betrayed to be crucified.

Matthew 27:34–35 They gave him vinegar to drink mingled with gall: and when he had tasted thereof, he would not drink.

And they crucified him, and parted his garments, casting lots: that it might be fulfilled which was spoken by the prophets, They parted my garments among them, and upon my vesture did they cast lots.

Matthew 27:46 And about the ninth hour Jesus cried with a loud voice, saying, Eli, Eli, Jama sabachthani? that is to say, My God, my God, why hast thou forsaken me?

Mark 8:31 And he began to teach them, that the Son of man must suffer many things, and be rejected of the elders, and of the chief priests, and scribes, and be killed.

Mark 15:24, 36 And when they had crucified him, they parted his garments, casting lots upon them, what every man should take. . . .

And one ran and filled a spunge full of vinegar, and put it on a reed, and gave him to drink.

Luke 23:33–34, 36 And when they were come to the place, which is called Calvary, there they crucified him, and the malefactors, one on the right hand, and the other on the left.

And they parted his raiment, and cast lots.
And the soldier also mocked him, coming to him, and offering him vinegar.

Luke 23:52–53 This man [Joseph of Arimathæa] went unto Pilate, and begged the body of Jesus.
And he took it down, and wrapped it in linen, and laid it in a sepulchre that was hewn in stone, wherein never man before was laid.

John 19:24, 29 They said therefore among themselves, Let us not rend it, but cast lots for it, whose it shall be: that the scripture might be fulfilled which saith, They parted my raiment among them, and for my vesture they did cast lots. These things therefore the soldiers did.
Now there was set a vessel full of vinegar: and they filled a spunge with vinegar, and put it upon hyssop, and put it to his mouth.

Romans 5:6, 8 For when we were yet without strength, in due time Christ died for the ungodly.
But God commendeth his love toward us, in that, while we were yet sinners, Christ died for us.

1 Corinthians 15:3–4
For I delivered unto you first of all that which I also received, how that Christ died for our sins according to the scriptures;
And that he was buried, and that he rose again the third day according to the scriptures.

Book of Mormon

Six hundred years before the birth of Christ, Lehi and his posterity not only had been instructed regarding the birth of the Savior, but they also had received revelation regarding his eventual death and crucifixion.

1 Nephi 10:11 And it came to pass after my father had spoken these words he spake unto my brethren concerning the gospel which should be preached among the Jews. . . . And after they had slain the Messiah, who

should come, and after he had been slain he should rise from the dead.

1 Nephi 19:10 — And the God of our fathers, who were led out of Egypt, out of bondage, and also were preserved in the wilderness by him, yea, the God of Abraham, and of Isaac, and the God of Jacob, yieldeth himself, according to the words of the angel, as a man, into the hands of wicked men, to be lifted up, according to the words of Zenock, and to be crucified, according to the words of Neum, and to be buried in a sepulchre, according to the words of Zenos, which he spake concerning the three days of darkness, which should be a sign given of the death unto those who should inhabit the isles of the sea, more especially given unto those who are of the house of Israel.

2 Nephi 10:3, 5 — Wherefore, as I said unto you, it must needs be expedient that Christ . . . should come among the Jews . . . and they shall crucify him. . . .

But because of priestcrafts and iniquities, they at Jerusalem will stiffen their necks against him, that he be crucified.

They had the writings of Isaiah wherein he referred to Christ's death.

Mosiah 14:4–9 — Surely he has borne our griefs, and carried our sorrows; yet we did esteem him stricken, smitten of God, and afflicted.

But he was wounded for our transgressions, he was bruised for our iniquities; the chastisement of our peace was upon him; and with his stripes we are healed. . . .

And the Lord hath laid on him the iniquities of us all.

He was oppressed, and he was afflicted, yet he opened not his mouth; he is brought as a lamb to the slaughter, and as a sheep before her shearers is dumb so he opened not his mouth.

He was taken from prison and from judgment;

	and who shall declare his generation? For he was cut off out of the land of the living; for the transgressions of my people was he stricken. And he made his grave with the wicked, and with the rich in his death; because he had done no evil, neither was any deceit in his mouth.
Alma 7:11–12	And he shall go forth, suffering pains and afflictions and temptations of every kind; and this that the word might be fulfilled which saith he will take upon him the pains and the sicknesses of his people. And he will take upon him death, that he may loose the bands of death which bind his people.
3 Nephi 6:20	And they did testify boldly of his [Jesus Christ's] death and sufferings.

Doctrine and Covenants

Christ appeared to modern-day prophets and declared his own death and resurrection.

D&C 6:2, 37	Behold, I am God; give heed unto my word. . . . Behold the wounds which pierced my side, and also the prints of the nails in my hands and feet.
D&C 20:23	He was crucified, died, and rose again the third day.
D&C 35:2	I am Jesus Christ, the Son of God, who was crucified for the sins of the world.
D&C 138:35	And so it was made known among the dead, both small and great, the unrighteous as well as the faithful, that redemption had been wrought through the sacrifice of the Son of God upon the cross.

(E) Christ's Second Coming was also prophesied

The plan for man's salvation was laid out from the beginning of creation: the Fall of Adam; Christ's birth and his atonement for us; his death and resurrection; and his coming again in the latter days in glory to rule and reign upon the earth. The Second Coming of the Savior was prophesied by both ancient and modern prophets just as the other aspects of the plan of salvation were.

Old Testament

Job 19:25	For I know that my redeemer liveth, and that he shall stand at the latter day upon the earth.
Psalm 24:7	Lift up your heads, O ye gates; and be ye lift up, ye everlasting doors; and the King of glory shall come in.
Isaiah 40:5	And the glory of the Lord shall be revealed, and all flesh shall see it together: for the mouth of the Lord hath spoken it.
Isaiah 45:23	I have sworn by myself, the word is gone out of my mouth in righteousness, and shall not return, That unto me every knee shall bow, every tongue shall swear.
Isaiah 52:10	The Lord hath made bare his holy arm in the eyes of all the nations; and all the ends of the earth shall see the salvation of our God.
Daniel 7:13–14	I saw in the night visions, and, behold, one like the Son of man came with the clouds of heaven, and came to the Ancient of days, and they brought him near before him. And there was given him dominion, and glory, and a kingdom, that all people, nations, and languages, should serve him: his dominion is an everlasting dominion, which shall not pass away, and his kingdom that which shall not be destroyed.
Micah 1:3	For, behold, the Lord cometh forth out of his place, and will come down, and tread upon the high places of the earth. And the mountains shall be molten under him, and the valleys shall be cleft, as wax before the fire, and as the waters that are poured down a steep place.
Zechariah 12:9–10	And it shall come to pass in that day, that I will

seek to destroy all the nations that come against Jerusalem.

And I will pour upon the house of David, and upon the inhabitants of Jerusalem, the spirit of grace and of supplications: and they shall look upon me whom they have pierced, and they shall mourn for him, as one mourneth for his only son, and shall be in bitterness for him, as one that is in bitterness for his firstborn.

Zechariah 13:6 And one shall say unto him, What are these wounds in thine hands? Then he shall answer, Those with which I was wounded in the house of my friends.

Zechariah 14:4–7, 9 And his feet shall stand in that day upon the mount of Olives, which is before Jerusalem on the east, and the mount of Olives shall cleave in the midst thereof toward the east and toward the west, and there shall be a very great valley; and half of the mountain shall remove toward the north, and half of it toward the south. . . .

And the Lord my God shall come, and all the saints with thee.

And it shall come to pass in that day, that the light shall not be clear, nor dark:

But it shall be one day which shall be known to the Lord, not day, not night: but it shall come to pass, that at evening time it shall be light. . . .

And the Lord shall be king over all the earth: in that day shall there be one Lord, and his name one.

Malachi 3:2–3 But who may abide the day of his coming? and who shall stand when he appeareth? for he is like a refiner's fire, and like fullers' soap;

And he shall sit as a refiner and purifier of silver: and he shall purify the sons of Levi, and purge them as gold and silver, that they may offer unto the Lord an offering in righteousness.

New Testament

Matthew 16:27	For the Son of man shall come in the glory of his Father with his angels; and then he shall reward every man according to his works.
Matthew 24:27	For as the lightning cometh out of the east, and shineth even unto the west; so shall also the coming of the Son of man be.
Matthew 25:31–33	When the Son of man shall come in his glory, and all the holy angels with him, then shall he sit upon the throne of his glory: And before him shall be gathered all nations: and he shall separate them one from another, as a shepherd divideth his sheep from the goats: And he shall set the sheep on his right hand, but the goats on the left.
Matthew 26:64	Jesus saith unto him, Thou hast said: nevertheless I say unto you, Hereafter shall ye see the Son of man sitting on the right hand of power, and coming in the clouds of heaven.
Luke 21:25–27	And there shall be signs in the sun, and in the moon, and in the stars; and upon the earth distress of nations, with perplexity; the sea and the waves roaring; Men's hearts failing them for fear, and for looking after those things which are coming on the earth: for the powers of heaven shall be shaken. And then shall they see the Son of man coming in a cloud with power and great glory.
Acts 1:10–11	And while they looked stedfastly toward heaven as he went up, behold, two men stood by them in white apparel; Which also said, Ye men of Galilee, why stand ye gazing up into heaven? this same Jesus, which is taken up from you into heaven, shall so come in like manner as ye have seen him go into heaven.

Acts 3:20–21	And he shall send Jesus Christ, which before was preached unto you: Whom the heaven must receive until the times of restitution of all things, which God hath spoken by the mouth of all his holy prophets since the world began.
JST, 1 Thessalonians 4:16–17	For the Lord himself shall descend from heaven with a shout, with the voice of the archangel, and with the trump of God: and the dead in Christ shall rise first: Then they who are alive, shall be caught up together into the clouds with them who remain, to meet the Lord in the air; and so shall we ever be with the Lord.
2 Thessalonians 1:7	And to you who are troubled rest with us, when the Lord Jesus shall be revealed from heaven with his mighty angels,
2 Peter 3:10	But the day of the Lord will come as a thief in the night; in the which the heavens shall pass away with a great noise, and the elements shall melt with fervent heat, the earth also and the works that are therein shall be burned up.
Jude 1:14–15	And Enoch also, the seventh from Adam, prophesied of these, saying, Behold, the Lord cometh with ten thousands of his saints, To execute judgment upon all, and to convince all that are ungodly among them of all their ungodly deeds which they have ungodly committed, and of all their hard speeches which ungodly sinners have spoken against him.
Revelation 1:7	Behold, he cometh with clouds; and every eye shall see him, and they also which pierce him: and all kindreds of the earth shall wail because of him. Even so, Amen.

Revelation 3:11	Behold, I come quickly; hold that fast which thou hast, that no man take thy crown.

Book of Mormon

1 Nephi 21:11	And I will make all my mountains a way, and my highways shall be exalted.
3 Nephi 24:2–3	But who may abide the day of his coming, and who shall stand when he appeareth? For he is like a refiner's fire, and like fuller's soap. And he shall sit as a refiner and purifier of silver; and he shall purify the sons of Levi, and purge them as gold and silver, that they may offer unto the Lord an offering in righteousness.

Jesus told the Nephites that the day would come when he would return to earth to judge the world.

3 Nephi 27:16	And it shall come to pass, that whoso repenteth and is baptized in my name shall be filled; and if he endureth to the end, behold, him will I hold guiltless before my Father at that day when I shall stand to judge the world.

Doctrine and Covenants

Modern-day prophets have received the same warnings.

D&C 1:12	Prepare ye, prepare ye for that which is to come, for the Lord is nigh;
D&C 29:10–12	For the hour is nigh, and that which was spoken by mine apostle must be fulfilled; for as they spoke so shall it come to pass; For I will reveal myself from heaven with power and great glory, with all the hosts thereof, and dwell in righteousness with men on earth a thousand years, and the wicked shall not stand. And again, verily, verily, I say unto you, and it hath gone forth in a firm decree, by the will of the Father, that mine apostles, the Twelve which were with me in my ministry at Jerusalem, shall stand at

my right hand at the day of my coming in a pillar of fire, being clothed with robes of righteousness, with crowns upon their heads, in glory even as I am, to judge the whole house of Israel, even as many as have loved me and kept my commandments, and none else.

D&C 33:18 — For behold, verily, verily, I say unto you, that I come quickly.

D&C 36:8 — I am Jesus Christ, the Son of God; wherefore, gird up your loins and I will suddenly come to my temple.

D&C 38:8 — But the day soon cometh that ye shall see me, and know that I am; for the veil of darkness shall soon be rent, and he that is not purified shall not abide the day.

D&C 41:4 — And I will be your ruler when I come; and behold, I come quickly, and ye shall see that my law is kept.

D&C 43:29 — For in mine own due time will I come upon the earth in judgment, and my people shall be redeemed and shall reign with me on earth.

D&C 45:48–52 — And then shall the Lord set his foot upon this mount, and it shall cleave in twain, and the earth shall tremble, and reel to and fro, and the heavens also shall shake.

And the Lord shall utter his voice, and all the ends of the earth shall hear it; and the nations of the earth shall mourn, and they that have laughed shall see their folly.

And calamity shall cover the mocker, and the scorner shall be consumed; and they that have watched for iniquity shall be hewn down and cast into the fire.

And then shall the Jews look upon me and say: What are these wounds in thine hands and in thy feet?

Then shall they know that I am the Lord; for I

will say unto them: These wounds are the wounds with which I was wounded in the house of my friends. I am he who was lifted up. I am Jesus that was crucified. I am the Son of God.

D&C 49 6–7 — And they have done unto the Son of Man even as they listed; and he has taken his power on the right hand of his glory, and now reigneth in the heavens, and will reign till he descends on the earth to put all enemies under his feet, which time is nigh at hand—

I, the Lord God, have spoken it; but the hour and the day no man knoweth, neither the angels in heaven, nor shall they know until he comes.

D&C 54:10 — And again, be patient in tribulation until I come; and, behold, I come quickly.

D&C 63:34–35 — And the saints also shall hardly escape; nevertheless, I, the Lord, am with them, and will come down in heaven from the presence of my Father and consume the wicked with unquenchable fire.

And, behold, this is not yet, but by and by.

D&C 76:63 — These are they whom he shall bring with him, when he shall come in the clouds of heaven to reign on the earth over his people.

D&C 88:104 — And this shall be the sound of his trump, saying to all people, both in heaven and in earth, and that are under the earth—for every ear shall hear it, and every knee shall bow, and every tongue shall confess, while they hear the sound of the trump, saying: Fear God, and give glory to him who sitteth upon the throne, forever and ever; for the hour of his judgment is come.

D&C 110:16 — Therefore, the keys of this dispensation are committed into your hands; and by this ye may know that the great and dreadful day of the Lord is near, even at the doors.

D&C 128:24	Behold, the great day of the Lord is at hand; and who can abide the day of his coming, and who can stand when he appeareth? For he is like a refiner's fire, and like fuller's soap; and he shall sit as a refiner and purifier of silver, and he shall purify the sons of Levi, and purge them as gold and silver, that they may offer unto the Lord an offering in righteousness.
D&C 130:1	When the Savior shall appear we shall see him as he is. We shall see that he is a man like ourselves.
D&C 133:2, 20, 25	The Lord who shall suddenly come to his temple; the Lord who shall come down upon the world with a curse to judgment; yea, upon the nations that forget God, and upon all the ungodly among you. For he shall make bare his holy arm in the eyes of all the nations, and all the ends of the earth shall see the salvation of their God. For behold, he shall stand upon the mount of Olivet, and upon the mighty ocean, even the great deep, and upon the islands of the sea, and upon the land of Zion. And the Lord, even the Savior, shall stand in the midst of his people, and shall reign over all flesh.

Chapter 6

Death and Resurrection

TENET: There are two different kinds of death: physical death and spiritual death. When Adam and Eve were first created and placed in the Garden of Eden, they were not subject to death. God commanded them not to partake of the fruit of the tree of knowledge and told them that if they did, they would surely die. In other words, they would become subject to the laws of mortality and would eventually suffer physical death. They also became separated from Heavenly Father, thus suffering spiritual death. The offspring of Adam and Eve are all subject to the laws of mortality and will suffer physical death. Because we are cut off from the presence of our Heavenly Father, we also experience spiritual death. Both of these deaths are rectified by the atonement, death, and resurrection of the Savior: all mankind will be resurrected and overcome physical death and all mankind can, through repentance, be reunited with our Heavenly Father and thus overcome spiritual death. Following the judgment, those who refuse to repent, even after suffering the Lord's wrath, will experience a second death as they will be forever cut off from the presence of the Lord and will not be redeemed.

(A) Death

Old Testament

Genesis 2:16–17 And the Lord God commanded the man, saying, Of every tree of the garden thou mayest freely eat:

But of the tree of the knowledge of good and

	evil, thou shalt not eat of it: for in the day that thou eatest thereof thou shalt surely die.
Genesis 3:2–3	And the woman said unto the serpent, We may eat of the fruit of the trees of the garden: But of the fruit of the tree which is in the midst of the garden, God hath said, Ye shall not eat of it, neither shall ye touch it, lest ye die.

Death was ushered in, as the Lord said it would, when Adam partook of the forbidden fruit.

Job 34:15	All flesh shall perish together, and man shall turn again unto dust.
Psalm 37:9	For evildoers shall be cut off.
Proverbs 14:32	The wicked is driven away in his wickedness [from his Maker]: but the righteous hath hope in his death.
Ecclesiastes 12:7	Then shall the dust return to the earth as it was: and the spirit shall return unto God who gave it.
Jeremiah 31:30	But every one shall die for his own iniquity.

New Testament

When Adam and Eve became mortal, their mortal, carnal natures became subject to temptations and sin and the consequences of sin (physical and spiritual death), as did all of their posterity.

Romans 5:12, 14	Wherefore, as by one man sin entered into the world, and death by sin; and so death passed upon all men, for that all have sinned. . . . Nevertheless death reigned from Adam to Moses, even over them that had not sinned after the similitude of Adam's transgression, who is the figure of him that was to come.
Romans 6:23	For the wages of sin is death.
Romans 8:6	For to be carnally minded is death.
Hebrews 9:27	And as it is appointed unto men once to die, but after this the judgment.

Revelation 2:11	He that hath an ear, let him hear what the Spirit saith unto the churches; He that overcometh shall not be hurt of the second death.

Book of Mormon

Alma, the son of Alma, instructed his son Corianton regarding death.

Alma 42:6–13

But behold, it was appointed unto man to die—therefore, as they were cut off from the tree of life they should be cut off from the face of the earth—and man became lost forever, yea, they became fallen man.

And now ye see by this that our first parents were cut off both temporally and spiritually from the presence of the Lord; and thus we see they became subjects to follow after their own will.

Now behold, it was not expedient that man should be reclaimed from this temporal death, for that would destroy the great plan of happiness.

Therefore, as the soul could never die, and the fall had brought upon all mankind a spiritual death as well as a temporal, that is, they were cut off from the presence of the Lord, it was expedient that mankind should be reclaimed from this spiritual death.

Therefore, as they had become carnal, sensual, and devilish, by nature, this probationary state became a state for them to prepare; it became a preparatory state.

And now remember, my son, if it were not for the plan of redemption, (laying it aside) as soon as they were dead their souls were miserable, being cut off from the presence of the Lord.

And now, there was no means to reclaim men from this fallen state, which man had brought upon himself because of his own disobedience;

Therefore, according to justice, the plan of redemption could not be brought about, only on conditions of repentance of men in this probationary state, yea, this preparatory state; for except it were for these conditions, mercy could not take effect except it should destroy the work of justice. Now the work of justice could not be destroyed; if so, God would cease to be God.

Samuel the Lamanite also taught the people regarding physical (temporal) and spiritual death.

Helaman 14:16 Yea, behold, this [Christ's] death bringeth to pass the resurrection, and redeemeth all mankind from the first death—that spiritual death; for all mankind, by the fall of Adam being cut off from the presence of the Lord, are considered as dead, both as to things temporal and to things spiritual.

Doctrine and Covenants

Revelations contained in the Doctrine and Covenant are consistent with the teachings of the Bible (the stick of Judah) and the Book of Mormon (the stick of Joseph).

D&C 29:41, 43–44 Wherefore, I, the Lord God, caused that he [Adam] should be cast out from the Garden of Eden, from my presence, because of his transgression, wherein he became spiritually dead, which is the first death, even that same death which is the last death, which is spiritual, which shall be pronounced upon the wicked when I shall say: Depart, ye cursed. . . .

And thus did I, the Lord God, appoint unto man the days of his probation—that by his natural death he might be raised in immortality unto eternal life, even as many as would believe;

And they that believe not unto eternal damnation; for they cannot be redeemed from their spiritual fall, because they repent not.

Pearl of Great Price

The same message is revealed in the Pearl of Great Price.

Moses 3:16–17 And I, the Lord God, commanded the man, saying: Of every tree of the garden thou mayest freely eat,

But of the tree of the knowledge of good and

evil, thou shalt not eat of it, nevertheless, thou mayest choose for thyself, for it is given unto thee; but, remember that I forbid it, for in the day thou eatest thereof thou shalt surely die.

Moses 6:48–49 — And he said unto them: Because that Adam fell, we are; and by his fall came death; and we are made partakers of misery and woe.

Behold Satan hath come among the children of men, and tempteth them to worship him; and men have become carnal, sensual, and devilish, and are shut out from the presence of God.

Moses 6:58–59 — Therefore I give unto you a commandment, to teach these things freely unto your children, saying:

That by reason of transgression cometh the fall, which fall bringeth death.

(B) Resurrection

1. All shall be resurrected

The scriptures tell us that everyone—the righteous and the wicked, the young and the old, the male and the female—will be resurrected.

Old Testament

Isaiah 25:8 — He will swallow up death in victory: and the Lord God will wipe away tears from off all faces; and the rebuke of his people shall he take away from off all the earth: for the Lord hath spoken it.

Isaiah 26:19 — Thy dead men shall live, together with my dead body shall they arise. Awake and sing, ye that dwell in dust: for thy dew is as the dew of herbs, and the earth shall cast out her dead.

Ezekiel 37:12 — Therefore prophesy and say unto them, Thus saith the Lord God; Behold, O my people, I will open your graves, and cause you to come up out of your graves, and bring you into the land of Israel.

Daniel 12:1–2 — And at that time thy people shall be delivered, every

	one that shall be found written in the book. And many of them that sleep in the dust of the earth shall awake, some to everlasting life, and some to shame and everlasting contempt.
Hosea 13:14	I will ransom them from the power of the grave; I will redeem them from death: O death, I will be thy plagues; O grave, I will be thy destruction.

New Testament

John 5:28–29	Marvel not at this: for the hour is coming, in the which all that are in the graves shall hear his voice, And shall come forth; they that have done good, unto the resurrection of life; and they that have done evil, unto the resurrection of damnation.
Acts 24:14–15	But this I confess unto thee, that after the way which they call heresy, so worship I the God of my fathers, believing all things which are written in the law and in the prophets: And have hope toward God, which they themselves also allow, that there shall be a resurrection of the dead, both of the just and the unjust.
Romans 5:10–11	For if, when we were enemies, we were reconciled to God by the death of his Son, much more, being reconciled, we shall be saved by his life. And not only so, but we also joy in God through our Lord Jesus Christ, by whom we have now received the atonement.
1 Corinthians 6:14	And God hath both raised up the Lord, and will also raise up us by his own power.
1 Corinthians 15:21–22	For since by man came death, by man came also the resurrection of the dead. For as in Adam all die, even so in Christ shall all be made alive.
1 Corinthians 15:52	In a moment, in the twinkling of an eye, at the

last trump: for the trumpet shall sound, and the dead shall be raised incorruptible, and we shall be changed.

Revelation 20:13 — And the sea gave up the dead which were in it; and death and hell delivered up the dead which were in them: and they were judged every man according to their works.

Book of Mormon

2 Nephi 9:11–12 — And because of the way of deliverance of our God, the Holy One of Israel, this death, of which I have spoken, which is the temporal, shall deliver up its dead; which death is the grave.

And this death of which I have spoken, which is the spiritual death, shall deliver up its dead; which spiritual death is hell; wherefore, death and hell must deliver up their dead, and hell must deliver up its captive spirits, and the grave must deliver up its captive bodies, and the bodies and the spirits of men will be restored one to the other; and it is by the power of the resurrection of the Holy One of Israel.

Mosiah 16: 6–8 — And now if Christ had not come into the world, speaking of things to come as though they had already come, there could have been no redemption.

And if Christ had not risen from the dead, or have broken the bands of death that the grave should have no victory, and that death should have no sting, there could have been no resurrection.

But there is a resurrection, therefore the grave hath no victory, and the sting of death is swallowed up in Christ.

Alma 11:41–43 — For behold, the day cometh that all shall rise from the dead and stand before God, and be judged according to their works.

Now, there is a death which is called a temporal death; and the death of Christ shall loose the bands of this temporal death, that all shall be raised from this temporal death.

The spirit and the body shall be reunited again in its perfect form; both limb and joint shall be restored to its proper frame, even as we now are at this time; and we shall be brought to stand before God, knowing even as we know now, and have a bright recollection of all our guilt.

Alma 40:1–5

Now my son, here is somewhat more I would say unto thee; for I perceive that thy mind is worried concerning the resurrection of the dead.

Behold, I say unto you, that there is no resurrection—or, I would say, in other words, that this mortal does not put on immortality, this corruption does not put on incorruption—until after the coming of Christ.

Behold, he bringeth to pass the resurrection of the dead. But behold, my son, the resurrection is not yet. Now, I unfold unto you a mystery; nevertheless, there are many mysteries which are kept, that no one knoweth them save God himself. But I show unto you one thing which I have inquired diligently of God that I might know—that is concerning the resurrection.

Behold, there is a time appointed that all shall come forth from the dead. Now when this time cometh no one knows; but God knoweth the time which is appointed.

Now, whether there shall be one time, or a second time, or a third time, that men shall come forth from the dead, it mattereth not; for God knoweth all these things; and it sufficeth me to know that this is the case—that there is a time appointed that all shall rise from the dead.

Mormon 9:12–13

Behold, he created Adam, and by Adam came the fall of man. And because of the fall of man came Jesus Christ, even the Father and the Son; and because of

Jesus Christ came the redemption of man.

And because of the redemption of man, which came by Jesus Christ, they are brought back into the presence of the Lord; yea, this is wherein all men are redeemed, because the death of Christ bringeth to pass the resurrection, which bringeth to pass a redemption from an endless sleep, from which sleep all men shall be awakened by the power of God when the trump shall sound; and they shall come forth, both small and great, and all shall stand before his bar, being redeemed and loosed from this eternal band of death, which death is a temporal death.

Doctrine and Covenants

D&C 29:26–28 But, behold, verily I say unto you, before the earth shall pass away, Michael, mine archangel, shall sound his trump, and then shall all the dead awake, for their graves shall be opened, and they shall come forth—yea, even all.

And the righteous shall be gathered on my right hand unto eternal life; and the wicked on my left hand will I be ashamed to own before the Father;

Wherefore I will say unto them—Depart from me, ye cursed, into everlasting fire, prepared for the devil and his angels.

D&C 29:43–44 And thus did I, the Lord God, appoint unto man the days of his probation—that by his natural death he might be raised in immortality unto eternal life, even as many as would believe;

And they that believe not unto eternal damnation; for they cannot be redeemed from their spiritual fall, because they repent not.

D&C 63:49–52 Yea, and blessed are the dead that die in the Lord, from henceforth, when the Lord shall come, and old things shall pass away, and all things become new, they shall rise from the dead and shall not die after, and shall receive an inheritance before the Lord, in the holy city.

And he that liveth when the Lord shall come, and hath kept the faith, blessed is he; nevertheless, it is appointed to him to die at the age of man.

Wherefore, children shall grow up until they become old; old men shall die; but they shall not sleep in the dust, but they shall be changed in the twinkling of an eye.

Wherefore, for this cause preached the apostles unto the world the resurrection of the dead.

D&C 76:15–17 For while we were doing the work of translation, which the Lord had appointed unto us, we came to the twenty-ninth verse of the fifth chapter of John, which was given unto us as follows—

Speaking of the resurrection of the dead, concerning those who shall hear the voice of the Son of Man:

And shall come forth; they who have done good, in the resurrection of the just; and they who have done evil, in the resurrection of the unjust.

Pearl of Great Price

Moses 1:39 For behold, this is my work and my glory—to bring to pass the immortality and eternal life of man.

Moses 5:9, 15 And in that day the Holy Ghost fell upon Adam, which beareth record of the Father and the Son, saying: I am the Only Begotten of the Father from the beginning, henceforth and forever, that as thou hast fallen thou mayest be redeemed, and all mankind, even as many as will.

And as many as believed in the Son, and repented of their sins, should be saved; and as many as believed not and repented not, should be damned; and the words went forth out of the mouth of God in a firm decree; wherefore they must be fulfilled.

Moses 7:62 And righteousness will I send down out of heaven;

and truth will I send forth out of the earth, to bear testimony of mine Only Begotten; his resurrection from the dead; yea, and also the resurrection of all men.

2. First resurrection: the resurrection of the just

The righteous will come forth in the first resurrection. Those who are resurrected with celestial bodies "will come forth in the morning of the first resurrection" and will "be caught up to meet the Lord" when he comes the second time; those who are resurrected with terrestrial bodies will come forth in the afternoon of the first resurrection, "after our Lord has ushered in the millennium."[1]

New Testament

Matthew 27:52–53 And the graves were opened; and many bodies of the saints which slept arose,

And came out of the graves after his resurrection, and went into the holy city, and appeared unto many.

Luke 14:13–14 But when thou makest a feast, call the poor, the maimed, the lame, the blind:

And thou shalt be blessed; for they cannot recompense thee: for thou shalt be recompensed at the resurrection of the just.

John 6:54 Whoso eateth my flesh, and drinketh my blood, hath eternal life; and I will raise him up at the last day.

1 Corinthians 15:22–23

For as in Adam all die, even so in Christ shall all be made alive.

But every man in his own order: Christ the firstfruits; afterward they that are Christ's at his coming.

1 Thessalonians 4:16–17

For the Lord himself shall descend from heaven with a shout, with the voice of the archangel, and with the trump of God; and the dead in Christ shall rise first:

Then we which are alive and remain shall be caught up together with them in the clouds, to meet the Lord in the air: and so shall we ever be with the Lord.

Revelation 20:4–6 And I saw thrones, and they sat upon them, and judgment was given unto them: and I saw the souls of them that were beheaded for the witness of Jesus, and for the word of God, and which had not worshipped the beast, neither his image, neither had received his mark upon their foreheads, or in their hands; and they lived and reigned with Christ a thousand years.

But the rest of the dead lived not again until the thousand years were finished. This is the first resurrection.

Blessed and holy is he that hath part in the first resurrection: on such the second death hath no power, but they shall be priests of God and of Christ, and shall reign with him a thousand years.

Book of Mormon

Mosiah 15:20–25 But behold, the bands of death shall be broken, and the Son reigneth, and hath power over the dead; therefore, he bringeth to pass the resurrection of the dead.

And there cometh a resurrection, even a first resurrection; yea, even a resurrection of those that have been, and who are, and who shall be, even until the resurrection of Christ—for so shall he be called.

And now, the resurrection of all the prophets, and all those that have believed in their words, or all those that have kept the commandments of God, shall come forth in the first resurrection; therefore, they are the first resurrection.

They are raised to dwell with God who had redeemed them; thus they have eternal life through Christ, who has broken the bands of death.

And these are those who have part in the first

resurrection; and these are they that have died before Christ came, in their ignorance, not having salvation declared unto them. And thus the Lord bringeth about the restoration of these; and they have a part in the first resurrection, or have eternal life, being redeemed by the Lord.

And little children also have eternal life.

Helaman 14:25 — And many graves shall be opened, and shall yield up many of their dead; and many saints shall appear unto many.

3 Nephi 23:9–13 — Verily I say unto you, I commanded my servant Samuel, the Lamanite, that he should testify unto this people, that at the day that the Father should glorify his name in me that there were many saints who should arise from the dead, and should appear unto many, and should minister unto them. And he said unto them: Was it not so?

And his disciples answered him and said: Yea, Lord, Samuel did prophesy according to thy words, and they were all fulfilled.

And Jesus said unto them: How be it that ye have not written this thing, that many saints did arise and appear unto many and did minister unto them?

And it came to pass that Nephi remembered that this thing had not been written.

And it came to pass that Jesus commanded that it should be written; therefore it was written according as he commanded.

Doctrine and Covenants

D&C 45:54 — And then shall the heathen nations be redeemed, and they that knew no law shall have part in the first resurrection; and it shall be tolerable for them.

D&C 63:49–52 — Yea, and blessed are the dead that die in the Lord, from henceforth, when the Lord shall come, and old things shall pass away, and all things become new, they shall rise from the dead and shall not die after, and shall receive an inheritance before the Lord, in the holy city.

And he that liveth when the Lord shall come, and hath kept the faith, blessed is he; nevertheless, it is appointed to him to die at the age of man.

Wherefore, children shall grow up until they become old; old men shall die; but they shall not sleep in the dust, but they shall be changed in the twinkling of an eye.

Wherefore, for this cause preached the apostles unto the world the resurrection of the dead.

D&C 76:50–51 (vs. 52–63 summarized), 64–65, 70

And again we bear record—for we saw and heard, and this is the testimony of the gospel of Christ concerning them who shall come forth in the resurrection of the just—

They are they who received the testimony of Jesus, and believed on his name and were baptized after the manner of his burial, being buried in the water in his name, and this according to the commandment which he has given—

They kept the commandments and "are sealed by the Holy Spirit of promise." They are "they who are the church of the Firstborn." The Father has given them all things. They are "priest and kings" who have received of his fulness and glory; "priests of the Most High, after the order of Melchizedek. . . . They are gods, even the sons of God—wherefore, all things are theirs. . . . They shall overcome all things" and "glory in God." They will "dwell in the presence of God and his Christ forever and ever." Christ will bring them with him in "the clouds of heaven to reign on the earth over his people."

These are they who shall have part in the first resurrection.

These are they who shall come forth in the resurrection of the just. . . .

These are they whose bodies are celestial, whose

glory is that of the sun, even the glory of God, the highest of all, whose glory the sun of the firmament is written of as being typical.

D&C 76:71–77

And again, we saw the terrestrial world, and behold and lo, these are they who are of the terrestrial, whose glory differs from that of the church of the Firstborn who have received the fulness of the Father, even as that of the moon differs from the sun in the firmament.

Behold, these are they who died without law;

And also they who are the spirits of men kept in prison, whom the Son visited, and preached the gospel unto them, that they might be judged according to men in the flesh;

Who received not the testimony of Jesus in the flesh, but afterwards received it.

These are they who are honorable men of the earth, who were blinded by the craftiness of men.

These are they who receive of his glory, but not of his fulness.

These are they who receive of the presence of the Son, but not of the fulness of the Father.

D&C 88:96–99

And the saints that are upon the earth, who are alive, shall be quickened and be caught up to meet him.

And they who have slept in their graves shall come forth, for their graves shall be opened; and they also shall be caught up to meet him in the midst of the pillar of heaven—

They are Christ's, the first fruits, they who shall descend with him first, and they who are on the earth and in their graves, who are first caught up to meet him; and all this by the voice of the sounding of the trump of the angel of God.

And after this another angel shall sound, which is the second trump; and then cometh the redemption of those who are Christ's at his coming; who have received their part in that prison which is prepared for them, that they might receive the gospel, and be judged according to men in the flesh.

D&C 132:19 — And again, verily I say unto you, if a man marry a wife by my word, which is my law, and by the new and everlasting covenant, and it is sealed unto them by the Holy Spirit of promise, by him who is anointed, unto whom I have appointed this power and the keys of this priesthood; and it shall be said unto them—Ye shall come forth in the first resurrection; and if it be after the first resurrection, in the next resurrection.

D&C 133:56 — And the graves of the saints shall be opened; and they shall come forth and stand on the right hand of the Lamb, when he shall stand upon Mount Zion, and upon the holy city, the New Jerusalem; and they shall sing the song of the Lamb, day and night forever and ever.

3. The second resurrection

Following Christ's thousand years of millennial reign, the wicked will come forth later in a second resurrection.

Book of Mormon

Mosiah 15:26 — But behold, and fear, and tremble before God, for ye ought to tremble; for the Lord redeemeth none such that rebel against him and die in their sins; yea, even all those that have perished in their sins ever since the world began, that have wilfully rebelled against God, that have known the commandments of God, and would not keep them; these are they that have no part in the first resurrection.

Doctrine and Covenants

D&C 76:81–88, 102

And again, we saw the glory of the telestial, which glory is that of the lesser, even as the glory of the stars differs from that of the glory of the moon in the firmament.

These are they who received not the gospel of Christ, neither the testimony of Jesus.

These are they who deny not the Holy Spirit.

These are they who are thrust down to hell.

These are they who shall not be redeemed from the devil until the last resurrection, until the Lord, even Christ the Lamb, shall have finished his work.

These are they who receive not of his fulness in the eternal world, but of the Holy Spirit through the ministration of the terrestrial;

And the terrestrial through the ministration of the celestial.

And also the telestial receive it of the administering of angels who are appointed to minister for them, or who are appointed to be ministering spirits for them; for they shall be heirs of salvation. . . .

These are they who are liars, and sorcerers, and adulterers, and whoremongers, and whosoever loves and makes a lie.

D&C 88:100–101 And again, another trump shall sound, which is the third trump; and then come the spirits of men who are to be judged, and are found under condemnation;

And these are the rest of the dead; and they live not again until the thousand years are ended, neither again, until the end of the earth.

4. Sons of perdition

Those who know that Jesus is the Christ and have a testimony of it through the Holy Spirit and then deny Christ will receive no reward of glory but will become sons of perdition. For them, it will be as though no redemption had been made, other than that they will have resurrected bodies.

New Testament

John 17:12 While I was with them in the world, I kept them in thy name: those that thou gavest me I have kept, and none of them is lost, but the son of perdition; that the scripture might be fulfilled.

2 Thessalonians 2:3	Let no man deceive you by any means: for that day shall not come, except there come a falling away first, and that man of sin be revealed, the son of perdition.
1 Timothy 6:9	But they that will be rich fall into temptation and a snare, and into many foolish and hurtful lusts, which drown men in destruction and perdition.
Hebrews 10:39	But we are not of them who draw back unto perdition; but of them that believe to the saving of the soul.
2 Peter 3:7	But the heavens and the earth, which are now, by the same word are kept in store, reserved unto fire against the day of judgment and perdition of ungodly men.
Jude 1:6	And the angels which kept not their first estate, but left their own habitation [those spirits who were cast out of heaven with Satan in the premortal life], he hath reserved in everlasting chains under darkness unto the judgment of the great day.
Revelation 12:4	And his tail drew the third part of the stars of heaven [the angels which kept not their first estate], and did cast them to the earth.
Revelation 17:8	The beast that thou sawest was, and is not; and shall ascend out of the bottomless pit, and go into perdition: and they that dwell on the earth shall wonder, whose names were not written in the book of life from the foundation of the world, when they behold the beast that was, and is not, and yet is.
Revelation 20:14–15	And death and hell were cast into the lake of fire. This is the second death. And whosoever was not found written in the book of life was cast into the lake of fire.

Book of Mormon

2 Nephi 2:17–18	And I, Lehi, according to the things which I have

read, must needs suppose that an angel of God, according to that which is written, had fallen from heaven; wherefore, he became a devil, having sought that which was evil before God.

And because he had fallen from heaven, and had become miserable forever, he sought also the misery of all mankind. Wherefore, he said unto Eve, yea, even that old serpent, who is the devil, who is the father of all lies, wherefore he said: Partake of the forbidden fruit, and ye shall not die, but ye shall be as God, knowing good and evil.

Mosiah 2:36–39

And now, I say unto you, my brethren, that after ye have known and have been taught all these things, if ye should transgress and go contrary to that which has been spoken, that ye do withdraw yourselves from the Spirit of the Lord, that it may have no place in you to guide you in wisdom's paths that ye may be blessed, prospered, and preserved—

I say unto you, that the man that doeth this, the same cometh out in open rebellion against God; therefore he listeth to obey the evil spirit, and becometh an enemy to all righteousness; therefore, the Lord has no place in him, for he dwelleth not in unholy temples.

Therefore if that man repenteth not, and remaineth and dieth an enemy to God, the demands of divine justice do awaken his immortal soul to a lively sense of his own guilt, which doth cause him to shrink from the presence of the Lord, and doth fill his breast with guilt, and pain, and anguish, which is like an unquenchable fire, whose flame ascendeth up forever and ever.

And now I say unto you, that mercy hath no claim on that man; therefore his final doom is to endure a never-ending torment.

Mosiah 16:5

But remember that he that persists in his own carnal nature, and goes on in the ways of sin and rebellion against God, remaineth in his fallen state and the devil hath all power over him. Therefore he is as though there was no redemption made, being an enemy to God; and also is the devil an enemy to God.

Alma 12:16–18

And now behold, I say unto you then cometh a death, even a second death, which is a spiritual death; then is a time that whosoever dieth in his sins, as to a temporal death, shall also die a spiritual death; yea, he shall die as to things pertaining unto righteousness.

Then is the time when their torments shall be as a lake of fire and brimstone, whose flame ascendeth up forever and ever; and then is the time that they shall be chained down to an everlasting destruction, according to the power and captivity of Satan, he having subjected them according to his will.

Then, I say unto you, they shall be as though there had been no redemption made; for they cannot be redeemed according to God's justice; and they cannot die, seeing there is no more corruption.

Alma 13:31–32

Wherefore, he gave commandments unto men, they having first transgressed the first commandments as to things which were temporal, and becoming as Gods, knowing good from evil, placing themselves in a state to act, or being placed in a state to act according to their wills and pleasures, whether to do evil or to do good—

Therefore God gave unto them commandments, after having made known unto them the plan of redemption, that they should not do evil, the penalty thereof being a second death, which was an everlasting death as to things pertaining unto righteousness; for on such the plan of redemption could have no power, for the works of justice could not be destroyed, according to the supreme goodness of God.

Alma 13:30	And may the Lord grant unto you repentance, that ye may not bring down his wrath upon you, that ye may not be bound down by the chains of hell, that ye may not suffer the second death.
Helaman 14:17–18	But behold, the resurrection of Christ redeemeth mankind, yea, even all mankind, and bringeth them back into the presence of the Lord. Yea, and it bringeth to pass the condition of repentance, that whosoever repenteth the same is not hewn down and cast into the fire; but whosoever repenteth not is hewn down and cast into the fire; and there cometh upon them again a spiritual death, yea, a second death, for they are cut off again as to things pertaining to righteousness.
3 Nephi 27:32	But behold, it sorroweth me because of the fourth generation from this generation, for they are led away captive by him even as was the son of perdition; for they will sell me for silver and for gold, and for that which moth doth corrupt and which thieves can break through and steal. And in that day will I visit them, even in turning their works upon their own heads.
3 Nephi 29:7	Yea, and wo unto him that shall say at that day, to get gain, that there can be no miracle wrought by Jesus Christ; for he that doeth this shall become like unto the son of perdition, for whom there was no mercy according to the word of Christ!

Doctrine and Covenants

D&C 63:17–18	Wherefore, I, the Lord, have said that the fearful, and the unbelieving, and all liars, and whosoever loveth and maketh a lie, and the whoremonger, and the sorcerer, shall have their part in that lake which burneth with fire and brimstone, which is the second death. Verily I say, that they shall not have part in the first resurrection.

D&C 76:25–26, 30–38

And this we saw also, and bear record, that an angel of God who was in authority in the presence of God, who rebelled against the Only Begotten Son whom the Father loved and who was in the bosom of the Father, was thrust down from the presence of God and the Son,

And was called Perdition, for the heavens wept over him—he was Lucifer, a son of the morning. . . .

And we saw a vision of the sufferings of those with whom he made war and overcame, for thus came the voice of the Lord unto us:

Thus saith the Lord concerning all those who know my power, and have been made partakers thereof, and suffered themselves through the power of the devil to be overcome, and to deny the truth and defy my power—

They are they who are the sons of perdition, of whom I say that it had been better for them never to have been born;

For they are vessels of wrath, doomed to suffer the wrath of God, with the devil and his angels in eternity;

Concerning whom I have said there is no forgiveness in this world nor in the world to come—

Having denied the Holy Spirit after having received it, and having denied the Only Begotten Son of the Father, having crucified him unto themselves and put him to an open shame.

These are they who shall go away into the lake of fire and brimstone, with the devil and his angels—

And the only ones on whom the second death shall have any power;

Yea verily, the only ones who shall not be redeemed in the due time of the Lord, after the sufferings of his wrath.

D&C 76:40–46

And this is the gospel, the glad tidings, which the

voice out of the heavens bore record unto us—

That he came into the world, even Jesus, to be crucified for the world, and to bear the sins of the world, and to sanctify the world, and to cleanse it from all unrighteousness;

That through him all might be saved whom the Father had put into his power and made by him;

Who glorifies the Father, and saves all the works of his hands, except those sons of perdition who deny the Son after the Father has revealed him.

Wherefore, he saves all except them—they shall go away into everlasting punishment, which is endless punishment, which is eternal punishment, to reign with the devil and his angels in eternity, where their worm dieth not, and the fire is not quenched, which is their torment—

And the end thereof, neither the place thereof, nor their torment, no man knows;

Neither was it revealed, neither is, neither will be revealed unto man, except to them who are made partakers thereof.

D&C 88:102 And another trump shall sound, which is the fourth trump, saying: There are found among those who are to remain until that great and last day, even the end, who shall remain filthy still.

Pearl of Great Price

Moses 4:3–4 Wherefore, because that Satan rebelled against me, and sought to destroy the agency of man, which I, the Lord God, had given him, and also, that I should give unto him mine own power; by the power of mine Only Begotten, I caused that he should be cast down;

And he became Satan, yea, even the devil, the father of all lies, to deceive and to blind men, and to lead them captive at his will, even as many as would not hearken unto my voice.

Speaking to Cain, the Lord said:

Moses 5:23–24	If thou doest well, thou shalt be accepted. And if thou doest not well, sin lieth at the door, and Satan desireth to have thee; and except thou shalt hearken unto my commandments, I will deliver thee up, and it shall be unto thee according to his desire. And thou shall rule over him; For from this time forth thou shalt be the father of his lies; thou shalt be called Perdition; for thou wast also before the world.

In the premortal life, there was a council in heaven.

Abraham 3:27–28	And the Lord said: Whom shall I send? And one answered like unto the Son of Man: Here am I, send me. And another [Lucifer] answered and said: Here am I, send me. And the Lord said: I will send the first. And the second was angry, and kept not his first estate; and, at that day, many [a third of the host of heaven] followed after him.

Notes

1. Bruce R. McConkie, *Mormon Doctrine*. 2nd ed. (Salt Lake City: Bookcraft, 1966), 640.

Chapter 7

Grace, Faith, Works, Exaltation

"Saved" by Grace

TENET: We are all saved by the grace of Jesus Christ. Two words need to be looked at: *saved* and *grace. Grace* is all Jesus Christ has done for us that we could not possibly do for ourselves. The dictionary gives a theological definition of *grace* as: "the unmerited love and favor of God toward man . . . the divine influence acting in man to make him pure and morally strong . . . the condition of a person thus influenced . . . a special virtue given to a person by God."[1] *Saved* is defined theologically as "to deliver from sin and punishment . . . to exercise power to redeem from evil and sin."[2]

It is through the grace of Jesus Christ and through no effort on our part that every person who lives upon the earth, has lived upon the earth or will yet live upon the earth, will someday be *saved*—that is, they will be resurrected from the grave.

In the Book of Mormon, we read:

2 Nephi 25:23	For we labor diligently to write, to persuade our children, and also our brethren, to believe in Christ, and to be reconciled to God; for we know that it is by grace that we are saved, after all we can do.

There is a difference between being *saved* (being resurrected) and exaltation (attaining the highest degree of glory after the resurrection).

The scriptures all foretell of a pending day of judgment when all mankind will be judged and held accountable for our sins and rewarded for our righteousness. The demands of justice require that a penalty be paid for each sin. It is through the grace of Christ taking upon himself the sins of the world (something that we can not do for ourselves) that we are given the opportunity to avoid suffering for our own sins (may be delivered from sin and punishment) if we repent of them.

(A) All people will be "saved"

(All will be resurrected)

OLD TESTAMENT

In the Old Testament we read the song of Hannah, wife of Elkanah and mother of Samuel, as she rejoiced at the birth of her son, which points to the knowledge she (and others) had regarding the Savior's grace in our resurrection. It says, in part:

1 Samuel 2:6 — The Lord killeth, and maketh alive: he bringeth down to the grave, and bringeth up.

Isaiah's words give further evidence of this knowledge.

Isaiah 25:8 — He will swallow up death in victory; and the Lord God will wipe away tears from off all faces; and the rebuke of his people shall he take away from off all the earth: for the Lord hath spoken it.

Isaiah 33:22 — For the Lord is our judge, the Lord is our lawgiver, the Lord is our king; he will save us.

In Hosea, we read the Lord's lament:

Hosea 13:14 — I will ransom them from the power of the grave; I will redeem them from death: O death, I will be thy plagues; O grave, I will be thy destruction: repentance shall be hid from mine eyes.

NEW TESTAMENT

Matthew 1:21 — And she shall bring forth a son, and thou shalt call his name Jesus: for he shall save his people from their sins.

John 3:16–17 — For God so loved the world, that he gave his only

	begotten Son, that whosoever believeth in him should not perish, but have everlasting life. For God sent not his Son into the world to condemn the world; but that the world through him might be saved.
Romans 5:8–9	But God commendeth his love toward us, in that, while we were yet sinners, Christ died for us. Much more, then, being now justified by his blood, we shall be saved from wrath through him.

Because of Christ's death and resurrection, we will not remain in the grave.

In the New Testament, Peter taught the "men and brethren" these same truths:

Acts 15:11	We believe that through the grace of the Lord Jesus Christ we shall be saved [resurrected], even as they.

Paul speaks of the resurrection:

Acts 24:14–15	But this I confess unto thee, that after the way which they call heresy, so worship I the God of my fathers, believing all things which are written in the law and in the prophets: And have hope toward God, which they themselves also allow, that there shall be a resurrection of the dead, both of the just and unjust.

Book of Mormon

The Book of Mormon teachings echo those of the Bible:

2 Nephi 2:4	And the way is prepared from the fall of man, and salvation [being saved from the grave] is free.
2 Nephi 10:24	Wherefore, my beloved brethren, reconcile yourselves to the will of God, and not to the will of the devil and the flesh; and remember, after ye are reconciled unto God, that it is only in and through the grace of God that ye are saved [from the grave].
Alma 11:41	For behold, the day cometh that all shall rise from the dead.

Mormon 9:13 And because of the redemption of man, which came by Jesus Christ, they are brought back into the presence of the Lord; yea, this is wherein all men are redeemed, because the death of Christ bringeth to pass the resurrection, which bringeth to pass a redemption from an endless sleep, from which sleep all men shall be awakened by the power of God when the trump shall sound; and they shall come forth, both small and great, and all shall stand before his bar, being redeemed and loosed from this eternal band of death, which death is a temporal death.

Doctrine and Covenants

From before the birth of Christ to our day, the Lord consistently revealed the same doctrine. To Joseph Smith he revealed:

D&C 29:26 But, behold, verily I say unto you, before the earth shall pass away, Michael, mine arch-angel, shall sound his trump, and then shall all the dead awake, for their graves shall be opened, and they shall come forth—yea, even all.

D&C 76:40–43 And this is the gospel, the glad tidings, which the voice out of the heavens bore record unto us—

That he came into the world, even Jesus, to be crucified for the world, and to bear the sins of the world, and to sanctify the world, and to cleanse it from all unrighteousness;

That through him all might be saved whom the Father had put into his power and made by him;

Who glorifies the Father, and saves all the works of his hands, except those sons of perdition who deny the Son after the Father has revealed him.

The sons of perdition are "saved" from the grave, but they experience a second death when they are cast out into everlasting darkness.

(B) People will receive different rewards

Even though each of us will be resurrected and thus "saved" through the grace of Jesus Christ and through no effort on our part, the degree of glory we attain is dependent upon our behavior here on earth.

Old Testament

This doctrine was taught by the prophets of the Old Testament.

Ecclesiastes 12:14 For God shall bring every work into judgment, with every secret thing, whether it be good, or whether it be evil.

In Jeremiah, we read:

Jeremiah 17:10 I the Lord search the heart, I try the reins, even to give every man according to his ways, and according to the fruit of his doings.

New Testament

It was taught by Jesus while he was here on the earth:

Matthew 16:27 For the Son of man shall come in the glory of his Father with his angels; and then he shall reward every man according to his works.

It was taught by his apostles:

John 5:28–29 Marvel not at this: for the hour is coming, in the which all that are in the graves shall hear his voice,

And shall come forth; they that have done good, unto the resurrection of life; and they that have done evil, unto the resurrection of damnation.

2 Corinthians 5:10 For we must all appear before the judgment seat of Christ; that every one may receive the things done in his body, according to that he hath done, whether it be good or bad.

Galatians 6:7 Be not deceived; God is not mocked: for whatsoever a man soweth, that shall he also reap.

Revelation 22:10–12 And he saith unto me, Seal not the sayings of the prophecy of this book: for the time is at hand.

He that is unjust, let him be unjust still: and he which is filthy, let him be filthy still: and he that is righteous, let him be righteous still: and he that is holy, let him be holy still.

And, behold, I come quickly; and my reward is with me, to give every man according as his work shall be.

Book of Mormon

In the Book of Mormon, King Benjamin counseled his people (about 124 B.C.), saying:

Mosiah 3:23–25

And now I have spoken the words which the Lord God hath commanded me.

And thus saith the Lord: They shall stand as a bright testimony against this people, at the judgment day; whereof they shall be judged, every man according to his works, whether they be good, or whether they be evil.

And if they be evil they are consigned to an awful view of their own guilt and abominations, which doth cause them to shrink from the presence of the Lord into a state of misery and endless torment, from whence they can no more return; therefore they have drunk damnation to their own souls.

Alma 3:26–27

And in one year were thousands and tens of thousands of souls sent to the eternal world, that they might reap their rewards according to their works, whether they were good or whether they were bad, to reap eternal happiness or eternal misery, according to the spirit which they listed to obey, whether it be a good spirit or a bad one.

For every man receiveth wages of him whom he listeth to obey, and this according to the words of the spirit of prophecy; therefore let it be according to the truth.

Amulek's teachings echoed those of King Benjamin, as Alma pointed out to the people:

Alma 12:12–14

And Amulek hath spoken plainly concerning death, and being raised from this mortality to a state of immortality, and being brought before the bar of God, to be judged according to our works.

Then if our hearts have been hardened, yea, if we have hardened our hearts against the word, insomuch that it has not been found in us, then will our state be awful, for then we shall be condemned.

For our words will condemn us, yea, all our works will condemn us; we shall not be found spotless; and our thoughts will also condemn us; and in the awful state we shall not dare to look up to our God; and we would fain be glad if we could command the rocks and the mountains to fall upon us to hide us from his presence.

Doctrine and Covenants

The Lord revealed the same truths in these latter days. Joseph Smith and Oliver Cowdery received this counsel through the Urim and Thummim in April of 1829:

D&C 6:33 Fear not to do good, my sons, for whatsoever ye sow, that shall ye also reap; therefore, if ye sow good ye shall also reap good for your reward.

As the Lord built up his Church in these latter days, he made this promise to the faithful:

D&C 63:48 He that sendeth up treasures unto the land of Zion shall receive an inheritance in this world, and his works shall follow him, and also a reward in the world to come.

On February 16, 1832, Joseph Smith and Sidney Rigdon sought information from the Lord regarding the following passage in John 5:29 which indicates that men shall be rewarded according to their works:

D&C 76:16–17 And shall come forth—They who have done good, in the resurrection of the just; and they who have done evil, in the resurrection of the unjust.

They then received a vision of the Plan of Salvation.

D&C 112:34 Be faithful until I come, for I come quickly; and my reward is with me to recompense every man according as his work shall be. I am Alpha and Omega. Amen.

(C) There are different degrees of glory

As the scriptures have said, we will all be judged following the resurrection, and, according to our works, we will receive our just rewards. Therefore, there are obviously different degrees of rewards. Jesus told his apostles:

John 14:2 In my Father's house are many mansions: if it were not so, I would have told you. I go to prepare a place for you.

Old Testament

Daniel understood that people would be rewarded in the resurrection according to their works here on earth:

Daniel 12:1–2 And at that time shall Michael stand up, the great prince which standeth for the children of thy people: and there shall be a time of trouble, such as never was since there was a nation even to that same time: and at that time thy people shall be delivered, every one that shall be found written in the book.

And many of them that sleep in the dust of the earth shall awake, some to everlasting life, and some to shame and everlasting contempt.

New Testament

The Apostle taught the people that there are different degrees of glory.

1 Corinthians 15:40–42

There are also celestial bodies, and bodies terrestrial: but the glory of the celestial is one, and the glory of the terrestrial is another.

There is one glory of the sun, and another glory of the moon, and another glory of the stars: for one star differeth from another star in glory.

So also is the resurrection of the dead.

In his second epistle to the Corinthians, Paul also makes reference to "the third heaven" (2 Corinthians 12:2).

Book of Mormon

While the Book of Mormon prophets do not use the terms celestial kingdom, terrestrial kingdom, nor telestial kingdom, it is evident from their writings that they were fully aware of and taught the people that there are different degrees of glory.

The Prophet Abinadi taught:

Mosiah 15:20–24, 26

> But behold, the bands of death shall be broken, and the Son reigneth, and hath power over the dead; therefore, he bringeth to pass the resurrection of the dead.
>
> And there cometh a resurrection, even a first resurrection; yea, even a resurrection of those that have been, and who are, and who shall be, even until the resurrection of Christ—for so shall he be called.
>
> And now, the resurrection of all the prophets, and all those that have believed in their words, or all those that have kept the commandments of God, shall come forth in the first resurrection; therefore, they are the first resurrection.
>
> They are raised to dwell with God who has redeemed them; thus they have eternal life through Christ, who has broken the bands of death. . .
>
> And thus the Lord bringeth about the restoration of these; and they have a part in the first resurrection, or have eternal life, being redeemed by the Lord. . .
>
> But behold, and fear, and tremble before God . . . for the Lord redeemeth none such that rebel against him and die in their sins . . . that have wilfully rebelled against God, that have known the commandments of God, and would not keep them; these are they that have no part in the first resurrection.

Doctrine and Covenants

On February 16, 1832, the Prophet Joseph Smith and Sydney Rigdon received a vision wherein God's plan of salvation was revealed to them, which included knowledge pertaining to the three different degrees of glory referred to by Paul.

D&C 76:64, 68–79, 81, 89, 91–92, 111

> These are they who shall have part in the first resurrection.
>
> These are they whose names are written in heaven, where God and Christ are the judge of all.
>
> These are they who are just men made perfect through Jesus the mediator of the new covenant, who wrought out this perfect atonement through the shedding of his own blood.
>
> These are they whose bodies are celestial, whose glory is that of the sun, even the glory of God, the highest of all, whose glory the sun of the firmament is written of as being typical.
>
> And again, we saw the terrestrial world, and behold and lo, these are they who are of the terrestrial, whose glory differs from that of the church of the Firstborn who have received the fulness of the Father, even as that of the moon differs from the sun in the firmament.
>
> Behold, these are they who died without law;
>
> And also they who are the spirits of men kept in prison, whom the Son visited, and preached the gospel unto them, that they might be judged according to men in the flesh;
>
> Who received not the testimony of Jesus in the flesh, but afterwards received it.
>
> These are they who are honorable men of the earth, who were blinded by the craftiness of men.
>
> These are they who receive of his glory, but not of his fulness.
>
> These are they who receive of the presence of the Son, but not of the fulness of the Father.
>
> Wherefore, they are bodies terrestrial, and not bodies celestial, and differ in glory as the moon differs from the sun.

> These are they who are not valiant in the testimony of Jesus; wherefore, they obtain not the crown over the kingdom of our God. . . .
>
> And again, we saw the glory of the telestial, which glory is that of the lesser, even as the glory of the stars differs from that of the glory of the moon in the firmament. . . .
>
> And thus we saw, in the heavenly vision, the glory of the telestial, which surpasses all understanding. . . .
>
> And thus we saw the glory of the terrestrial which excels in all things the glory of the telestial, even in glory, and in power, and in might, and in dominion.
>
> And thus we saw the glory of the celestial, which excels in all things—where God, even the Father, reigns upon his throne forever and ever. . . .
>
> For they shall be judged according to their works, and every man shall receive according to his own works, his own dominion, in the mansions which are prepared.

The admonition that the Lord gave to Joseph Smith a month later also pertains to everyone:

D&C 78:7

> For if you will that I give unto you a place in the celestial world, you must prepare yourselves by doing the things which I have commanded you and required of you.

The Lord further explained to Joseph Smith:

D&C 88:21–24

> And they who are not sanctified through the law which I have given unto you, even the law of Christ, must inherit another kingdom, even that of a terrestrial kingdom, or that of a telestial kingdom.
>
> For he who is not able to abide the law of a celestial kingdom cannot abide a celestial glory.
>
> And he who cannot abide the law of a terrestrial kingdom cannot abide a terrestrial glory.

And he who cannot abide the law of a telestial kingdom cannot abide a telestial glory; therefore he is not meet for a kingdom of glory. Therefore he must abide a kingdom which is not a kingdom of glory.

In addition, the Lord revealed to Joseph Smith that within the celestial glory there are three heavens, or degrees of glory. He also revealed to Joseph the requirements to attain the highest degree of glory.

D&C 131:1–4 In the celestial glory there are three heavens or degrees;

And in order to obtain the highest, a man must enter into this order of the priesthood [meaning the new and everlasting covenant of marriage];

And if he does not, he cannot obtain it.

He may enter into the other, but that is the end of his kingdom; he cannot have an increase.

Pearl of Great Price

Moses was also instructed to freely teach the people about the plan of salvation and what one must do to "enjoy the words of eternal life in this world, and eternal life in the world to come, even immortal glory" (Moses 6:59).

Abraham 3:26 And they who keep their first estate shall be added upon; and they who keep not their fist estate shall not have glory in the same kingdom with those who keep their first estate; and they who keep their second estate shall have glory added upon their heads for ever and ever.

The scriptures (the Bible, Book of Mormon, Doctrine and Covenants, and Pearl of Great Price) all provide evidence that the Lord has consistently instructed the people here on the earth that we will be judged according to our works in this life, that there are different degrees of glory, and that the degree of glory we receive after the resurrection will be according to our works—our faithfulness and obedience in this life.

(D) Christ atoned for our sins

(Conditional on our repentance)

It is through the grace of Christ who atoned for the sins of the world that we will not have to suffer for our own sins if we repent of them, and we will someday be reunited with our Heavenly Father. However, if we do not repent of our sins, that aspect of the atonement will have no effect on us and we will have to suffer for our sins ourselves.

Old Testament

Long before the birth of Christ, knowledge of an eventual atonement was known among the people. The Lord instructed Moses:

Leviticus 17:11	For the life of the flesh is in the blood: and I have given it to you upon the altar to make an atonement for your souls: for it is the blood that maketh an atonement for the soul.

It is evident in the writings of the Old Testament prophets that they understood that we must repent and follow Christ if we do not want to have to pay the penalty for our own sins.

Proverbs 28:26	He that trusteth in his own heart is a fool: but whoso walketh wisely, he shall be delivered.

In Ecclesiastes we also read:

Ecclesiastes 8:2, 5	I counsel thee to keep the king's commandment, and that in regard of the oath of God. . . . Whoso keepeth the commandment shall feel no evil thing.

The great Prophet Isaiah, referring to Jesus Christ, wrote:

Isaiah 53:5–8	But he was wounded for our transgressions, he was bruised for our iniquities: the chastisement of our peace was upon him; and with his stripes we are healed. All we like sheep have gone astray; we have turned everyone to his own way; and the Lord hath laid on him the iniquity of us all. He was oppressed, and he was afflicted, yet he opened not his mouth: he is brought as a lamb to the slaughter, and as a sheep before her shearers is dumb, so he openeth not his mouth. He was taken from prison and from judgment:

and who shall declare his generation? for he was cut off out of the land of the living: for the transgression of my people was he stricken.

Another prophet declared:

Joel 2:32 — And it shall come to pass, that whosoever shall call on the name of the Lord [follow his teachings] shall be delivered.

New Testament

Jesus reminded his apostles that he came into this life to atone for the sins of the people:

Matthew 20:28 — Even as the Son of man came not to be ministered unto, but to minister, and to give his life a ransom for many.

Matthew 26:28 — For this is my blood of the new testament, which is shed for many for the remission of sins.

John 10:15 — As the Father knoweth me, even so know I the Father: and I lay down my life for the sheep.

Acts 4:12 — Neither is there salvation in any other: for there is none other name under heaven given among men, whereby we must be saved.

Philippians 2:12 — Wherefore, my beloved, as ye have always obeyed, not as in my presence only, but now much more in my absence, work out your own salvation with fear and trembling. [Note: salvation means receiving an inheritance in the Celestial Kingdom of God.]

The Apostle wrote two epistles to the Thessalonian saints. In his second epistle, it is clear that he understood that the wicked would have to suffer for their own sins. He counseled them:

2 Thessalonians 1:6–10

Seeing it is a righteous thing with God to recompense tribulation to them that trouble you;

And to you who are troubled rest with us, when the Lord Jesus shall be revealed from heaven with his mighty angels,

In flaming fire taking vengeance on them that know not God, and that obey not the gospel of our Lord Jesus Christ:

Who shall be punished with everlasting destruction from the presence of the Lord, and from the glory of his power;

When he shall come to be glorified in his saints, and to be admired in all them that believe (because our testimony among you was believed) in that day.

Paul also wrote to the Hebrews:

Hebrews 5:9 And being made perfect, he became the author of eternal salvation unto all them that obey him.

Book of Mormon

Prior to the birth of Christ (between 600–592 B.C.), the atonement of the Savior was also revealed to Nephi.

1 Nephi 11:33 And I, Nephi, saw that he was lifted up upon the cross and slain for the sins of the world.

Nephi's father Lehi expanded upon that doctrine:

2 Nephi 2:6–7 Wherefore, redemption cometh in and through the Holy Messiah; for he is full of grace and truth.

Behold, he offereth himself a sacrifice for sin, to answer the ends of the law, unto all those who have a broken heart and a contrite spirit; and unto none else can the ends of the law be answered.

Several centuries later (about 124 B.C.), king Benjamin preached the same doctrine.

Mosiah 3:11–12, 17 For behold, and also his blood atoneth for the sins of those who have fallen by the transgression of Adam, who have died not knowing the will of God concerning them, or who have ignorantly sinned.

But wo, wo, unto him who knoweth that he rebelleth against God! For salvation cometh to none such except it be through repentance and faith on the Lord Jesus Christ. . . .

> And moreover, I say unto you, that there shall be no other name given nor any other way nor means whereby salvation can come unto the children of men, only in and through the name of Christ, the Lord Omnipotent.

In these verses, receiving salvation means receiving an inheritance in the Celestial Kingdom of God.

Approximately 42 years later (about 82 B.C.), Amulek taught the people:

Alma 11:40–41

> And he [Christ] shall come into the world to redeem his people; and he shall take upon him the transgressions of those who believe on his name; and these are they that shall have eternal life, and salvation cometh to none else.
>
> Therefore the wicked remain as though there had been no redemption made, except it be the loosing of the bands of death; for behold, the day cometh that all shall rise from the dead and stand before God, and be judged according to their works.

A few years later (about 74 B.C.), Amulek testified:

Alma 34:8, 37

> And now, behold, I will testify unto you of myself that these things are true. Behold, I say unto you, that I do know that Christ shall come among the children of men, to take upon him the transgressions of his people, and that he shall atone for the sins of the world; for the Lord God hath spoken it. . . .
>
> And now, my beloved brethren, I desire that ye should remember these things, and that ye should work out your salvation with fear before God, and that ye should no more deny the coming of Christ.

Following the Savior's death and resurrection, he appeared to his "sheep" on the American continent (about A.D. 34) and said to them:

3 Nephi 11:14

> Arise and come forth unto me, that ye may thrust your hands into my side, and also that ye may feel the prints of the nails in my hands and in my feet, that ye may know that I am the God of Israel, and

the God of the whole earth, and have been slain for the sins of the world.

Doctrine and Covenants

In June 1829, the Lord gave a revelation through Joseph Smith wherein he said:

D&C 18:11	For, behold, the Lord your Redeemer suffered death in the flesh; wherefore he suffered the pain of all men, that all men might repent and come unto him.

A few months later, the Lord again gave a revelation through the Prophet Joseph Smith, wherein he said:

D&C 19:16–18	For behold, I, God, have suffered these things for all, that they might not suffer if they would repent; But if they would not repent they must suffer even as I; Which suffering caused myself, even God, the greatest of all, to tremble because of pain, and to bleed at every pore, and to suffer both body and spirit—and would that I might not drink the bitter cup, and shrink [March 1830].

Years later, on October 3, 1918, President Joseph F. Smith, president of The Church of Jesus Christ of Latter-day Saints at that time, had a vision wherein the Savior again revealed that we are redeemed from our sins on condition of repentance.

D&C 138:19	And there [in the spirit prison] he preached to them the everlasting gospel, the doctrine of the resurrection and the redemption of mankind from the fall, and from individual sins on conditions of repentance.

Reiterating what the scriptures declare, Joseph Fielding Smith, tenth president of the Church wrote:

> So I say there never was a sin committed that was not atoned for. Christ paid the debt of my sins on one condition, and that is that I will believe in him and keep his commandments. He did that for you and for every other person in the world; but he never paid any debt

on the cross, or before he went on the cross, for the sins of any of us, if we will be rebellious. If we are rebellious, we will have to pay the price ourselves.[3]

Notes

1. *Webster's New World Dictionary*, 2nd College ed. (Cleveland, OH: World Publishing, 1976), 605.
2. Ibid., 1267.
3. Joseph Fielding Smith, *Doctrines of Salvation*, compiled by Bruce R. McConkie, vol. 1. (Salt Lake City: Bookcraft, 1954–56), 131.

Chapter 8

Repentance and Forgiveness

TENET: The scriptures, ancient and modern, call all mankind to repentance. Because Adam and Eve partook of the forbidden fruit and became separated from God—suffering a spiritual death—all mankind are subject to the sins of mortality and are dead spiritually; that is, we are separated from God. And since "no whoremonger, nor unclean person, nor covetous man, who is an idolater, hath any inheritance in the kingdom of Christ and of God" (Ephesians 5:5), we must repent in order to become clean and be reunited (or reconciled) with God. Upon repentance, we are forgiven of our sins and receive blessings in this life as well as in the next.

(A) Repentance

Old Testament

Old Testament scriptures call the people to repentance.

Ezra 10:10–11 — And Ezra the priest stood up, and said unto them, Ye have transgressed, and have taken strange wives, to increase the trespass of Israel.

Now therefore make confession unto the Lord God of your fathers, and do his pleasure: and separate yourselves from the people of the land, and from the strange wives.

Proverbs 28:13 — He that covereth his sins shall not prosper: but whoso confesseth and forsaketh them shall have mercy.

Isaiah 1:16 — Wash you, make you clean; put away the evil of your doings from before mine eyes; cease to do evil.

Isaiah 55:7 — Let the wicked forsake his way, and the unrighteous man his thoughts: and let him return unto the Lord, and he will have mercy upon him; and to our God, for he will abundantly pardon.

Jeremiah 35:15 — I have sent also unto you all my servants the prophets, rising up early and sending them, saying, Return ye now every man from his evil way, and amend your doings, and go not after other gods to serve them, and ye shall dwell in the land which I have given to you and to your fathers: but ye have not inclined your ear, nor hearkened unto me.

New Testament

The New Testament scriptures continue the call people to repentance.

Matthew 3:1–2 — In those days came John the Baptist, preaching in the wilderness of Judea,

And saying, Repent ye: for the kingdom of heaven is at hand.

The Savior himself said that he had come to call sinners to repentance.

Matthew 9:13 — But when Jesus heard that, he said unto them, They that be whole need not a physician, but they that are sick.

But go ye and learn what that meaneth, I will have mercy, and not sacrifice: for I am not come to call the righteous, but sinners to repentance.

Mark 6:7, 12 — He [the Savior] called unto him the twelve, and began to send them forth by two and two; and gave them power over unclean spirits. . . .

And they went out, and preached that men should repent.

Referring to the Galilæans "whose blood Pilate had mingled with their sacrifices," Jesus warned the people:

Luke 13:3	Except ye repent, ye shall all likewise perish.

Paul reminded the people that God:

Acts 17:30	Commandeth all men every where to repent.

Peter also taught that we all need to repent:

2 Peter 3:9	The Lord is not slack concerning his promise, as some men count slackness; but is longsuffering to us-ward, not willing that any should perish, but that all should come to repentance.

Book of Mormon

The doctrine that all men must repent is repeated in the Book of Mormon.

1 Nephi 10:21	Wherefore, if ye have sought to do wickedly in the days of your probation, then ye are found unclean before the judgment-seat of God; and no unclean thing can dwell with God; wherefore, ye must be cast off forever.
2 Nephi 2:21	And the days of the children of men were prolonged, according to the will of God, that they might repent while in the flesh; wherefore, their state became a state of probation, and their time was lengthened, according to the commandments which the Lord God gave unto the children of men. For he gave commandment that all men must repent; for he showed unto all men that they were lost, because of the transgression of their parents.

Alma, referring to people who refuse to repent, said:

Alma 5:31–32	Wo unto such an one, for he is not prepared, and the time is at hand that he must repent or he cannot be saved! [He cannot receive an inheritance in the celestial kingdom.] Yea, even wo unto all ye workers of iniquity; repent, repent, for the Lord God hath spoken it!

Doctrine and Covenants

In June 1829 in a revelation given to Joseph Smith the Lord reiterated the importance of repentance:

D&C 16:6 — And now, behold, I say unto you, that the thing which will be of the most worth unto you will be to declare repentance unto this people, that you may bring souls unto me, that you may rest with them in the kingdom of my Father.

A few months later, in March 1830, the Lord told Joseph Smith:

D&C 19:4–5 — Surely every man must repent or suffer, for I, God, am endless.

Wherefore, I revoke not the judgments which I shall pass, but woes shall go forth, weeping, wailing and gnashing of teeth, yea, to those who are found on my left hand.

In September 1830 the Lord asked Joseph Smith:

D&C 29:49 — And, again, I say unto you, that whoso having knowledge, have I not commanded to repent?

This question confirms that the Lord is the same yesterday, today, and tomorrow and that people throughout the generations of time as recorded in all the scriptures have been commanded to repent.

The Lord again stressed the need for repentance in another revelation given to Joseph Smith on February 19, 1831:

D&C 42:28 — Thou knowest my laws concerning these things are given in my scriptures; he that sinneth and repenteth not shall be cast out.

(B) Forgiveness

God's grace is evident in his willingness to forgive us of our sins when we repent.

Old Testament

Centuries before the birth of the Savior, King David recognized that when we confess our sins and repent, God will forgive us.

Psalm 32:5	I acknowledged my sin unto thee, and mine iniquity have I not hid. I said, I will confess my transgressions unto the Lord; and thou forgavest the iniquity of my sin.

David continued:

Psalm 86:5	For thou, Lord, art good, and ready to forgive; and plenteous in mercy unto all them that call upon thee.

This doctrine is reinforced in the writings of Isaiah.

Isaiah 1:18–20	Come now, and let us reason together, saith the Lord: though your sins be as scarlet, they shall be as white as snow; though they be red like crimson, they shall be as wool. If ye be willing and obedient, ye shall eat the good of the land: But if ye refuse and reel, ye shall be devoured with the sword: for the mouth of the Lord hath spoken it.

The Prophet Ezekiel recorded the words of the Lord as he received them.

Ezekiel 18:20–21	The soul that sinneth, it shall die. The son shall not bear the iniquity of the father, neither shall the father bear the iniquity of the son: the righteousness of the righteous shall be upon him, and the wickedness of the wicked shall be upon him. But if the wicked will turn from all his sins that he hath committed, and keep all my statutes, and do that which is lawful and right, he shall surely live, he shall not die. All his transgressions that he hath committed, they shall not be mentioned unto him: in his righteousness that he hath done he shall live.

New Testament

When Christ was upon the earth, he told the scribes:

Matthew 9:6	The Son of man hath power on earth to forgive sins.

Christ also taught the Pharisees, "Wherefore I say unto you, All manner of sin and blasphemy shall be forgiven unto men." But then he added a caveat:

Matthew 12:31–32 But the blasphemy against the Holy Ghost shall not be forgiven unto men.

And whosoever speaketh a word against the Son of man, it shall be forgiven him: but whosoever speaketh against the Holy Ghost, it shall not be forgiven him, neither in this world, neither in the world to come.

In his teachings recorded in the book of Acts, Paul says:

Acts 13:38–39 Be it known unto you therefore, men and brethren, that through this man [Jesus] is preached unto you the forgiveness of sins:

And by him all that believe are justified from all things, from which ye could not be justified by the law of Moses.

In his epistle to the Ephesians, Paul praised God the Father and the Lord Jesus Christ:

Ephesians 1:7 In whom we have redemption through his blood, the forgiveness of sins, according to the riches of his grace.

John recorded:

1 John 1:9 If we confess our sins, he is faithful and just to forgive us our sins, and to cleanse us from all unrighteousness.

Book of Mormon

Prior to the birth of Christ (about 124 B.C.), King Benjamin addressed the Nephite nation residing in America; he called them to repentance and spoke of the Savior's willingness to forgive their sins if they repented. The people took his message to heart:

Mosiah 4:2–3 And they had viewed themselves in their own carnal state, even less than the dust of the earth. And they all cried aloud with one voice, saying: O have mercy, and apply the atoning blood of Christ that we may receive forgiveness of our sins, and our hearts may be purified; for we believe in Jesus Christ, the Son of God, who created heaven and earth, and all things; who shall come down among the children of men.

And it came to pass that after they had spoken these words the Spirit of the Lord came upon them, and they were filled with joy, having received a remission of their sins, and having peace of conscience, because of the exceeding faith which they had in Jesus Christ who should come, according to the words which king Benjamin had spoken unto them.

The Lord instructed the Prophet Alma regarding forgiveness:

Mosiah 26:29 Therefore I say unto you, Go; and whosoever transgresseth against me, him shall ye judge according to the sins which he had committed; and if he confess his sins before thee and me, and repenteth in the sincerity of his heart, him shall ye forgive, and I will forgive him also.

Moroni, the last prophet of the Book of Mormon, recorded for future generations to read that the command to forgive those who repent was followed in the church at that time. Thus, the Lord was also bound by his word to forgive them.

Moroni 6:8 But as oft as they repented and sought forgiveness, with real intent, they were forgiven.

Doctrine and Covenants

The truths taught in ancient days have been given to mankind again in these latter days. Joseph Smith was given a revelation in which the Lord said:

D&C 1:31–32 For I the Lord cannot look upon sin with the least degree of allowance;

Nevertheless, he that repents and does the commandments of the Lord shall be forgiven [November 1, 1831].

Three months earlier, the Lord had told the prophet:

D&C 58:42 Behold, he who has repented of his sins, the same is forgiven, and I, the Lord, remember them no more.

Joseph Smith was also given a vision wherein the Lord showed him the fate of those who know his power and deliberately reject him.

D&C 76:34–35 Concerning whom I have said there is no forgiveness in this world nor in the world to come—

Having denied the Holy Spirit after having received it, and having denied the Only Begotten Son of the Father, having crucified him unto themselves and put him to an open shame [February 16, 1832].

This echoes the Savior's message as recorded in Matthew 12:31–32, quoted earlier in the chapter.

The scriptures all present the same message: if we repent, through God's grace, we will be forgiven and Christ's atonement will answer the demands of justice in our behalf—we will not have to suffer for our own sins. If we do not repent, we will have to suffer for our sins.

Chapter 9

Christ's Grace Impacts Us in This Life as Well as in the Next

TENET: Forgiveness for our sins not only has an eternal perspective to it, but also a mortal perspective: true repentance and Christ's forgiveness free us from guilt feelings in this life, give us peace of mind and allow us to progress in this mortal sphere, and give us hope. When we are in harmony with the Lord, we can receive inspiration from him and be directed to truth, both as relating to spiritual matters as well as relating to temporal matters.

(A) Peace

Old Testament

King David, referring to those who "give unto the Lord glory and strength" (Psalm 29:1), wrote:

Psalm 29:11	The Lord will give strength unto his people; the Lord will bless his people with peace.

King David also taught his people:

Psalm 37:37	Mark the perfect man, and behold the upright: for the end of that man is peace.
Psalm 119:165	Great peace have they which love thy law: and nothing shall offend them.

The great Prophet Isaiah also admonished the people:

Isaiah 32:17 And the work of righteousness shall be peace; and the effect of righteousness quietness and assurance for ever.

He also reminded the wicked (those who refuse to repent and remain in their sins) that:

Isaiah 48:22 There is no peace, saith the Lord, unto the wicked.

New Testament

Prior to Christ's crucifixion, he consoled his apostles by reminding them that "the Holy Ghost, whom the Father will send in my name," would be a Comforter and would teach them all things and bring all things to their remembrance "whatsoever I have said unto you" (John 14:26). Then he told them, "Peace I leave with you, my peace I give unto you: not as the world giveth, give I unto you. Let not your heart be troubled, neither let it be afraid (14:27).

Christ comforted his disciples and said:

John 16: 33 These things I have spoken unto you, that in me ye might have peace. In the world ye shall have tribulation: but be of good cheer; I have overcome the world.

Paul wrote to the Roman saints:

Romans 8:6 For to be carnally minded is death, but to be spiritually minded is life and peace.

He continued in his epistle to the Romans:

Romans 14:17 For the kingdom of God is not meat and drink; but righteousness, and peace, and joy in the Holy Ghost.

Paul wrote to the Corinthian saints that:

1 Corinthians 14:33 God is not the author of confusion, but of peace.

In his letter to the Galatians, Paul reminded them:

Galatians 5:22 But the fruit of the Spirit is love, joy, peace, longsuffering, gentleness, goodness, faith.

James' teachings echo those of Paul:

James 3:17–18 But the wisdom that is from above is first pure, then peaceable, gentle, and easy to be intreated, full of mercy and good fruits, without partiality, and without hypocrisy.

And the fruit of righteousness is sown in peace of them that make peace.

Book of Mormon

In the Book of Mormon, Nephi, the son of Lehi, recognized that yielding to temptation results in the loss of peace.

2 Nephi 4:27 And why should I yield to sin, because of my flesh? Yea, why should I give way to temptations, that the evil one have place in my heart to destroy my peace and afflict my soul.

King Benjamin spoke to the Nephites about the atonement and obtaining a remission of their sins:

Mosiah 4:1–3 He cast his eyes round about on the multitude, and behold they had fallen to the earth, for the fear of the Lord had come upon them.

And they had viewed themselves in their own carnal state, even less than the dust of the earth. And they all cried aloud with one voice, saying: O have mercy, and apply the atoning blood of Christ that we may receive forgiveness of our sins, and our hearts may be purified; for we believe in Jesus Christ, the Son of God, who created heaven and earth, and all things; who shall come down among the children of men.

And it came to pass that after they had spoken these words the Spirit of the Lord came upon them, and they were filled with joy, having received a remission of their sins, and having peace of conscience, because of the exceeding faith which they had in Jesus Christ who should come, according to the words which king Benjamin had spoken unto them.

Alma explained to his son Shiblon about his own conversion—his anguish due to sin, his subsequent repentance, and the resultant forgiveness and peace he found.

Alma 38:8	And it came to pass that I was three days and three nights in the most bitter pain and anguish of soul; and never, until I did cry out unto the Lord Jesus Christ for mercy, did I receive a remission of my sins. But behold, I did cry unto him and I did find peace to my soul.
Alma 58:11	Yea, and it came to pass that the Lord our God did visit us with assurances that he would deliver us; yea, insomuch that he did speak peace to our souls.

Doctrine and Covenants

In more recent times, Joseph Smith was also reminded by the Lord:

D&C 59:23	But learn that he who doeth the works of righteousness shall receive his reward, even peace in this world, and eternal life in the world to come [August 17, 1831].

(B) Knowledge and inspiration

It is through the grace of the Lord that people are inspired to accomplish the things that they accomplish and are blessed with wisdom and knowledge.

Old Testament

Speaking of Bezaleel of the tribe of Judah who the Lord appointed to work on the tabernacle, the Lord told Moses:

Exodus 31:3–5	And I have filled him with the spirit of God, in wisdom, and in understanding, and in knowledge, and in all manner of workmanship, To devise cunning works, to work in gold, and in silver, and in brass, And in cutting of stones, to set them, and in carving of timber, to work in all manner of workmanship.

Solomon recognized that knowledge and wisdom come from God:

2 Chronicles 1:10 Give me now wisdom and knowledge, that I may go out and come in before this people: for who can judge this thy people, that is so great.

The Lord responded:

2 Chronicles 1:11–12

Because this was in thine heart, and thou hast not asked riches, wealth, or honour, nor the life of thine enemies, neither yet hast asked long life; but hast asked wisdom and knowledge for thyself, that thou mayest judge my people, over whom I have made thee king:

Wisdom and knowledge is granted unto thee.

In Proverbs, we read:

Proverbs 14:18 The simple inherit folly: but the prudent are crowned with knowledge.

This truism is repeated:

Proverbs 18:15 The heart of the prudent getteth knowledge; and the ear of the wise seeketh knowledge.

Referring to Daniel and his four friends who refused to eat or drink that which the Lord had commanded they not eat or drink, we read in Daniel that:

Daniel 1:17 As for these four children, God gave them knowledge and skill in all learning and wisdom: and Daniel had understanding in all visions and dreams.

New Testament

In the New Testament, we read Paul's words to the Romans:

Romans 15:13–14 Now the God of hope fill you with all joy and peace in believing, that ye may abound in hope, through the power of the Holy Ghost.

And I myself also am persuaded of you, my brethren, that ye also are full of goodness, filled with all knowledge, able also to admonish one another.

Emphasizing that the Lord is the giver of all knowledge and gifts, and that these gifts and knowledge are to bless our mortal lives as well as the lives of others, Paul wrote to the Corinthians (reminding them that all gifts are important):

1 Corinthians 12:6–11

> And there are diversities of operations, but it is the same God which worketh all in all.
>
> But the manifestation of the Spirit is given to every man to profit withal.
>
> For to one is given by the Spirit the word of wisdom; to another the word of knowledge by the same Spirit;
>
> To another faith by the same Spirit; to another the gifts of healing by the same Spirit;
>
> To another the working of miracles; to another prophecy; to another discerning of spirits; to another divers kinds of tongues; to another the interpretation of tongues:
>
> But all these worketh that one and the selfsame Spirit, dividing to every man severally as he will [see verses 12–31].

Paul reminded the Colossians that in God the Father and Jesus Christ "are hid all the treasures of wisdom and knowledge" (Colossians 2:3).

Peter counseled the people that if we live righteously (repent of our sins), we will be blessed in this life and will have a greater knowledge of Jesus Christ.

2 Peter 1:2–9

> Grace and peace be multiplied unto you through the knowledge of God, and of Jesus our Lord,
>
> According as his divine power hath given unto us all things that pertain unto life and godliness, through the knowledge of him that hath called us to glory and virtue:
>
> Whereby are given unto us exceeding great and precious promises: that by these ye might be partakers of the divine nature, having escaped the corruption that is in the world through lust.

And beside this, given all diligence, add to your faith virtue; and to virtue knowledge;

And to knowledge temperance; and to temperance patience; and to patience godliness;

And to godliness brotherly kindness; and to brotherly kindness charity.

For if these things be in you, and abound, they make you that ye shall neither be barren nor unfruitful in the knowledge of our Lord Jesus Christ.

But he that lacketh these things is blind, and cannot see afar off, and hath forgotten that he was purged from his old sins.

Book of Mormon

The Book of Mormon teaches the same concepts. Because of Nephi's righteousness, the Lord blessed him with knowledge.

2 Nephi 4:23 Behold, he hath heard my cry by day, and he hath given me knowledge by visions in the night-time.

Ammon, the son of king Mosiah, also received knowledge through the Spirit.

Alma 18:35 And a portion of that Spirit dwelleth in me, which giveth me knowledge, and also power according to my faith and desires which are in God.

Doctrine and Covenants

On November 1, 1831, the Prophet Joseph Smith received instruction from the Lord wherein the Lord pointed out in our dispensation that when people are righteous and repent, they receive inspiration.

D&C 1:24–28 Behold, I am God and have spoken it; these commandment are of me, and were given unto my servants in their weakness, after the manner of their language, that they might come to understanding.

And inasmuch as they erred it might be made known;

And inasmuch as they sought wisdom they might be instructed;

And inasmuch as they sinned they might be

chastened, that they might repent;

And inasmuch as they were humble they might be made strong, and blessed from on high, and receive knowledge from time to time.

Earlier, on February 9, 1831, the Lord told Joseph Smith:

D&C 42:61 If thou shalt ask, thou shalt receive revelation upon revelation, knowledge upon knowledge, that thou mayest know the mysteries and peaceable things—that which bringeth joy, that which bringeth life eternal.

The Lord also instructed Joseph Smith:

D&C 88:77–80 Teach one another the doctrine of the kingdom.

Teach ye diligently and my grace shall attend you, that you may be instructed more perfectly in theory, in principle, in doctrine, in the law of the gospel, in all things that pertain unto the kingdom of God, that are expedient for you to understand;

Of things both in heaven and in the earth, and under the earth; things which have been, things which are, things which must shortly come to pass; things which are at home, things which are abroad; the wars and the perplexities of the nations, and the judgments which are on the land; and a knowledge also of countries and of kingdoms—

That ye may be prepared in all things when I shall send you again to magnify the calling whereunto I have called you, and the mission with which I have commissioned you.

The Lord gave a promise to all his children that if they obey his words of wisdom regarding the foods and drinks which they ingest, they will be blessed.

D&C 89:18–20 And all saints who remember to keep and do these sayings, walking in obedience to the commandments, shall receive health in their navel and marrow to their bones;

And shall find wisdom and great treasures of knowledge, even hidden treasures;

And shall run and not be weary, and shall walk and not faint.

(C) Hope

Hope is a feeling that what is wanted will happen, a desire accompanied by expectation. It is the thing that one has a hope for, a reason for hope, a person or thing on which one may base some hope. Repentance and Christ's subsequent forgiveness of our sins allows us to have hope that we can receive eternal exaltation as promised to the righteous. It is coupled with faith and charity. It provides motivation to keep the commandments. The wicked and unrepentant have no such hope.

Old Testament

Job 27:8 — For what is the hope of the hypocrite, though he hath gained, when God taketh away his soul?

Psalm 16:8–9 — I have set the Lord always before me: because he is at my right hand, I shall not be moved.

Therefore my heart is glad, and my glory rejoiceth: my flesh also shall rest in hope.

Proverbs 10:28 — The hope of the righteous shall be gladness: but the expectation of the wicked shall perish.

Proverbs 14:32 — The wicked is driven away in his wickedness: but the righteous hath hope in his death.

Jeremiah 17:7 — Blessed is the man that trusteth in the Lord, and whose hope the Lord is.

Joel 3:16 — The Lord will be the hope of his people.

New Testament

Paul touched upon the subject of hope in many of his epistles to the various congregations of saints (the Romans and Galatians, Timothy, Titus, and others).

Romans 5:1–2, 5 — Therefore being justified by faith, we have peace with God through our Lord Jesus Christ:

By whom also we have access by faith into this grace wherein we stand, and rejoice in hope of the glory of God. . . .

And hope maketh not ashamed; because the love of God is shed abroad in our hearts by the Holy Ghost which is given unto us.

Romans 15:4 — For whatsoever things were written aforetime were written for our learning, that we through patience and comfort of the scriptures might have hope.

Galatians 5:5 — For we through the Spirit wait for the hope of righteousness by faith.

1 Timothy 1:1 — Paul, an apostle of Jesus Christ by the commandment of God our Saviour, and Lord Jesus Christ, which is our hope.

Titus 1:2 — In hope of eternal life, which God, that cannot lie, promised before the world began.

Titus 3:7 — That being justified by his grace, we should be made heirs according to the hope of eternal life.

Hebrews 11:1 — Now faith is the substance of things hoped for, the evidence of things not seen.

Peter also speaks of the hope we have through Jesus Christ.

1 Peter 1:3–5 — Blessed be the God and Father of our Lord Jesus Christ, which according to his abundant mercy hath begotten us again unto a lively hope by the resurrection of Jesus Christ from the dead,

To an inheritance incorruptible, and undefiled, and that fadeth not away, reserved in heaven for you,

Who are kept by the power of God through faith unto salvation ready to be revealed in the last time.

Book of Mormon

Book of Mormon prophets also taught that if we follow the Savior (repent of our sins and receive forgiveness), we will have hope in eternal life.

2 Nephi 31:20	Wherefore, ye must press forward with a steadfastness in Christ, having a perfect brightness of hope, and a love of God and of all men. Wherefore, if ye shall press forward, feasting upon the word of Christ, and endure to the end, behold, thus saith the Father: Ye shall have eternal life.
Alma: 7:24	And see that ye have faith, hope, and charity, and then ye will always abound in good works.
Alma 32:21	And now as I said concerning faith—faith is not to have a perfect knowledge of things; therefore if ye have faith ye hope for things which are not seen, which are true.

The ancient Jaredites also understood the importance of hope in faith, and faith in hope. Ether taught:

Ether 12:4	Wherefore, whoso believeth in God might with surety hope for a better world, yea, even a place at the right hand of God, which hope cometh of faith, maketh an anchor to the souls of men, which would make them sure and steadfast, always abounding in good works being led to glorify God.

The Lord told the Jaredites:

Ether 12:28	Behold, I will show unto the Gentiles their weakness and I will show unto them that faith, hope and charity bringeth unto me—the fountain of all righteousness.

Moroni, the last prophet of the Book of Mormon, wrote:

Ether 12:32	And I also remember that thou hast said that thou hast prepared a house for man, yea, even among the mansions of thy Father, in which man might have a more excellent hope; wherefore man must hope, or he cannot receive an inheritance in the place which thou hast prepared.

Moroni recorded some of the teachings of his father, Mormon:

Moroni 7:40–43 — And again, my beloved brethren, I would speak unto you concerning hope. How is it that ye can attain unto faith, save ye shall have hope?

And what is it that ye shall hope for? Behold I say unto you that ye shall have hope through the atonement of Christ and the power of his resurrection, to be raised unto life eternal, and this because of your faith in him according to the promise.

Wherefore, if a man have faith he must needs have hope; for without faith there cannot be any hope.

And again, behold I say unto you that he cannot have faith and hope, save he shall be meek, and lowly of heart.

Moroni 8:26 — And the remission of sins bringeth meekness, and lowliness of heart; and because of meekness and lowliness of heart cometh the visitation of the Holy Ghost, which Comforter filleth with hope and perfect love, which love endureth by diligence unto prayer, until the end shall come, when all the saints shall dwell with God.

Moroni's final entry in his writings reminds us again of the importance of faith, hope, and charity:

Moroni 10:20–22 — Wherefore, there must be faith; and if there must be faith there must also be hope; and if there must be hope there must also be charity.

And except ye have charity ye can in nowise be saved in the kingdom of God; neither can ye be saved in the kingdom of God if ye have not faith; neither can ye if ye have no hope.

And if ye have no hope ye must needs be in despair; and despair cometh because of iniquity.

Doctrine and Covenants

The Lord stressed the importance of faith, hope, and charity again in these latter days.

D&C 4:5 And faith, hope, charity and love, with an eye single to the glory of God, qualify him for the work.

D&C 18:19 And if you have not faith, hope, and charity, you can do nothing.

Joseph Smith wrote an epistle to the Church affirming the hope we have in Christ's teachings:

D&C 128:21 And again, the voice of God in the chamber of old Father Whitmer, in Fayette, Seneca county, and at sundry times, and in divers places through all the travels and tribulations of this Church of Jesus Christ of Latter-day Saints! And the voice of Michael, the archangel; the voice of Gabriel, and of Raphael, and of divers angels, from Michael or Adam down to the present time, all declaring their dispensations, their rights, their keys, their honors, their majesty and glory, and the power of their priesthood; giving line upon line, precept upon precept; here a little, and thee a little; giving us consolation by holding forth that which is to come, confirming our hope!

To the peoples of the Old Testament, New Testament, Book of Mormon, and our day: the Lord has shown his grace in blessing the righteous with peace, inspiration, knowledge, and hope that benefits them here in mortality and will also bless them throughout the eternities.

Chapter 10

God Communicates with His Children

TENET: Beginning with Adam and Eve, the Lord has communicated with his children. He communicates with them in a variety of ways: (A) In person; (B) Out of the whirlwind; (C) Through the Holy Ghost; (D) Through angels; (E) Through prophets; (F) Through similitudes; (G) Through the Urim and Thummim and other devices; (H) Through visions and dreams.

As recorded in the Old Testament, "Surely the Lord God will do nothing, but he revealeth his secret unto his servants the prophets" (Amos 3:7). In Paul's epistle to the Hebrews, he reminded the people that "Jesus Christ [is] the same yesterday, and today, and for ever" (Hebrews 13:8). Thus, it stands to reason that God continues to communicate with his children today.

Sometimes he initiates the communication; sometimes it is in response to prayer. However, he doesn't respond when people are wicked.

(A) In person

Old Testament

Genesis 17:1	And when Abram was ninety years old and nine, the Lord appeared to Abram.
Genesis 35:1, 15	And God said unto Jacob, Arise, go up to Bethel, and dwell there: and make there an altar unto God,

that appeared unto thee when thou fleddest from the face of Esau thy brother.

And Jacob called the name of the place where God spake with him, Bethel.

Exodus 33:11 — And the Lord spake unto Moses face to face, as a man speaketh unto his friend.

Numbers 11:25 — And the Lord came down in a cloud, and spake unto him [unto Moses].

Numbers 12:5–8 — And the Lord came down in the pillar of the cloud, and stood in the door of the tabernacle, and called Aaron and Miriam: and they both came forth.

And he said, Hear now my words: If there be a prophet among you, I the Lord will make myself known unto him in a vision, and will speak unto him in a dream.

My servant Moses is not so, who is faithful in all mine house.

With him will I speak mouth to mouth, even apparently, and not in dark speeches; and the similitude of the Lord shall he behold: wherefore then were ye not afraid to speak against my servant Moses?

Deuteronomy 1:6 — The Lord our God spake unto us in Horeb, saying, Ye have dwelt long enough in this mount.

1 Samuel 3:10–11, 21

And the Lord came, and stood, and called as at other times, Samuel, Samuel, Then Samuel answered, Speak; for thy servant heareth.

And the Lord said to Samuel, Behold, I will do a thing in Israel, at which both the ears of every one that heareth it shall tingle. . . .

And the Lord appeared again in Shiloh: for the Lord revealed himself to Samuel in Shiloh by the word of the Lord.

Psalm 99:6–7 — Moses and Aaron among his priests, and Samuel among them that call upon his name; they called upon the Lord, and he answered them.

He spake unto them in the cloudy pillar: they kept his testimonies and the ordinance that he gave them.

New Testament

Mark 12:26 — Have ye not read in the book of Moses, how in the bush God spake unto him, saying, I am the God of Abraham, and the God of Isaac, and the God of Jacob?

John 9:29 — We know that God spake unto Moses.

Acts 9:4–6 — And he [Saul] fell to the earth, and heard a voice saying unto him, Saul, Saul, why persecutest thou me?

And he said, Who art thou, Lord? And the Lord said, I am Jesus whom thou persecutest: it is hard for thee to kick against the pricks.

And he trembling and astonished said, Lord, what wilt thou have me to do? And the Lord said unto him, Arise, and go into the city, and it shall be told thee what thou must do.

Book of Mormon

1 Nephi 11:11 — And I said unto him: To know the interpretation thereof—for I spake unto him as a man speaketh; for I beheld that he was in the form of a man; yet nevertheless, I knew that it was the Spirit of the Lord; and he spake unto me as a man speaketh with another.

3 Nephi 17:17 — And no tongue can speak, neither can there be written by any man, neither can the hearts of men conceive so great and marvelous things as we both saw and heard Jesus speak; and no one can conceive of the joy which filled our souls at the time we heard him pray for us unto the Father.

Ether 3:6, 9–13 — And it came to pass that when the brother of Jared had said these words, behold, the Lord stretched forth his hand and touched the stones one by one with his finger. And the veil was taken from off the eyes of the brother of Jared, and he saw the finger of the Lord; and it was as the finger of a man, like unto flesh, and blood; and the brother of Jared fell down before the Lord, for he was struck with fear. . . .

And the Lord said unto him: Because of thy faith thou hast seen that I shall take upon me flesh and blood; and never has man come before me with such exceeding faith as thou hast; for were it not so ye could not have seen my finger. Sawest thou more than this?

And he answered: Nay; Lord, show thyself unto me.

And the Lord said unto him: Believest thou the words which I shall speak?

And he answered: Yea, Lord, I know that thou speakest the truth, for thou art a God a truth, and canst not lie.

And when he had said these words, behold, the Lord showed himself unto him.

Doctrine and Covenants

The Lord also appeared to Joseph Smith and Oliver Cowdery in these latter days.

D&C 110:2–4 We saw the Lord standing upon the breastwork of the pulpit, before us; and under his feet was a paved work of pure gold, in color like amber.

His eyes were as a flame of fire; the hair of his head was white like the pure snow; his countenance shone above the brightness of the sun; and his voice was as the sound of the rushing of great waters, even the voice of Jehovah, saying:

I am the first and the last; I am he who liveth, I am he who was slain; I am your advocate with the Father.

Pearl of Great Price

God has communicated in person with his children from the time of Adam.

Moses 1:1–3	The words of God, which he spake unto Moses at a time when Moses was caught up into an exceedingly high mountain, And he saw God face to face, and talked with him, and the glory of God was upon Moses; therefore Moses could endure his presence. And God spake unto Moses, saying, Behold, I am the Lord God Almighty, and Endless is my name; for I am without beginning of days or end of years; and is not this endless?
Moses 6:22	And this is the genealogy of the sons of Adam, who was the son of God, with whom God himself conversed.

(B) Out of the whirlwind

Old Testament

Job 38:1–2	Then the Lord answered Job out of the whirlwind, and said, Who is this that darkeneth counsel by words without knowledge?

New Testament

Acts 2:1–4	And when the day of Pentecost was fully come, they were all with one accord in one place, And suddenly there came a sound from heaven as of a rushing mighty wind, and it filled all the house where they were sitting, And there appeared unto them cloven tongues like as of fire, and it sat upon each of them. And they were all filled with the Holy Ghost, and began to speak with other tongues, as the Spirit gave them utterance.

Doctrine and Covenants

In the prayer offered at the dedication of the temple of the Church of

Jesus Christ of Latter-day Saints at Kirtland, Ohio, March 27, 1836, the Prophet Joseph Smith prayed:

D&C 109: 36–37 Let it be fulfilled upon them, as upon those on the day of Pentecost; let the gift of tongues be poured out upon thy people, even cloven tongues as of fire, and the interpretation thereof.

And let thy house be filled, as with a rushing mighty wind, with thy glory.

The response to that petition written by Joseph Smith is recorded:

> Brother George A. Smith arose and began to prophesy, when a noise was heard like the sound of a rushing mighty wind, which filled the Temple, and all the congregation simultaneously arose, being moved upon by an invisible power; many began to speak in tongues and prophesy; others saw glorious visions; and I beheld the Temple was filled with angels, which fact I declared to the congregation. The people of the neighborhood came running together (hearing an unusual sound within, and seeing a bright light like a pillar of fire resting upon the Temple), and were astonished at what was taking place.[1]

(C) Through the Holy Ghost—through a still, small voice

Old Testament

Numbers 11:25 And the Lord came down in a cloud, and spake unto him, and took of the spirit that was upon him, and gave it unto the seventy elders: and it came to pass, that, when the spirit rested upon them, they prophesied, and did not cease.

New Testament

As long as Jesus was upon the earth, the Holy Ghost could not come and comfort them nor bear witness of Christ's divinity to them, but Christ told them when he went away, he would send the Holy Ghost.

John 16:7, 13 Nevertheless I tell you the truth; It is expedient for you that I go away: for if I go not away the Comforter will not come unto you; but if I depart, I will send him unto you. . . .

Howbeit when he, the Spirit of truth, is come, he will guide you into all truth: for he shall not speak of himself; but whatsoever he shall hear, that shall he speak: and he will shew you things to come.

Acts 1:8 — But ye shall receive power, after that the Holy Ghost is come upon you: and ye shall be witnesses unto me both in Jerusalem, and in all Judæa, and in Samaria, and unto the uttermost part of the earth.

Acts 1:16 — Men and brethren, this scripture must needs have been fulfilled, which the Holy Ghost by the mouth of David spake before concerning Judas, which was guide to them that took Jesus.

Acts 2:17–18 — And it shall come to pass in the last days, saith God, I will pour out of my Spirit upon all flesh: and your sons and your daughters shall prophesy. . . .

And on my servants and on my handmaidens I will pour out in those days of my Spirit; and they shall prophesy.

Acts 28:24–26 — And some believed the things which were spoken, and some believed not.

And when they agreed not among themselves, they departed, after that Paul had spoken one word, Well spake the Holy Ghost by Esaias the prophet unto our fathers,

Saying Go unto this people, and say, Hearing ye shall hear, and shall not understand; and seeing ye shall see, and not perceive.

1 Corinthians 12:7–11

But the manifestation of the Spirit is given to every man to profit withal.

For to one is given by the Spirit the word of wisdom; to another the word of knowledge by the same Spirit;

To another faith by the same Spirit; to another the gifts of healing by the same Spirit;

To another the working of miracles; to another

prophecy; to another discerning of spirits; to another divers kinds of tongues; to another the interpretation of tongues:

But all these worketh that one and the selfsame Spirit, dividing to every man severally as he will.

1 Timothy 4:1–3 — Now the Spirit speaketh expressly, that in the latter times some shall depart from the faith, giving heed to seducing spirits, and doctrines of devils;

Speaking lies in hypocrisy; having their conscience seared with a hot iron;

Forbidding to marry, and commanding to abstain from meats, which God hath created to be received with thanksgiving of them which believe and know the truth.

Book of Mormon

1 Nephi 10:19 — For he that diligently seeketh shall find; and the mysteries of God shall be unfolded unto them, by the power of the Holy Ghost, as well in these times as in times of old, and as well in times of old as in times to come; wherefore, the course of the Lord is one eternal round.

2 Nephi 31:13 — Yea, by following your Lord and your Savior down into the water, according to his word, behold, then shall ye receive the Holy Ghost, yea, then cometh the baptism of fire and of the Holy Ghost; and then can ye speak with the tongue of angels, and shout praises unto the Holy One of Israel.

Alma 5:46–47 — Behold, I say unto you they are made known unto me by the Holy Spirit of God. Behold, I have fasted and prayed many days that I might know these things of myself. And now I do know of myself that they are true; for the Lord God hath made them manifest unto me by his Holy Spirit; and this is the spirit of revelation which is in me.

And moreover, I say unto you that it has thus been revealed unto me, that the words which have

	been spoken by our fathers are true, even so according to the spirit of prophecy which is in me, which is also by the manifestation of the Spirit of God.
Alma 58:11	Yea, and it came to pass that the Lord our God did visit us with assurances that he would deliver us; yea, insomuch that he did speak peace to our souls.
Helaman 5:18	And it came to pass that Nephi and Lehi did preach unto the Lamanites with such great power and authority, for they had power and authority, given unto them that they might speak, and they also had what they should speak given unto them.
Helaman 5:46–47	And it came to pass that there came a voice unto them, yea, a pleasant voice, as if it were a whisper, saying: Peace, peace be unto you, because of your faith in my Well Beloved, who was from the foundation of the world.
3 Nephi 19:13	And it came to pass when they were all baptized and had come up out of the water, the Holy Ghost did fall upon them, and they were filled with the Holy Ghost and with fire.

Moroni 10:8–17 [11–16 condensed]

And again I exhort you, my brethren, that ye deny not the gifts of God, for they are many; and they come from the same God. And there are different ways that these gifts are administered: but it is the same God who worketh all in all; and they are given by the manifestations of the Spirit of God, unto men, to profit them.

For behold, to one is given by the Spirit of God, that he may teach the word of wisdom;

And to another, that he may teach he word of knowledge by the same Spirit;

And to another . . . great faith . . . the gifts of healing. . . . work mighty miracles . . . . prophesy concerning all things. . . . the beholding of angels and ministering spirits. . . . all kinds of tongues . . . interpretation of languages and of divers kinds of tongues.

And all these gifts come by the Spirit of Christ: and they come unto every man severally, according as he will.

Doctrine and Covenants

The Lord continues to communicate with his children today through the Holy Ghost.

D&C 11:10–11 Behold, thou hast a gift, or thou shalt have a gift if thou wilt desire of me in faith, with an honest heart, believing in the power of Jesus Christ, or in my power which speaketh unto thee;

For, behold, it is I that speak; behold, I am the light which shineth in darkness, and by my power I give these words unto thee.

D&C 18:34–36 These words are not of men nor of man, but of me; wherefore, you shall testify they are of me and not of man;

For it is my voice which speaketh them unto you; for they are given by my Spirit unto you, and by my power you can read them one to another; and save it were by my power you could not have them;

Wherefore, you can testify that you have heard my voice, and know my words.

The Savior revealed to Joseph Smith that his (Christ's) atonement applied to:

D&C 20:26 Not only those who believed after he came in the meridian of time, in the flesh, but all those from the beginning, even as many as were before he came, who believed in the words of the holy prophets, who spake as they were inspired by the gift of the Holy Ghost, who truly testified of him in all things, should have eternal life.

D&C 24:5–6 And thou shalt continue in calling upon God in my name, and writing the things which shall be given

	thee by the Comforter, and expounding all scriptures unto the church. And it shall be given thee in the very moment what thou shalt speak and write, and they shall hear it, or I will send unto them a cursing instead of a blessing.
D&C 28:4	And if thou art led at any time by the Comforter to speak or teach, or at all times by the way of commandment unto the church, thou mayest do it.

In a revelation received in November of 1831, the Lord confirms that he communicates with his children through the Holy Ghost:

D&C 68:3–4	And this is the ensample unto them [four elders to whom he was referring], that they shall speak as they are moved upon by the Holy Ghost. And whatsoever they shall speak when moved upon by the Holy Ghost shall be scripture, shall be the will of the Lord, shall be the mind of the Lord, shall be the word of the Lord, shall be the voice of the Lord, and the power of God unto salvation.
D&C 84:64	Therefore, as I said unto mine apostles I say unto you again, that every soul who believeth on your words, and is baptized by water for the remission of sins, shall receive the Holy Ghost.
D&C 100:5–6	Therefore, verily I say unto you, lift up your voices unto this people; speak the thoughts that I shall put into your hearts, and you shall not be confounded before men; For it shall be given you in the very hour, yea, in the very moment, what ye shall say.

(D) Through angels

Old Testament

In every dispensation of time, God has communicated with his children through angels.

Genesis 21:17	And God heard the voice of the lad; and the angel

of God called to Hagar out of heaven, and said unto her, What aileth thee, Hagar? fear not; for God hath heard the voice of the lad where he is.

Genesis 31:11 And the angel of God spake unto me in a dream, saying, Jacob: And I said, Here am I.

Judges 6:11–12, 22–23

And there came an angel of the Lord, and sat under an oak which was in Ophrah, that pertained unto Joash the Abi-ezrite: and his son Gideon threshed wheat by the winepress, to hide it from the Midianites.

And the angel of the Lord appeared unto him, and said unto him, The Lord is with thee, thou mighty man of valour. . . .

And when Gideon perceived that he was an angel of the Lord, Gideon said, Alas, O Lord God! for because I have seen an angel of the Lord face to face.

And the Lord said unto him, Peace be unto thee; fear not: thou shalt not die.

Judges 13:3, 6, 18, 20

And the angel of the Lord appeared unto the woman, and said unto her, Behold now, thou art barren, and bearest not: but thou shalt conceive, and bear a son. . . .

Then the woman came and told her husband, saying, A man of God came unto me, and his countenance was like the countenance of an angel of God, very terrible: but I asked him not whence he was, neither told me his name. . . .

And the angel of the Lord said unto him [Manoah], Why askest thou thus after my name, seeing it is secret? . . .

For it came to pass, when the flame went up toward heaven from off the altar, that the angel of the Lord ascended in the flame of the altar. And Manoah and his wife looked on it, and fell on their faces to the ground.

1 Kings 19:5, 7	And as he [Elijah] slept under a juniper tree, behold, then an angel touched him, and said unto him, Arise and eat. . . . And the angel of the Lord came again the second time, and touched him, and said, Arise and eat; because the journey is too great for thee.

Sometimes the Lord uses the services of unseen angels:

2 Kings 6:15–17	And when the servant of the man of God [Elisha] was risen early, and gone forth, behold, an host compassed the city both with horses and chariots. And his servant said unto him, Alas, my master! how shall we do? And he answered, Fear not: for they that be with us are more than they that be with them. And Elisha prayed, and said, Lord, I pray thee, open his eyes, that he may see. And the Lord opened the eyes of the young man; and he saw: and, behold, the mountain was full of horses and chariots of fire round about Elisha.

An angel conversed with Zechariah:

Zechariah 1:9	Then said I, O my lord, what are these? And the angel that talked with me said unto me, I will shew thee what these be.

New Testament

Angels ministered unto the Savior when he was on the earth:

Matthew 4:11	Then the devil leaveth him, and, behold, angels came and ministered unto him.

Jesus Christ declared that in the latter days:

Matthew 13:41	The Son of man shall send forth his angels, and they shall gather out of his kingdom all things that offend, and them which do iniquity.

Sometimes God's messengers are translated beings.

Matthew 17:1–3	And after six days Jesus taketh Peter, James, and

John his brother, and bringeth them up into an high mountain apart,

And was transfigured before them: and his face did shine as the sun, and his raiment was white as the light.

And behold, there appeared unto them Moses and Elias talking with him.

Luke 1:11, 13, 19 — And there appeared unto him [Zacharias] an angel of the Lord standing on the right side of the altar of incense.

But the angel said unto him, Fear not, Zacharias: for thy prayer is heard; and thy wife Elisabeth shall bear thee a son, and thou shalt call his name John.

And the angel answering said unto him, I am Gabriel, that stand in the presence of God; and am sent to speak unto thee, and to shew thee these glad tidings.

John 20:11–12 — But Mary stood without at the sepulchre weeping: and as she wept, she stooped down, and looked into the sepulchre,

And seeth two angels in white sitting, the one at the head, and the other at the feet, where the body of Jesus had lain.

Acts 5:19–20 — But the angel of the Lord by night opened the prison doors, and brought them [Peter and John] forth, and said,

Go, stand and speak in the temple to the people all the words of this life.

Hebrews 13:2 — Be not forgetful to entertain strangers: for thereby some have entertained angels unawares.

John revealed that in the latter days, angels would again be sent to earth to communicate with God's children.

Revelation 14:6 — And I saw another angel fly in the midst of heaven, having the everlasting gospel to preach unto them that dwell on the earth, and to every nation, and kindred, and tongue, and people.

Revelation 22:16	I Jesus have sent mine angel to testify unto you these things in the churches.

Book of Mormon

Book of Mormon records reveal that the Lord also used angels to communicate with his children here in America between 600 B.C. and A.D. 400.

Nephi reprimanded his brothers for their wickedness:

1 Nephi 17:45	Ye are swift to do iniquity but slow to remember the Lord your God. Ye have seen an angel, and he spake unto you; yea, ye have heard his voice from time to time; and he hath spoken unto you in a still small voice, but ye were past feeling, that ye could not feel his words; wherefore, he has spoken unto you like unto the voice of thunder, which did cause the earth to shake as if it were to divide asunder.

Later, Nephi explained to his brothers:

2 Nephi 32:3	Angels speak by the power of the Holy Ghost; wherefore, they speak the words of Christ.

Jacob, Nephi's brother, described an encounter with Sherem who declared that there would be no Christ:

Jacob 7:5	And he had hope to shake me from the faith, notwithstanding the many revelations and the many things which I had seen concerning these things; for I truly had seen angels, and they had ministered unto me. And also, I had heard the voice of the Lord speaking unto me in very word, from time to time; wherefore, I could not be shaken [between 544 and 421 B.C.]

An angel appeared unto King Benjamin, about 124 B.C., and taught him about the eventual birth of the Savior.

Mosiah 3:2–5	And the things which I shall tell you are made known unto me by an angel from God. And he said

unto me: Awake; and I awoke, and behold he stood before me.

And he said unto me: Awake, and hear the words which I shall tell thee; for behold, I am come to declare unto you the glad tiding of great joy.

For the Lord hath heard thy prayers, and hath judged of thy righteousness, and hath sent me to declare unto thee that thou mayest rejoice; and that thou mayest declare unto thy people, that they may also be filled with joy.

For behold, the time cometh, and is not far distant, that with power, the Lord Omnipotent who reigneth, who was, and is from all eternity to all eternity, shall come down from heaven among the children of men, and shall dwell in a tabernacle of clay, and shall go forth amongst men, working mighty miracles.

In Mormon's abridgement of the records, he reported that the unbelieving sons of King Mosiah and their friend, the son of Alma, rebelled against God.

Mosiah 27:11–14

And as I said unto you, as they were going about rebelling against God, behold, the angel of the Lord appeared unto them; and he descended as it were in a cloud; and he spake as it were with a voice of thunder, which caused the earth to shake upon which they stood;

And so great was their astonishment, that they fell to the earth, and understood not the words which he spake unto them.

Nevertheless he cried again, saying: Alma, arise and stand forth, for why persecutest thou the church of God? For the Lord hath said: This is my church, and I will establish it; and nothing shall overthrow it, saved it is the transgression of my people.

And again, the angel said: Behold, the Lord hath heard the prayers of his people, and also the prayers of his servant, Alma, who is thy father; for he has prayed with much faith concerning thee that thou mightest be brought to the knowledge of the truth; therefore, for this purpose have I come to convince thee of the power and authority of God, that the prayers of his servants might be answered according to their faith [between 100 and 92 B.C.].

After Alma the son of Alma had been chastised by an angel and had become converted, he spent his life teaching the word of the Lord.

Alma 8:14–16

And it came to pass that while he was journeying thither, being weighed down with sorrow, wading through much tribulation and anguish of soul, because of the wickedness of the people who were in the city of Ammonihah . . . behold an angel of the Lord appeared unto him, saying:

Blessed art thou, Alma; therefore, lift up thy head and rejoice, for thou hast great cause to rejoice. . . .

And behold, I am sent to command thee that thou return to the city of Ammonihah, and preach again unto the people of the city.

Alma 13:21–22, 24–26

And now it came to pass that when Alma had said these words unto them, he stretched forth his hand unto them and cried with a mighty voice, saying: Now is the time to repent, for the day of salvation draweth nigh;

Yea, and the voice of the Lord, by the mouth of angels, doth declare it unto all nations. . . .

For behold, angels are declaring it unto many at this time in our land. . . .

And now we only wait to hear the joyful news declared unto us by the mouth of angels, of his coming. . . .[Christ's birth]

And it shall be made known unto just and holy men, by the mouth of angels, at the time of his coming, that the words of our fathers may be fulfilled, according to that which they have spoken concerning him, which was according to the spirit of prophecy which was in them [about 82 B.C.].

Alma the Younger explained his conversion to his son Shiblon.

Alma 38:7	But behold, the Lord in his great mercy sent his angel to declare unto me that I must stop the work of destruction among his people; yea, and I have seen an angel face to face, and he spake with me, and his voice was as thunder, and it shook the whole earth [about 73 B.C.].

The Prophet Mormon, who abridged the records that comprise the book that bears his name, the Book of Mormon, intermittently narrates the events that were recorded:

Helaman 5:48–49	And now, when they heard this they cast up their eyes as if to behold from whence the voice came; and behold, they saw the heavens open; and angels came down out of heaven and ministered unto them. And there were about three hundred souls who saw and heard these things; and they were bidden to go forth and marvel not, neither should they doubt [about 30 B.C.].

Following the birth, death, and resurrection of the Savior, angels continued to minister unto the people. Moroni, the last prophet of the Book of Mormon, recorded some of the words of his father, Mormon:

Moroni 7:29–31	And because he [Jesus Christ] hath done this, my beloved brethren, have miracles ceased? Behold I say unto you, Nay; neither have angels ceased to minister unto the children of men. For behold, they are subject unto him, to minister according to the word of his command, showing themselves unto them of strong faith and a firm mind in every form of godliness. And the office of their ministry is to call men unto repentance, and to fulfill and to do the work of the covenants of the Father, which he hath made unto the children of men, to prepare the way among

the children of men, by declaring the word of Christ unto the chosen vessels of the Lord, that they may bear testimony of him [between A.D. 400 and 421].

Doctrine and Covenants

Just as angels and other messengers have administered to people throughout the various dispensations, including the appearance of Moses and Elias to Christ's apostles on the mount of transfiguration, angels and other messengers have communicated with prophets and apostles in these latter days.

D&C 13:1 Upon you my fellow servants, in the name of Messiah I [Gabriel] confer the Priesthood of Aaron, which holds the keys of the ministering of angels, and of the gospel of repentance, and of baptism by immersion for the remission of sins; and this shall never be taken again from the earth, until the sons of Levi do offer again an offering unto the Lord in righteousness.

D&C 110:11–16 After this vision closed, the heavens were again opened unto us; and Moses appeared before us [Joseph Smith and Oliver Cowdery], and committed unto us the keys of the gathering of Israel from the four parts of the earth, and the leading of the ten tribes from the land of the north.

After this, Elias appeared, and committed the dispensation of the gospel of Abraham, saying that in us and our seed all generations after us should be blessed.

After this vision had closed, another great and glorious vision burst upon us; for Elijah the prophet, who was taken to heaven without tasting death, stood before us, and said:

Behold, the time has fully come, which was spoken of by the mouth of Malachi—testifying that he [Elijah] should be sent, before the great and dreadful day of the Lord come—

To turn the hearts of the fathers to the children,

and the children to the fathers, lest the whole earth be smitten with a curse—

Therefore, the keys of this dispensation are committed into your hands; and by this ye may know that the great and dreadful day of the Lord is near, even at the doors.

D&C 129:1–9

There are two kinds of beings in heaven, namely: Angels, who are resurrected personages, having bodies of flesh and bones—

For instance, Jesus said: Handle me and see, for a spirit hath not flesh and bones, as ye see me have.

Secondly, The spirits of just men made perfect, they who are not resurrected, but inherit the same glory.

When a messenger comes saying he has a message from God, offer him your hand and request him to shake hands with you.

If he be an angel he will do so, and you will feel his hand.

If he be the spirit of a just man made perfect he will come in his glory; for that is the only way he can appear—

Ask him to shake hands with you, but he will not move, because it is contrary to the order of heaven for a just man to deceive; but he will still deliver his message.

If it be the devil as an angel of light, when you ask him to shake hands he will offer you his hand, and you will not feel anything; you may therefore detect him.

These are three grand keys whereby you may know whether any administration is from God.

Pearl of Great Price

Moses 5:6–7

And after many days an angel of the Lord appeared unto Adam, saying: Why dost thou offer sacrifices unto the Lord? And Adam said unto him: I know not, save the Lord commanded me.

And the angel spake, saying: This thing is a similitude of the sacrifice of the Only Begotten of the Father, which is full of grace and truth.

Moses 7:27 — And Enoch beheld angels descending out of heaven, bearing testimony of the Father and Son, and the Holy Ghost fell on many, and they were caught up by the powers of heaven into Zion.

Joseph Smith recorded the events surrounding the appearance of the Angel Moroni on September 21, 1823.

JS—H 1:30, 33 — While I was thus in the act of calling upon God, I discovered a light appearing in my room, which continued to increase until the room was lighter than at noonday, when immediately a personage appeared at my bedside, standing in the air, for his feet did not touch the floor. . . .

He called me by name, and said unto me that he was a messenger sent from the presence of God to me, and that his name was Moroni; that God had a work for me to do; and that my name should be had for good and evil among all nations, kindreds, and tongues, or that it should be both good and evil spoken of among all people.

(E) Through prophets

The Lord has always revealed his word through his prophets. The Prophet Amos declared:

Amos 3:7 — Surely the Lord God will do nothing, but he revealeth his secret unto his servants the prophets.

That was true in Old Testament times, in New Testament times, in Book of Mormon times, and it is true in our day. He reveals his word through prophets, seers, and revelators.

Old Testament

Exodus 4:11–12 — And the Lord said unto him [Moses], Who hath made man's mouth? or who maketh the dumb, or deaf, or the seeing, or the blind? have not I the Lord?

	Now therefore go, and I will be with thy mouth, and teach thee what thou shalt say.
Deuteronomy 18:18	I will raise them up a Prophet from among their brethren, like unto thee, and will put my words in his mouth; and he shall speak unto them all that I shall command him.
1 Samuel 3:20–21	And all Israel from Dan even to Beer-sheba knew that Samuel was established to be a prophet of the Lord. And the Lord appeared again in Shiloh: for the Lord revealed himself to Samuel in Shiloh by the word of the Lord.
1 Samuel 9:9	Beforetime in Israel, when a man went to inquire of God, thus he spake, Come, and let us go to the seer: for he that is now called a Prophet was beforetime called a Seer.
2 Samuel 23:1–2	Now these be the last words of David. David the son of Jesse said, and the man who was raised up on high, the anointed of the God of Jacob, and the sweet psalmist of Israel, said, The Spirit of the Lord spake by me, and his word was in my tongue.
2 Kings 17:13	Yet the Lord testified against Israel, and against Judah, by all the prophets, and by all the seers, saying, Turn ye from your evil ways, and keep my commandments and my statutes, according to all the law which I commanded your fathers, and which I sent to you by my servants the prophets.

The Lord told Jeremiah:

Jeremiah 1:5	Before I formed thee in the belly I knew thee; and before thou camest forth out of the womb I sanctified thee, and I ordained thee a prophet unto the nations.
Jeremiah 7:25	Since the day that your fathers came forth out of the

land of Egypt unto this day I have even sent unto you all my servants the prophets, daily rising up early and sending them.

Hosea 12:10 — I have also spoken by the prophets, and I have multiplied visions, and used similitudes, by the ministry of the prophets.

New Testament

Matthew 11:13 — For all the prophets and the law prophesied until John.

Luke 1:70 — As he spake by the mouth of his holy prophets, which have been since the world began.

John the Baptist testified:

John 3:34 — For he whom God hath sent [Christ] speaketh the words of God: for God giveth not the Spirit by measure unto him.

John 6:14 — Then those men, when they had seen the miracle that Jesus did, said, This is of a truth that prophet that should come into the world.

Acts 3:20–21 — And he shall send Jesus Christ, which before was peached unto you:

Whom the heaven must receive until the times of restitution of all things, which God hath spoken by the mouth of all his holy prophets since the world began.

Acts 15:32 — And Judas and Silas, being prophets also themselves, exhorted the brethren with many words, and confirmed them.

1 Corinthians 12:28 — And God hath set some in the church, first apostles, secondarily prophets, thirdly teachers, after that miracles, then gifts of healings, helps, governments, diversities of tongues.

Ephesians 2:19–20 — Now therefore ye are no more strangers and foreigners, but fellowcitizens with the saints, and of the household of God;

And are built upon the foundation of the apostles and prophets, Jesus Christ himself being the chief corner stone.

Ephesians 4:11–12 — And he gave some, apostles; and some, prophets; and some, evangelists; and some, pastors and teachers;

For the perfecting of the saints, for the work of the ministry, for the edifying of the body of Christ.

Hebrews 1:1–2 — God, who at sundry times and in divers manners spake in time past unto the fathers by the prophets,

Hath in these last days spoken unto us by his Son, whom he hath appointed heir of all things, by whom also he made the worlds.

2 Peter 1:21 — For the prophecy came not in old time by the will of man: but holy men of God spake as they were moved by the Holy Ghost.

Book of Mormon

Nephi recounted the words of his father, Lehi:

1 Nephi 10:4–5, 7 — Yea, even six hundred years from the time that my father left Jerusalem, a prophet would the Lord God raise up among the Jews—even a Messiah, or, in other words, a Savior of the world.

And he also spake concerning the prophets, how great a number had testified of these things, concerning this Messiah, of whom he had spoken, or this Redeemer of the world. . . .

And he spake also concerning a prophet who should come before the Messiah, to prepare the way of the Lord.

1 Nephi 22:2 — And I, Nephi, said unto them: Behold they were manifest unto the prophet by the voice of the Spirit; for by the Spirit are all things made known unto the prophets, which shall come upon the children of men according to the flesh.

2 Nephi 25:18–19	For there is save one Messiah spoken of by the prophets, and that Messiah is he who should be rejected of the Jews. For according to the words of the prophets, the Messiah cometh in six hundred years from the time that my father left Jerusalem; and according to the words of the prophets, and also the word of the angel of God, his name shall be Jesus Christ, the Son of God.
Jacob 4:13	Behold, my brethren, he that prophesieth, let him prophesy to the understanding of men; for the Spirit speaketh the truth and lieth not. Wherefore, it speaketh of things as they really are, and of things as they really will be; wherefore, these things are manifested unto us plainly, for the salvation of our souls. But behold, we are not witnesses alone in these things; for God also spake them unto prophets of old.
Mosiah 8:15–17	And the king said that a seer is greater than a prophet. And Ammon said that a seer is a revelator and a prophet also; and a gift which is greater can no man have except he should possess the power of God, which no man can; yet a man may have great power given him from God. But a seer can know of things which are past, and also of things which are to come, and by them shall all things be revealed, or, rather, shall secret things be made manifest, and hidden things shall come to light, and things which are not known shall be made known by them, and also things shall be made known by them which otherwise could not be known.
Helaman 5:18	And it came to pass that Nephi and Lehi did preach unto the Lamanites with such great power and authority, for they had power and authority given unto them that they might speak, and they also had what they should speak given unto them.

3 Nephi 1:13	Lift up your head and be of good cheer; for behold, the time is at hand, and on this night shall the sign be given, and on the morrow come I into the world, to show unto the world that I will fulfill all that which I have caused to be spoken by the mouth of my holy prophets.

Doctrine and Covenants

D&C 45:15	Wherefore, hearken and I will reason with you, and I will speak unto you and prophesy, as unto men in days of old.

On December 25, 1832, the Prophet Joseph Smith received the following revelation:

D&C 87:1–4	Verily, thus saith the Lord concerning the wars that will shortly come to pass, beginning at the rebellion of South Carolina, which will eventually terminate in the death and misery of many souls; And the time will come that war will be poured out upon all nations, beginning at this place. For behold, the Southern States shall be divided against the Northern States, and the Southern States will call on other nations, even the nation of Great Britain, as it is called, and they shall also call upon other nations, in order to defend themselves against other nations; and then war shall be poured out upon all nations. And it shall come to pass, after many days, slaves shall rise up against their masters, who shall be marshaled and disciplined for war. [Note: the fulfillment of this prophecy occurred almost 30 years later when the Civil War began in 1861.]

(F) Through the Urim and Thummim and other devices

Just as we mortal parents use the technology we have to communicate with our children—telephone, email, text messaging, letters, and so forth—the Lord uses special devices to guide and instruct his children: the Urim and Thummim, for instance, as well as other devices.

Old Testament

Exodus 28:30 — And thou shalt put in the breastplate of judgment the Urim and the Thummim; and they shall be upon Aaron's heart, when he goeth in before the Lord: and Aaron shall bear the judgment of the children of Israel upon his heart before the Lord continually.

Leviticus 8:8 — And he put the breastplate upon him: also he put in the breastplate the Urim and the Thummim.

Numbers 27:21 — And he shall stand before Eleazar the priest, who shall ask counsel for him after the judgment of Urim before the Lord.

Deuteronomy 33:8 — And of Levi he said, Let thy Thummim and thy Urim be with thy holy one, whom thou didst prove at Massah, and with whom thou didst strive at the waters of Meribah.

When people are unworthy, the Lord does not answer them.

1 Samuel 28:6 — And when Saul inquired of the Lord, the Lord answered him not, neither by dreams, nor by Urim, nor by prophets.

Ezra 2:63; Nehemiah 7:65

And the Tirshatha said unto them, that they should not eat of the most holy things, till there stood up a priest with Urim and with Thummim.

New Testament

Revelation 2:17 — He that hath an ear, let him hear what the Spirit saith unto the churches; To him that overcometh will I give to eat of the hidden manna, and will give him a white stone, and in the stone a new name written, which no man knoweth saving he that receiveth it.

Book of Mormon

1 Nephi 16:10, 16, 28–29

And it came to pass that as my father arose in the morning, and went forth to the tent door, to his great astonishment he beheld upon the ground a round ball of curious workmanship; and it was of fine brass. And within the ball were two spindles; and the one pointed the way whither we should go into the wilderness. . . .

And we did follow the directions of the ball, which led us in the more fertile parts of the wilderness. . . .

And it came to pass that I, Nephi, beheld the pointers which were in the ball, that they did work according to the faith and diligence and heed which we did give unto them.

And there was also written upon them a new writing, which did give us understanding concerning the ways of the Lord; and it was written and changed from time to time, according to the faith and diligence which we gave unto it.

1 Nephi 18:12, 21 — And it came to pass that after they had bound me insomuch that I could not move, the compass, which had been prepared of the Lord, did cease to work. . . .

And it came to pass after they had loosed me, behold, I took the compass, and it did work whither I desired it.

2 Nephi 5:12 — And I, Nephi, had also brought the records which were engraven upon the plates of brass; and also the ball, or compass, which was prepared for my father by the hand of the Lord, according to that which is written.

Omni 1:20 — And it came to pass in the days of Mosiah, there was a large stone brought unto him with engravings on it; and he did interpret the engravings by the gift and power of God.

Mosiah 8:13 — Now Ammon said unto him: I can assuredly tell thee, O king, of a man that can translate the records; for he has wherewith that he can look, and translate all records that are of ancient date; and it is a gift from God. And the things are called interpreters, and no man can look in them except he be commanded, lest he should look for that he ought not and he should perish. And whosoever is commanded to look in them, the same is called a seer.

Mosiah 28:20 — And now, as I said unto you, that after King Mosiah had done these things, he took the plates of brass, and all the things which he had kept, and conferred them upon Alma, who was the son of Alma; yea, all the records, and also the interpreters, and conferred them upon him, and commanded him that he should keep and preserve them.

Alma 37:21, 24, 38–40

And now, I will speak unto you concerning those twenty-four plates, that ye keep them . . . and that ye preserve these interpreters. . . .

And now, my son, these interpreters were prepared that the word of God might be fulfilled. . . .

And now, my son, I have somewhat to say concerning the thing which our fathers call a ball, or director—or our fathers called it Liahona, which is, being interpreted, a compass; and the Lord prepared it.

And behold, there cannot any man work after the manner of so curious a workmanship. And behold, it was prepared to show unto our fathers the course which they should travel in the wilderness.

And it did work for them according to their faith in God; therefore, if they had faith to believe that God could cause that those spindles should point the way they should go, behold, it was done; therefore they had this miracle, and also many other miracles wrought by the power of God, day by day.

Following the confounding of languages at the tower of Babel, the Lord said unto the brother of Jared:

Ether 3:23–24 — And behold, these two stones will I give unto thee, and ye shall seal them up also with the things which ye shall write.

For behold, the language which ye shall write I have confounded; wherefore I will cause in my own due time that these stones shall magnify to the eyes of men these things which ye shall write.

Doctrine and Covenants

At the beginning of this dispensation of time, the Urim and Thummim were again given to a prophet for the purpose of receiving revelation and for translating ancient records.

D&C 10:1 — Now, behold, I say unto you, that because you delivered up those writings which you had power given unto you to translate by the means of the Urim and Thummim, into the hands of a wicked man, you have lost them.

The Lord gave the following revelation through Joseph Smith through the Urim and Thummim to Oliver Cowdery, David Whitmer, and Martin Harris in June of 1829:

D&C 17:1 — Behold, I say unto you, that you must rely upon my word, which if you do with full purpose of heart, you shall have a view of the plates, and also of the breastplate, the sword of Laban, the Urim and Thummim, which were given to the brother of Jared upon the mount, when he talked with the Lord face to face, and the miraculous directors which were given to Lehi while in the wilderness, on the borders of the Red Sea.

The Prophet Joseph Smith taught:

D&C 130:8–11 — The place where God resides is a great Urim and Thummim.

This earth, in its sanctified and immortal state, will be made like unto crystal and will be a Urim and Thummim to the inhabitants who dwell thereon, whereby all things pertaining to an inferior kingdom, or all kingdoms of a lower order, will be manifest to those who dwell on it; and this earth will be Christ's.

Then the white stone mentioned in Revelation 2:17, will become a Urim and Thummim to each individual who receives one, whereby things pertaining to a higher order of kingdoms will be made known;

And a white stone is given to each of those who come into the celestial kingdom, whereon is a new name written, which no man knoweth save he that receiveth it. The new name is the key word [April 2, 1843].

Pearl of Great Price

Consistent with the Old Testament, we read in the Pearl of Great Price that Abraham had the Urim and Thummim.

Abraham 3:1 — And I, Abraham, had the Urim and Thummim, which the Lord my God had given unto me, in Ur of the Chaldees.

We also read in Joseph Smith's history that the Urim and Thummim were entrusted to him so he could carry out the work of the restoration of the Church.

JS—H 1:34–35 — He [the Angel Moroni] said there was a book deposited, written upon gold plates, giving an account of the former inhabitants of this continent. . . .

Also, that there were two stones in silver bows—and these stones, fastened to a breastplate, constituted what is called the Urim and Thummim—deposited with the plates; and the possession and use of these stones were what constituted "seers" in ancient or former times; and that God had prepared them for the purpose of translating the book.

Following Angel Moroni's instructions, Joseph Smith went to the hill Cumorah. He said:

JS—H 1:52, 59, 62 — Having removed the earth, I obtained a lever, which I got fixed under the edge of the stone, and with a little exertion raised it up. I looked in, and there indeed did I behold the plates, the Urim and Thummim, and the breastplate, as stated by the messenger. . . .

At length the time arrived for obtaining the plates, the Urim and Thummim, and the breastplate. On the twenty-second day of September, one thousand eight hundred and twenty-seven, having gone as usual at the end of another year to the place where they were deposited, the same heavenly messenger delivered them up to me with this charge: that I should be responsible for them; that if I should let them go carelessly, or through any neglect of mine, I should be cut off; but that if I would use all my endeavors to preserve them, until he, the messenger, should call for them, they should be protected. . . .

By this timely aid was I enabled to reach the place of my destination in Pennsylvania; and immediately after my arrival there I commenced copying the characters off the plates. I copied a considerable number of them, and by means of the Urim and Thummim I translated some of them.

(G) Through dreams

Less tangible, but equally real, the Lord communicates with his children through dreams.

Old Testament

Genesis 20:3 — But God came to Abimelech in a dream by night.

Genesis 31:11–12, 24

And the angel of God spake unto me in a dream, saying, Jacob: And I said, Here am I.

And he said, Lift up now thine eyes, and see, all the rams which leap upon the cattle are ringstraked, speckled, and grisled: for I have seen all that Laban doeth unto thee. . . .

And God came to Laban the Syrian in a dream by night, and said unto him, Take heed that thou speak not to Jacob either good or bad.

Genesis 37:5, 9 — And Joseph dreamed a dream [of the sheaves], and he told it his brethren: and they hated him yet the more. . . .

And he dreamed yet another dream, and told it his brethren, and said, Behold, I have dreamed a dream more; and, behold, the sun and the moon and the eleven stars made obeisance to me.

Genesis 40:8 — And they [the king's imprisoned chief butler and chief baker] said unto him [Joseph], We have dreamed a dream, and there is no interpreter of it.

Joseph interpreted their dreams—in three days the chief butler would be restored to his position and in three days the chief baker would be hanged.

Genesis 41:1–7 — And it came to pass at the end of two full years, that Pharaoh dreamed: and, behold, he stood by the river.

And, behold, there came up out of the river seven well favoured kine and fatfleshed; and they fed in a meadow.

And, behold, seven other kine came up after them out of the river, ill favoured and leanfleshed; and stood by the other kine upon the brink of the river.

And the ill favoured and leanfleshed kine did eat up the seven well favoured and fat kine. So Pharaoh awoke.

And he slept and dreamed the second time: and, behold, seven ears of corn came up upon one stalk, rank and good.

And, behold, seven thin ears and blasted with the east wind sprung up after them.

And the seven thin ears devoured the seven rank and full ears. And Pharaoh awoke, and, behold, it was a dream.

Joseph interpreted the dreams: there would be seven years of plenty followed by seven years of famine (vs. 26–32):

Genesis 41:25	And Joseph said unto Pharaoh, The dream of Pharaoh is one: God hath shewed Pharaoh what he is about to do.
Numbers 12:6	And he said, Hear now my words: If there be a prophet among you, I the Lord will make myself known unto him in a vision, and will speak unto him in a dream.
Judges 7:13, 15	And when Gideon was come, behold, there was a man that told a dream unto his fellow, and said, Behold, I dreamed a dream, and, lo, a cake of barley bread tumbled into the host of Midian, and came unto a tent, and smote it that it fell, and overturned it, that the tent lay along. . . . And it was so, when Gideon heard the telling of the dream, and the interpretation thereof, that he worshipped, and returned into the host of Israel, and said, Arise; for the Lord hath delivered into your hand the host of Midian.
1 Kings 3:5	In Gibeon the Lord appeared to Solomon in a dream by night.
Daniel 2:1, 19	And in the second year of the reign of Nebuchadnezzar Nebuchadnezzar dreamed dreams, wherewith his spirit was troubled, and his sleep brake from him. . . . Then was the secret revealed unto Daniel in a night vision. Then Daniel blessed the God of heaven.
Daniel 7:1, 15–16	In the first year of Belshazzar king of Babylon Daniel had a dream and visions of his head upon his bed: then he wrote the dream, and told the sum of the matters. . . . I Daniel was grieved in my spirit in the midst of my body, and the visions of my head troubled me. I came near unto one of them that stood by, and

asked him the truth of all this. So he told me, and made me know the interpretation of the things.

Joel 2:28–29 — And it shall come to pass afterward, that I will pour out my spirit upon all flesh; and your sons and your daughters shall prophesy, your old men shall dream dreams, your young men shall see visions:

And also upon the servants and upon the handmaids in those days will I pour out my spirit.

New Testament

Matthew 1:20 — But while he thought on these things, behold, the angel of the Lord appeared unto him in a dream, saying, Joseph, thou son of David, fear not to take unto thee Mary thy wife: for that which is conceived in her is of the Holy Ghost.

Matthew 2: 12–13 — And being warned of God in a dream that they should not return to Herod, they [the wise men] departed into their own country another way.

And when they were departed, behold, the angel of the Lord appeareth to Joseph in a dream, saying, Arise, and take the young child and his mother, and flee into Egypt; and be thou there until I bring thee word: for Herod will seek the young child to destroy him.

Matthew 2:19–20 — But when Herod was dead, behold, an angel of the Lord appeareth in a dream to Joseph in Egypt,

Saying, Arise, and take the young child and his mother, and go into the land of Israel: for they are dead which sought the young child's life.

Book of Mormon

1 Nephi 1:16 — And now I, Nephi, do not make a full account of the things which my father hath written, for he hath written many things which he saw in visions and in dreams.

1 Nephi 2:2 — And it came to pass that the Lord commanded my

	father, even in a dream, that he should take his family and depart into the wilderness.
1 Nephi 3:2	And it came to pass that he spake unto me saying: Behold I have dreamed a dream, in the which the Lord hath commanded me that thou and thy brethren shall return to Jerusalem [to get the brass plates from Laban].
1 Nephi 8:2	And it came to pass that while my father tarried in the wilderness he spake unto us, saying: Behold, I have dreamed a dream; or, in other words, I have seen a vision.

This was a vision of the tree of life.

1 Nephi 15:21	And it came to pass that they [Nephi's brothers] did speak unto me again, saying: What meaneth this thing which our father saw in a dream? What meaneth the tree which he saw?
Ether 9:3	And the Lord warned Omer in a dream that he should depart out of the land; wherefore Omer departed out of the land with his family.

(H) Through visions

The Lord also communicates with his children through visions.

Old Testament

Genesis 15:1	After these things the word of the Lord came unto Abram in a vision, saying, Fear not, Abram: I am thy shield, and thy exceeding great reward.
Genesis 46:2–3	And God spake unto Israel in the visions of the night, and said, Jacob, Jacob. And he said, Here am I. And he said, I am God, the God of thy father: fear not to go down into Egypt; for I will there make of thee a great nation.
2 Chronicles 26:5	And he [Uzziah] sought God in the days of Zechariah, who had understanding in the visions of God: and as long as he sought the Lord, God made him to prosper.

Psalm 89:19	Then thou spakest in vision to thy holy one, and saidst, I have laid help upon one that is mighty; I have exalted one chosen out of the people.
Proverbs 29:18	Where there is no vision, the people perish: but he that keepeth the law, happy is he.
Isaiah 1:1	The vision of Isaiah the son of Amoz, which he saw concerning Judah and Jerusalem in the days of Uzziah, Jotham, Ahaz, and Hezekiah, kings of Judah.
Jeremiah 1:11–14	Moreover the word of the Lord came unto me, saying; Jeremiah, what seest thou? And I said, I see a rod of an almond tree. Then said the Lord unto me, Thou hast well seen: for I will hasten my word to perform it. And the word of the Lord came unto me the second time, saying, What seest thou? And I said, I see a seething pot; and the face thereof is toward the north. Then the Lord said unto me, Out of the north an evil shall break forth upon all the inhabitants of the land.
Ezekiel 1:1	Now it came to pass in the thirtieth year, in the fourth month, in the fifth day of the month, as I was among the captives by the river of Chebar, that the heavens were opened, and I saw visions of God.
Daniel 1:17	As for these four children, God gave them knowledge and skill in all learning and wisdom: and Daniel had understanding in all visions and dreams.

New Testament

Matthew 17:1–3, 9	And after six days Jesus taketh Peter, James, and John his brother, and bringeth them up into an high mountain apart, And was transfigured before them: and his face did shine as the sun, and his raiment was white as the light.

And, behold, there appeared unto them Moses and Elias talking with him. . . .

And as they came down from the mountain, Jesus charged them, saying, Tell the vision to no man, until the Son of man be risen again from the dead.

Luke 1:21–22

And the people waited for Zacharias, and marvelled that he tarried so long in the temple.

And when he came out, he could not speak unto them: and they perceived that he had seen a vision in the temple; for he beckoned unto them, and remained speechless.

Acts 7:55–56, 59

But he [Stephen], being full of the Holy Ghost, looked up stedfastly into heaven, and saw the glory of God, and Jesus standing of the right hand of God,

And said, Behold, I see the heavens opened, and the Son of man standing on the right hand of God. . . .

And they stoned Stephen, calling upon God, and saying, Lord Jesus, receive my spirit.

Acts 18:9–10

Then spake the Lord to Paul in the night by a vision, Be not afraid, but speak, and hold not thy peace:

For I am with thee, and no man shall set on thee to hurt thee: for I have much people in this city.

Book of Mormon

Visions were not limited to the peoples of the Old and New Testaments. Those residing upon the American continents also received visions.

1 Nephi 1:5–8

Wherefore it came to pass that my father, Lehi, as he went forth prayed unto the Lord, yea, even with all his heart, in behalf of his people.

And it came to pass as he prayed unto the Lord, there came a pillar of fire and dwelt upon a rock before him; and he saw and heard much; and because of the things which he saw and heard he did quake and tremble exceedingly.

And it came to pass that he returned to his own house at Jerusalem; and he cast himself upon his bed, being overcome with the Spirit and the things which he had seen.

And being thus overcome with the Spirit, he was carried away in a vision, even that he saw the heavens open, and he thought he saw God sitting upon his throne, surrounded with numberless concourses of angels in the attitude of singing and praising their God.

He also saw the eventual birth of the Savior and the calling of the Twelve Apostles.

1 Nephi 5:4 — And it had come to pass that my father spake unto her, saying: I know that I am a visionary man; for if I had not seen the things of God in a vision I should not have known the goodness of God, but had tarried at Jerusalem, and had perished with my brethren.

1 Nephi 10:17 — And it came to pass after I, Nephi, having heard all the words of my father, concerning the things which he saw in a vision, and also the things which he spake by the power of the Holy Ghost, which power he received by faith on the Son of God—and the Son of God was the Messiah who should come—I, Nephi, was desirous also that I might see, and hear, and know of these things, by the power of the Holy Ghost, which is the gift of God unto all those who diligently seek him, as well in times of old as in the time that he should manifest himself unto the children of men.

1 Nephi 11:1 — For it came to pass after I had desired to know the things that my father had seen, and believing that the Lord was able to make them known unto me, as I sat pondering in mine heart I was caught away in the Spirit of the Lord, yea, into an exceeding high

mountain, which I never had before seen, and upon which I never had before set my foot.

Nephi was shown in vision what his father was shown in vision (the tree of life) and given the interpretation thereof (1 Nephi 11–14).

2 Nephi 1:4 — For, behold, said he [Lehi], I have seen a vision, in which I know that Jerusalem is destroyed; and had we remained in Jerusalem we should also have perished.

Alma 8:20 — And the man [Amulek] said unto him [Alma]: I am a Nephite, and I know that thou art a holy prophet of God, for thou art the man whom an angel said in a vision: Thou shalt receive. Therefore, go with me into my house and I will impart unto thee of my food; and I know that thou wilt be a blessing unto me and my house.

Alma 19:16 — And it came to pass that they did call on the name of the Lord, in their might, even until they had all fallen to the earth, save it were one of the Lamanitish women, whose name was Abish, she having been converted unto the Lord for many years, on account of a remarkable vision of her father.

Doctrine and Covenants

Because the Lord is the same yesterday, today, and tomorrow, he continues to communicate with his children through visions.

D&C 76:5, 10–14 — For thus saith the Lord—I, the Lord, am merciful and gracious unto those who fear me, and delight to honor those who serve me in righteousness and in truth unto the end. . . .

For by my Spirit will I enlighten them, and by my power will I make known unto them the secrets of my will—yea, even those things which eye has not seen, nor ear heard, nor yet entered into the heart of man.

We, Joseph Smith, Jun., and Sidney Rigdon, being in the Spirit on the sixteenth day of February, in the year of our Lord one Thousand eight hundred and thirty-two—

By the power of the Spirit our eyes were opened and our understandings were enlightened, so as to see and understand the things of God—

Even those things which were from the beginning before the world was, which were ordained of the Father, through his Only Begotten Son, who was in the bosom of the Father, even from the beginning;

Of whom we bear record; and the record which we bear is the fulness of the gospel of Jesus Christ, who is the Son, whom we saw and with whom we conversed in the heavenly vision.

D&C 76:47 — Nevertheless, I, the Lord, show it by vision unto many, but straightway shut it up again.

D&C 76:50 — And again we bear record—for we saw and heard, and this is the testimony of the gospel of Christ concerning them who shall come forth in the resurrection of the just.

Joseph Smith and Sidney Rigdon received a vision regarding the eventual resurrection of both the just and the unjust, the expulsion of Lucifer from heaven, and his evil activities as Satan on the earth; the terrible fate of those who become sons of perdition; the distinctive glories of the various kingdoms of glory: celestial, terrestrial, and telestial, and the qualifications of those who attain each of those glories; and heard the Savior declare that all shall be judged and rewarded according to their works and that every knee shall bow and every tongue confess "to him who sits upon the throne forever and ever" (D&C 76:110).

On January 21, 1836, the Prophet Joseph Smith received another vision wherein he saw his deceased brother Alvin in the celestial kingdom; and learned from the Lord the doctrine of salvation for the dead and that:

D&C 137:10 — All children who die before they arrive at the years of accountability are saved in the celestial kingdom of heaven.

D&C 138: 11, 60 And as I [Joseph F. Smith] pondered over these things which are written, the eyes of my understanding were opened, and the Spirit of the Lord rested upon me, and I saw the hosts of the dead, both small and great. . . . [The vision is then explained.]

Thus was the vision of the redemption of the dead revealed to me, and I bear record, and I know that this record is true, through the blessing of our Lord and Savior, Jesus Christ, even so. Amen.

Pearl of Great Price

Moses 1:27–29 And it came to pass, as the voice was still speaking, Moses cast his eyes and beheld the earth, yea, even all of it; and there was not a particle of it which he did not behold, discerning it by the spirit of God.

And he beheld also the inhabitants thereof, and there was not a soul which he beheld not; and he discerned them by the Spirit of God; and their numbers were great, even numberless as the sand upon the sea shore.

And he beheld many lands; and each land was called earth, and there were inhabitants on the face thereof.

Moses 7:21–28 And it came to pass that the Lord showed unto Enoch all the inhabitants of the earth; and he beheld, and lo, Zion, in process of time, was taken up into heaven. And the Lord said unto Enoch: Behold mine abode forever.

And Enoch also beheld the residue of the people which were the sons of Adam; and they were a mixture of all the seed of Adam save it was the seed of Cain, for the seed of Cain were black, and had not place among them.

And after that Zion was taken up into heaven, Enoch beheld, and lo, all the nations of the earth were before him;

And there came generation upon generation; and Enoch was high and lifted up, even in the bosom of the Father, and of the Son of Man; and behold, the power of Satan was upon all the face of the earth.

And he saw angels descending out of heaven; and he heard a voice saying: Wo, wo be unto the inhabitants of the earth.

And he beheld Satan; and he had a great chain in his hand, and it veiled the whole face of the earth with darkness; and he looked up and laughed, and his angels rejoiced.

And Enoch beheld angels descending out of heaven, bearing testimony of the Father and Son; and the Holy Ghost fell on many, and they were caught up by the powers of heaven into Zion.

And it came to pass that the God of heaven looked upon the residue of the people, and he wept; and Enoch bore record of it, saying: How is it that the heavens weep, and shed forth their tears as the rain upon the mountains?

Abraham 1:15–16

And as they lifted up their hands upon me, that they might offer me up and take away my life, behold, I lifted up my voice unto the Lord my God, and the Lord hearkened and heard, and he filled me with the vision of the Almighty, and the angel of his presence stood by me, and immediately unloosed my bands;

And his voice was unto me: Abraham, Abraham, behold, my name is Jehovah, and I have heard thee, and have come down to deliver thee, and to take thee away from thy father's house, and from all thy kinsfolk, into a strange land which thou knowest not of.

JS—H 1:17

It no sooner appeared that I found myself delivered from the enemy which held me bound. When the light rested upon me I saw two Personages, whose brightness and glory defy all description, standing above me in the air. One of them spake unto me, calling me by name and said, pointing to the other—This is My Beloved Son. Hear Him!

JS—H 1:21 Some few days after I had this vision, I happened to be in company with one of the Methodist preachers, who was very active in the before mentioned religious excitement; and, conversing with him on the subject of religion, I took occasion to give him an account of the vision which I had had. I was greatly surprised at his behavior; he treated my communication not only lightly, but with great contempt, saying it was all of the devil, that there were no such things as visions or revelations in these days; that all such things had ceased with the apostles, and that there would never be any more of them.

JS—H 1:24–25 However, it was nevertheless a fact that I had beheld a vision. I have thought since, that I felt much like Paul, when he made his defense before King Agrippa, and related the account of the vision he had when he saw a light, and heard a voice; but still there were but few who believed him; some said he was dishonest, others said he was mad; and he was ridiculed and reviled. But all this did not destroy the reality of his vision. He had seen a vision, he knew he had, and all the persecution under heaven could not make it otherwise; and though they should persecute him unto death, yet he knew, and would know to his latest breath, that he had both seen a light and heard a voice speaking unto him, and all the world could not make him think or believe otherwise.

So it was with me. I had actually seen a light, and in the midst of that light I saw two Personages, and they did in reality speak to me; and though I was hated and persecuted for saying that I had seen a vision, yet it was true; and while they were persecuting me, reviling me, and speaking all manner of evil against me falsely for so saying, I was led to say in my heart: Why persecute me for telling the truth? I have actually seen a vision; and who am I that I can withstand God, or why does the world think to make me deny what I have actually seen? For I had seen a vision; I knew it, and I knew that God knew it, and I could not deny it, neither dared I do it; at least I knew that by so doing I would offend God, and come under condemnation.

Notes

1. Joseph Smith, *History of The Church of Jesus Christ of Latter-day Saints,* edited by B. H. Roberts, 2nd ed., rev., vol. 2. (Salt Lake City: The Church of Jesus Christ of Latter-day Saints), 428.

Chapter 11

Born Again

TENET: When Adam and Eve partook of the forbidden fruit in the Garden of Eden, they became subject to mortal death and also died spiritually; that is, they became separated from Heavenly Father and became subject to Satan's temptations. Man's fallen state is naturally carnal and sensual. Therefore, in order for a person to be saved in the kingdom of God (be reunited with our Father in Heaven), he must be "born again." He must become "dead" to carnal and sensual things, and be "born" to spiritual desires. Just as our birth into mortality involved three elements—water, blood, and Spirit—being born spiritually also involves three elements—water (baptism by immersion, which represents Christ's death, burial, and resurrection as well as our willingness to accept Christ, join his Church, and take upon us his name; being cleansed from our sins and being "born" as a new person—receiving a "new heart," that is, having our heart focused on spiritual things rather than carnal and sensual things); blood (accepting the Savior's blood atonement for us as evidenced by our keeping the commandments and following his teachings); and Spirit (receiving the Holy Ghost, which is the baptism of Fire, the Holy Ghost being the Sanctifier).

Old Testament

1 Samuel 10:9	And it was so, that when he [Saul] had turned his back to go from Samuel, God gave him another heart: and all those signs came to pass that day.

Jeremiah 24:7 — And I will give them an heart to know me, that I am the Lord: and they shall be my people, and I will be their God: for they shall return unto me with their whole heart.

Ezekiel 11:19–21 — And I will give them one heart, and I will put a new spirit within you; and I will take the stony heart out of their flesh, and will give them an heart of flesh:

That they may walk in my statutes, and keep mine ordinances, and do them: and they shall be my people, and I will be their God.

But as for them whose heart walketh after the heart of their detestable things and their abominations, I will recompense their way upon their own heads saith the Lord God.

Ezekiel 18:31 — Cast away from you all your transgressions, whereby ye have transgressed; and make you a new heart and a new spirit: for why will ye die, O house of Israel?

New Testament

Matthew 3:11 — I indeed baptize you with water unto repentance: but he that cometh after me is mightier than I, whose shoes I am not worthy to bear: he shall baptize you with the Holy Ghost, and with fire.

Luke 3:16 — John answered, saying unto them all, I indeed baptize you with water; but one mightier than I cometh, the latchet of whose shoes I am not worthy to unloose: he shall baptize you with the Holy Ghost and with fire.

Nicodemus was puzzled by Christ's teaching that a man must be born again and asked:

John 3:4 — How can a man be born when he is old? can he enter the second time into his mother's womb, and be born?

People today continue to be confused as to what it means to be born again. Christ responded that a man must:

John 3:5–6

Be born of water and of the Spirit, or he cannot enter into the kingdom of God.

That which is born of the flesh is flesh; and that which is born of the Spirit is spirit.

Paul explained this in more detail to the Roman saints.

Romans 6:3–12

Know ye not, that so many of us as were baptized into Jesus Christ were baptized into his death?

Therefore we are buried [immersed in water] with him by baptism into death: that like as Christ was raised up from the dead by the glory of the Father, even so we also should walk in newness of life.

For if we have been planted together in the likeness of his death, we shall be also in the likeness of his resurrection:

Knowing this, that our old man is crucified with him, that the body of sin might be destroyed, that henceforth we should not serve sin.

For he that is dead is freed from sin.

Now if we be dead with Christ, we believe that we shall also live with him:

Knowing that Christ being raised from the dead dieth no more; death hath no more dominion over him.

For in that he died, he died unto sin once: but in that he liveth, he liveth unto God.

Likewise reckon ye also yourselves to be dead indeed unto sin, but alive unto God through Jesus Christ our Lord.

Let not sin therefore reign in your mortal body, that ye should obey it in the lusts thereof.

Romans 12:2

And be not conformed to this world: but be ye transformed by the renewing of our mind, that ye may prove what is that good, and acceptable, and perfect, will of God.

Paul taught the same doctrine to the Corinthians.

2 Corinthians 5:17 Therefore if any man be in Christ, he is a new creature: old things are passed away; behold, all things are become new.

He encouraged the Ephesians to "put on the new man."

Ephesians 4:17–24 This I say therefore, and testify in the Lord, that ye henceforth walk not as other Gentiles walk, in the vanity of their mind,

Having the understanding darkened, being alienated from the life of God through the ignorance that is in them, because of the blindness of their heart:

Who being past feeling have given themselves over unto lasciviousness, to work all uncleanness with greediness.

But ye have not so learned Christ;

If so be that ye have heard him, and have been taught by him, as the truth is in Jesus;

That ye put off concerning the former conversation the old man, which is corrupt according to the deceitful lusts;

And be renewed in the spirit of your mind;

And that ye put on the new man, which after God is created in righteousness and true holiness.

He used the same phrase, to "put on the new man," in his epistle to the Colossians.

Colossians 3:8–10 But now ye also put off all these; anger, wrath, malice, blasphemy, filthy communication out of your mouth.

Lie not one to another, seeing that ye have put off the old man with his deeds;

And have put on the new man, which is renewed in knowledge after the image of him that created him:

In Peter's epistle, he equates being born again with purifying our souls, obeying truth, loving our fellow man, living by the word of God.

1 Peter 1:22–23	Seeing ye have purified your souls in obeying the truth through the Spirit unto unfeigned love of the brethren, see that ye love one another with a pure heart fervently: Being born again, not of corruptible seed, but of incorruptible, by the word of God, which liveth and abideth for ever.
1 Peter 2:1–2	Wherefore laying aside all malice, and all guile, and hypocrisies, and envies, and all evil speakings, As newborn babes, desire the sincere milk of the word, that ye may grow thereby.

John's words echo those of Peter and Paul.

1 John 2:29	If ye know that he is righteous, ye know that every one that doeth righteousness is born of him.
JST, 1 John 3:9	Whosoever is born of God doth not continue in sin; for the Spirit of God remaineth in him; and he cannot sin, because he is born of God, having received that holy Spirit of promise.
1 John 3:14	We know that we have passed from death unto life, because we love the brethren. He that loveth not his brother abideth in death.
1 John 4:7	Beloved, let us love one another: for love is of God; and ever one that loveth is born of God, and knoweth God.
1 John 5:1, 4	Whosoever believeth that Jesus is the Christ is born of God: and every one that loveth him that begat loveth him also that is begotten of him. . . . For whatsoever is born of God overcometh the world: and this is the victory that overcometh the world, even our faith.
1 John 5:18	We know that whosoever is born of God sinneth not; but he that is begotten of God keepeth himself, and that wicked one toucheth him not.

Book of Mormon

Prophets of the Book of Mormon preached the importance of being "born again" and explained the doctrine very explicitly.

2 Nephi 31:13	Wherefore, my beloved brethren, I know that if ye shall follow the Son, with full purpose of heart, acting no hypocrisy and no deception before God, but with real intent, repenting of your sins, witnessing unto the Father that ye are willing to take upon you the name of Christ, by baptism—Yea, by following your Lord and your Savior down into the water [be baptized by immersion], according to his word, behold, then shall ye receive the Holy Ghost; yea, then cometh the baptism of fire and of the Holy Ghost.
Mosiah 3:19	For the natural man is an enemy to God, and has been from the fall of Adam, and will be, forever and ever, unless he yields to the enticings of the Holy Spirit, and putteth off the natural man and becometh a saint through the atonement of Christ the Lord, and becometh as a child, submissive, meek, humble, patient, full of love, willing to submit to all things which the Lord seeth fit to inflict upon him, even as a child doth submit to his father.
Mosiah 5:2	And they all cried with one voice, saying: Yea, we believe all the words which thou hast spoken unto us; and also, we know of their surety and truth, because of the Spirit of the Lord Omnipotent, which has wrought a mighty change in us, or in our hearts, that we have no more disposition to do evil, but to do good continually.
Mosiah 5:7	And now, because of the covenant which ye have made ye shall be called the children of Christ, his sons, and his daughters; for behold, this day he hath spiritually begotten you; for ye say that your hearts are changed through faith on his name; therefore, ye are born of him and have become his sons and his daughters.

Mosiah 27:24–29	For, said he, I have repented of my sins, and have been redeemed of the Lord; behold I am born of the Spirit. And the Lord said unto me: Marvel not that all mankind, yea, men and women, all nations, kindreds, tongues and people, must be born again; yea, born of God, changed from their carnal and fallen state, to a state of righteousness, being redeemed of God, becoming his sons and daughters; And thus they become new creatures; and unless they do this, they can in nowise inherit the kingdom of God. I say unto you, unless this be the case, they must be cast off; and this I know, because I was like to be cast off. Nevertheless, after wading through much tribulation, repenting nigh unto death, the Lord in mercy hath seen fit to snatch me out of an everlasting burning, and I am born of God. My soul hath been redeemed from the gall of bitterness and bonds of iniquity. I was in the darkest abyss; but now I behold the marvelous light of God. My soul was racked with eternal torment; but I am snatched, and my soul is pained no more.
Alma 5:12–14	And according to his faith there was a mighty change wrought in his heart. Behold I say unto you that this is all true. And behold, he preached the word unto your fathers, and a mighty change was also wrought in their hearts, and they humbled themselves and put their trust in the true and living God. And behold, they were faithful until the end; therefore they were saved. And now behold, I ask of you, my brethren of the church, have ye spiritually been born of God? Have ye received his image in your countenances? Have ye experienced this mighty change in your hearts?

Alma 5:49	And now I say unto you that this is the order after which I am called, yea, to preach unto my beloved brethren, yea, and every one that dwelleth in the land; yea, to preach unto all, both old and young, both bond and free; yea, I say unto you the aged, and also the middle aged, and the rising generation; yea, to cry unto them that they must repent and be born again.
Alma 7:14	Now I say unto you that ye must repent, and be born again; for the Spirit saith if ye are not born again ye cannot inherit the kingdom of heaven; therefore come and be baptized unto repentance, that ye may be washed from your sins, that ye may have faith on the Lamb of God, who taketh away the sins of the world, who is mighty to save and to cleanse from all unrighteousness.
Alma 19:33	And it came to pass that when Ammon arose he also administered unto them, and also did all the servants of Lamoni; and they did all declare unto the people the self-same thing—that their hearts had been changed; that they had no more desire to do evil.
Alma 22:15–16	And it came to pass that after Aaron had expounded these things unto him, the king said: What shall I do that I may have this eternal life of which thou hast spoken? Yea, what shall I do that I may be born of God, having this wicked spirit rooted out of my breast, and receive his Spirit, that I may be filled with joy, that I may not be cast off at the last day? Behold, said he, I will give up all that I possess, yea, I will forsake my kingdom, that I may receive this great joy. But Aaron said unto him: If thou desirest this thing, if thou wilt bow down before God, yea, if thou wilt repent of all thy sins, and will bow down before God, and call on his name in faith, believing that ye shall receive, then shalt thou receive the hope which thou desirest.

Alma 36:23–24	But behold, my limbs did receive their strength again, and I stood upon my feet, and did manifest unto the people that I had been born of God. Yea, and from that time even until now, I have labored without ceasing, that I might bring souls unto repentance; that I might bring them to taste of the exceeding joy of which I did taste; that they might also be born of God, and be filled with the Holy Ghost.
Alma 38:6	Now, my son, I would not that ye should think that I know these things of myself, but it is the Spirit of God which is in me which maketh these things known unto me; for if I had not been born of God I should not have known these things.
Helaman 5:45	And behold, the Holy Spirit of God did come down from heaven, and did enter into their hearts, and they were filled as if with fire, and they could speak forth marvelous words.
Helaman 15:7–8	And behold, ye do know of yourselves, for ye have witnessed it, that as many of them as are brought to the knowledge of the truth, and to know of the wicked and abominable traditions of their fathers, and are led to believe the holy scriptures, yea, the prophecies of the holy prophets, which are written, which leadeth them to faith on the Lord, and unto repentance, which faith and repentance bringeth a change of heart unto them— Therefore, as many as have come to this, ye know of yourselves are firm and steadfast in the faith, and in the thing wherewith they have been made free.

Doctrine and Covenants

The Savior confirmed in these latter days that being born again involves blood (a person must believe in Christ's atonement, as evidenced by their righteous actions), water (baptism by immersion), and Spirit (receiving the Gift of the Holy Ghost).

D&C 5:16	And behold, whosoever believeth on my words, them will I visit with the manifestation of my Spirit; and they shall be born of me, even of water and of the Spirit.
D&C 18:17–25	Behold, you have my gospel before you, and my rock, and my salvation. Ask the Father in my name, in faith believing that you shall receive, and you shall have the Holy Ghost, which manifesteth all things which are expedient unto the children of men. And if you have not faith, hope, and charity, you can do nothing. Contend against no church, save it be the church of the devil. Take upon you the name of Christ, and speak the truth in soberness. And as many as repent and are baptized in my name, which is Jesus Christ, and endure to the end, the same shall be saved. Behold, Jesus Christ is the name which is given of the Father, and there is none other name given whereby man can be saved; Wherefore, all men must take upon them the name which is given of the Father, for in that name shall they be called at the last day; Wherefore, if they know not the name by which they are called, they cannot have place in the kingdom of my Father.
D&C 19:31	And of tenets thou shalt not talk, but thou shalt declare repentance and faith on the Savior, and remission of sins by baptism, and by fire, yea, even the Holy Ghost.
D&C 76:69	These are they who are just men made perfect through Jesus the mediator of the new covenant, who wrought out this perfect atonement through the shedding of his own blood.

Pearl of Great Price

From Adam's day to our day, men have been commanded to repent and be born again. Enoch recorded:

Moses 6:50–53, 57–60

> But God hath made known unto our fathers that all men must repent.
>
> And he called upon our father Adam by his own voice, saying: I am God; I made the world, and men before they were in the flesh.
>
> And he also said unto him: If thou wilt turn unto me, and hearken unto my voice, and believe, and repent of all thy transgressions, and be baptized, even in water, in the name of mine Only Begotten Son, who is full of grace and truth, which is Jesus Christ, the only name which shall be given under heaven, whereby salvation shall come unto the children of men, ye shall receive the gift of the Holy Ghost, asking all things in his name and whatsoever ye shall ask, it shall be given you.
>
> And our father Adam spake unto the Lord, and said: Why is it that men must repent and be baptized in water? And the Lord said unto Adam: Behold I have forgiven thee thy transgression in the Garden of Eden. . . .
>
> Wherefore teach it unto your children, that all men, everywhere, must repent, or they can in nowise inherit the kingdom of God, for no unclean thing can dwell there, or dwell in his presence; for, in the language of Adam, Man of Holiness is his name, and the name of his Only Begotten is the Son of Man, even Jesus Christ, a righteous Judge, who shall come in the meridian of time.
>
> Therefore I give unto you a commandment, to teach these things freely unto your children, saying;
>
> That by reason of transgression cometh the fall, which fall bringeth death, and inasmuch as ye were born into the world by water, and blood, and the spirit, which I have made, and so became of dust

a living soul, even so ye must be born again into the kingdom of heaven, of water, and of the Spirit, and be cleansed by blood, even the blood of mine Only Begotten; that ye might be sanctified from all sin, and enjoy the words of eternal life in this world, and eternal life in the world to come, even immortal glory;

For by the water ye keep the commandment; by the Spirit ye are justified, and by the blood ye are sanctified.

Moses 6:64–66

And it came to pass, when the Lord had spoken with Adam, our father, that Adam cried unto the Lord, and he was caught away by the Spirit of the Lord, and was carried down into the water, and was laid under the water, and was brought forth out of the water.

And thus he was baptized, and the Spirit of God descended upon him, and thus he was born of the Spirit, and became quickened in the inner man.

And he heard a voice out of heaven, saying: Thou art baptized with fire, and with the Holy Ghost. This is the record of the Father, and the Son, from henceforth and forever.

Chapter 12

Baptism

TENET: Jesus taught that people must be baptized by water and by fire or they cannot enter into the kingdom of God. He set the example by being baptized. Baptism: (A) Is a commandment: everyone must be baptized in order to be saved; (B) Represents the burial and resurrection of our Savior, Jesus Christ; (C) Shows our willingness to follow God's commandments; (D) Brings us into membership in Christ's church; (E) Represents our repentance and willingness to keep the commandments; the burying of our sins; coming forth from the water clean; having no desire to do evil, but to have a change in heart, being born again—that is, born of the water and of the spirit (or fire); (F) Jesus set the example.

There are two baptisms: baptism of water and baptism by fire; both are necessary. Baptism is by immersion and must be performed by one having authority to do so. In order for those who die without having been appropriately baptized to receive the same blessings that those who are baptized receive, proxy baptism is done for the dead. Children do not need to be baptized until they reach the age of accountability (eight years old). Infants and children who die before they reach the age of accountability do not need baptism.

(A) Baptism is a commandment.

Everyone must be baptized in order to be saved

New Testament

Matthew 28:19–20	Go ye therefore, and teach all nations, baptizing them in the name of the Father, and of the Son, and of the Holy Ghost: Teaching them to observe all things whatsoever I have commanded you: and, lo, I am with you alway, even unto the end of the world. Amen.
Mark 16:16	He that believeth and is baptized shall be saved; but he that believeth not shall be damned.
John 3:5	Jesus answered, Verily, verily, I say unto thee. Except a man be born of water and of the Spirit, he cannot enter into the kingdom of God.
1 Peter 3:21	The like figure whereunto even baptism doth also now save us (not the putting away of the filth of the flesh, but the answer of a good conscience toward God,) by the resurrection of Jesus Christ.

Book of Mormon

2 Nephi 9:23–24	And he commandeth all men that they must repent, and be baptized in his name, having perfect faith in the Holy One of Israel, or they cannot be saved in the kingdom of God. And if they will not repent and believe in his name, and be baptized in his name, and endure to the end, they must be damned; for the Lord God, the Holy One of Israel, has spoken it.
2 Nephi 31:5	And now, if the Lamb of God, he being holy, should have need to be baptized by water, to fulfill all righteousness, O then, how much more need have we, being unholy, to be baptized, yea, even by water!
3 Nephi 11:33–34	And whoso believeth in me, and is baptized, the same shall be saved; and they are they who shall inherit the kingdom of God. And whoso believeth not in me, and is not baptized, shall be damned.

3 Nephi 27:20	Now this is the commandment: Repent, all ye ends of the earth, and come unto me and be baptized in my name, that ye may be sanctified by the reception of the Holy Ghost, that ye may stand spotless before me at the last day.
Ether 4:18–19	Therefore, repent all ye ends of the earth, and come unto me, and believe in my gospel, and be baptized in my name; for he that believeth and is baptized shall be saved; but he that believeth not shall be damned; and signs shall follow them that believe in my name. And blessed is he that is found faithful unto my name at the last day, for he shall be lifted up to dwell in the kingdom prepared for him from the foundation of the world. And behold it is I that hath spoken it. Amen.

Doctrine and Covenants

D&C 18:22	And as many as repent and are baptized in my name, which is Jesus Christ, and endure to the end, the same shall be saved.
D&C 18:41–42	And you must preach unto the world, saying: You must repent and be baptized, in the name of Jesus Christ; For all men must repent and be baptized, and not only men, but women, and children who have arrived at the years of accountability.
D&C 84:64, 74–75	Therefore, as I said unto mine apostles I say unto you again, that every soul who believeth on your words, and is baptized by water for the remission of sins, shall receive the Holy Ghost. . . . Verily, verily, I say unto you, they who believe not on your words, and are not baptized in water in my name, for the remission of their sins, that they may receive the Holy Ghost, shall be damned, and shall not come into my Father's kingdom where my Father and I am.

And this revelation unto you, and commandment, is in force from this very hour upon all the world, and the gospel is unto all who have not received it.

D&C 112:28–29 But purify your hearts before me; and then go ye into all the world, and preach my gospel unto every creature who has not received it;

And he that believeth and is baptized shall be saved, and he that believeth not, and is not baptized, shall be damned.

Pearl of Great Price

Moses 6:51–53 And he called upon our father Adam by his own voice, saying: I am God; I made the world, and men before they were in the flesh.

And he also said unto him: If thou wilt turn unto me, and hearken unto my voice, and believe, and repent of all thy transgressions, and be baptized, even in water, in the name of mine Only Begotten Son, who is full of grace and truth, which is Jesus Christ, the only name which shall be given under heaven, whereby salvation shall come unto the children of men, ye shall receive the gift of the Holy Ghost, asking all things in his name, and whatsoever ye shall ask, it shall be given you.

And our father Adam spake unto the Lord, and said: why is it that men must repent and be baptized in water? And the Lord said unto Adam: Behold I have forgiven thee thy transgression in the Garden of Eden.

Moses 7:11 And he gave unto me [Enoch] a commandment that I should baptize in the name of the Father, and of the Son, which is full of grace and truth, and of the Holy Ghost, which beareth record of the Father and the Son.

(B) Baptism represents the burial and resurrection of our Savior, Jesus Christ

New Testament

Romans 6:3–4 Know ye not, that so many of us as were baptized into Jesus Christ were baptized into his death?

Therefore we are buried with him by baptism into death: that like as Christ was raised up from the dead by the glory of the Father, even so we also should walk in newness of life.

Colossians 2:12 — Buried with him in baptism, wherein also ye are risen with him through the faith of the operation of God, who hath raised him from the dead.

Doctrine and Covenants

D&C 76:51 — They are they who received the testimony of Jesus, and believed on his name and were baptized after the manner of his burial, being buried in the water in his name, and this according to the commandment which he has given.

D&C 128:12 — Herein is glory and honor, and immortality and eternal life—The ordinance of baptism by water, to be immersed therein in order to answer to the likeness of the dead, that one principle might accord with the other; to be immersed in the water and come forth out of the water is in the likeness of the resurrection of the dead in coming forth out of their graves; hence, this ordinance was instituted to form a relationship with the ordinance of baptism for the dead, being in likeness of the dead.

(C) Baptism shows our willingness to follow God's commandments

New Testament

Acts 2:36–38 — Therefore let all the house of Israel know assuredly, that God hath made that same Jesus, whom ye have crucified, both Lord and Christ.

Now when they heard this, they were pricked in their heart, and said unto Peter and to the rest of the apostles, Men and brethren, what shall we do?

Then Peter said unto them, Repent, and be baptized every one of you in the name of Jesus Christ for the remission of sins, and ye shall receive the gift of the Holy Ghost.

Acts 19:4–5 Then said Paul, John verily baptized with the baptism of repentance, saying unto the people, that they should believe on him which should come after him, that is, on Christ Jesus.

When they heard this, they were baptized in the name of the Lord Jesus.

Book of Mormon

Mosiah 18:10 Now I say unto you, if this be the desire of your hearts, what have you against being baptized in the name of the Lord, as a witness before him that ye have entered into a covenant with him, that ye will serve him and keep his commandments, that he may pour out his Spirit more abundantly upon you?

Mosiah 21:35 They were desirous to be baptized as a witness and a testimony that they were willing to serve God with all their hearts.

3 Nephi 7:25 Therefore, there were ordained of Nephi, men unto this ministry, that all such as should come unto them should be baptized with water, and this as a witness and a testimony before God, and unto the people, that they had repented and received a remission of their sins.

(D) Baptism brings us into membership in Christ's Church

New Testament

Galatians 3:26–27 For ye are all the children of God by faith in Christ Jesus.

For as many of you as have been baptized into Christ have put on Christ.

Book of Mormon

Mosiah 18:17 And they [204 people baptized in the waters of Mormon by Alma] were called the church of God, or the church of Christ, from that time forward.

And it came to pass that whosoever was baptized by the power and authority of God was added to his church.

Alma 4:4 — And they began to establish the church more fully; yea, and many were baptized in the waters of Sidon and were joined to the church of God.

3 Nephi 18:5 — And when the multitude had eaten and were filled, he [the resurrected Christ] said unto the disciples: Behold there shall one be ordained among you, and to him will I give power that he shall break bread and bless it and give it unto the people of my church, unto all those who shall believe and be baptized in my name.

3 Nephi 21:22 — But if they will repent and hearken unto my words, and harden not their hearts, I [Christ] will establish my church among them, and they shall come in unto the covenant and be numbered among this the remnant of Jacob, unto whom I have given this land for their inheritance.

3 Nephi 26:21 — And they who were baptized in the name of Jesus were called the church of Christ.

4 Nephi 1:1 — And it came to pass that the thirty and fourth year passed away, and also the thirty and fifth, and behold the disciples of Jesus had formed a church of Christ in all the lands round about. And as many as did come unto them, and did truly repent of their sins, were baptized in the name of Jesus; and they did also receive the Holy Ghost.

Doctrine and Covenants

D&C 10:53, 67 — And for this cause have I said: If his generation harden not their hearts, I will establish my church among them. . . .

Behold, this is my doctrine—whosoever repenteth and cometh unto me, the same is my church.

D&C 18:21–25	Take upon you the name of Christ, and speak the truth in soberness. And as many as repent and are baptized in my name, which is Jesus Christ, and endure to the end, the same shall be saved. Behold, Jesus Christ is the name which is given of the Father, and there is none other name given whereby man can be saved; Wherefore, all men must take upon them the name which is given of the Father, for in that name shall they be called at the last day; Wherefore, if they know not the name by which they are called, they cannot have place in the kingdom of my Father.

(E) Baptism is necessary in order for us to receive a remission of our sins

Baptism is a witness of our repentance and willingness to keep the commandments; the burying of our sins and coming forth from the water clean—born of the water and of the spirit (or fire). It represents our being born again and that we no longer desire to do evil but have had a change in heart, that is, we have received a "new" heart.

New Testament

Matthew 3:11	I indeed baptize you with water unto repentance: but he that cometh after me is mightier than I, whose shoes I am not worthy to bear: he shall baptize you with the Holy Ghost, and with Fire.
Mark 1:4	John did baptize in the wilderness, and preach the baptism of repentance for the remission of sins.
Luke 3:3	And he came into all the country about Jordan, preaching the baptism of repentance for the remission of sins.
Acts 2:38	Then Peter said unto them, Repent, and be baptized every one of you in the name of Jesus Christ for the remission of sins, and ye shall receive the gift of the Holly Ghost.

Acts 22:16 — And now why tarriest thou? arise, and be baptized, and wash away thy sins, calling on the name of the Lord.

Book of Mormon

2 Nephi 31:13, 17 — Wherefore, my beloved brethren, I know that if ye shall follow the Son, with full purpose of heart, acting no hypocrisy and no deception before God, but with real intent, repenting of your sins, witnessing unto the Father that ye are willing to take upon you the name of Christ, by baptism—yea, by following your Lord and your Savior down into the water, according to his word, behold, then shall ye receive the Holy Ghost; yea, then cometh the baptism of fire and of the Holy Ghost. . . .

Wherefore, do the things which I have told you I have seen that your Lord and your Redeemer should do; for, for this cause have they been shown unto me, that ye might know the gate by which ye should enter. For the gate by which ye should enter is repentance and baptism by water; and then cometh a remission of your sins by fire and by the Holy Ghost.

Mosiah 18:10 — Now I say unto you, if this be the desire of your hearts, what have you against being baptized in the name of the Lord, as a witness before him that ye have entered into a covenant with him, that ye will serve him and keep his commandments, that he may pour out his Spirit more abundantly upon you?

Mosiah 21:35 — They were desirous to be baptized as a witness and a testimony that they were willing to serve God with all their hearts.

Alma 7:14–15 — Now I say unto you that ye must repent, and be born again; for the Spirit saith if ye are not born again ye cannot inherit the kingdom of heaven; therefore come and be baptized unto repentance, that ye may be washed from your sins, that ye may have faith on the Lamb of God, who taketh away the sins of the world, who is mighty to save and to cleanse from all unrighteousness.

Yea, I say unto you come and fear not, and lay aside every sin, which easily doth beset you, which doth bind you down to destruction, yea, come and go forth, and show unto your God that ye are willing to repent of your sins and enter into a covenant with him to keep his commandments, and witness it unto him this day by going into the waters of baptism.

3 Nephi 9:20 And ye shall offer for a sacrifice unto me a broken heart and a contrite spirit. And whoso cometh unto me with a broken heart and a contrite spirit, him will I baptize with fire and with the Holy Ghost.

3 Nephi 11:35–37 Verily, verily, I say unto you, that this is my doctrine, and I bear record of it from the Father; and whoso believeth in me believeth in the Father also; and unto him will the Father bear record of me, for he will visit him with fire and with the Holy Ghost.

And thus will the Father bear record of me, and the Holy Ghost will bear record unto him of the Father and me; for the Father, and I, and the Holy Ghost are one.

And again I say unto you, ye must repent, and become as a little child, and be baptized in my name, or ye can in nowise receive these things.

3 Nephi 12:1–2 Blessed are ye if ye shall give heed unto the words of these twelve whom I have chosen from among you to minister unto you, and to be your servants; and unto them I have given power that they may baptize you with water; and after that ye are baptized with water, behold, I will baptize you with fire and with the Holy Ghost. . . .

Yea, blessed are they who shall believe in your words, and come down into the depths of humility and be baptized, for they shall be visited with fire and with the Holy Ghost, and shall receive a remission of their sins.

3 Nephi 19:13 — And it came to pass when they were all baptized and had come up out of the water, the Holy Ghost did fall upon them, and they were filled with the Holy Ghost and with fire.

Moroni 8:10 — Behold I say unto you that this thing shall ye teach—repentance and baptism unto those who are accountable and capable of committing sin; yea, teach parents that they must repent and be baptized, and humble themselves as their little children, and they shall all be saved with their little children.

Moroni 8:25–26 — And the first fruits of repentance is baptism; and baptism cometh by faith unto the fulfilling the commandments; and the fulfilling the commandments bringeth remission of sins.

And the remission of sins bringeth meekness, and lowliness of heart; and because of meekness and lowliness of heart cometh the visitation of the Holy Ghost.

Doctrine and Covenants

D&C 19:31 — And of tenets thou shalt not talk, but thou shalt declare repentance and faith on the Savior, and remission of sins by baptism, and by fire, yea, even the Holy Ghost.

D&C 33:11 — Yea, repent and be baptized, every one of you, for a remission of your sins; yea, be baptized even by water, and then cometh the baptism of fire and of the Holy Ghost.

D&C 39:6 — And this is my gospel—repentance and baptism by water, and then cometh the baptism of fire and the Holy Ghost, which showeth all things, and teacheth the peaceable things of the kingdom.

D&C 55:1–2 — Behold, thus saith the Lord unto you, my servant

William, yea, even the Lord of the whole earth, thou are called and chosen; and after thou hast been baptized by water, which if you do with an eye single to my glory, you shall have a remission of your sins and a reception of the Holy Spirit by the laying on of hands. . .

And then thou shalt be ordained by the hand of my servant Joseph Smith, Jun., to be an elder unto this church, to preach repentance and remission of sins by way of baptism in the name of Jesus Christ, the Son of the living God.

D&C 68:27 — And their children shall be baptized for the remission of their sins when eight years old, and receive the laying on of the hands.

Pearl of Great Price

Moses 6:58–59 — Therefore I give unto you a commandment, to teach these things freely unto your children, saying:

That by reason of transgression cometh the fall, which fall bringeth death, and inasmuch as ye were born into the world by water, and blood, and the spirit, which I have made, and so became of dust a living soul, even so ye must be born again into the kingdom of heaven, of water, and of the Spirit, and be cleansed by blood, even the blood of mine Only Begotten; that ye might be sanctified from all sin, and enjoy the words of eternal life in this world, and eternal life in the world to come, even immortal glory.

(F) Jesus set the example

New Testament

Matthew 3:13–16 — Then cometh Jesus from Galilee to Jordan unto John, to be baptized of him.

But John forbad him, saying, I have need to be baptized of thee, and comest thou to me?

And Jesus answering said unto him, Suffer it to

be so now: for thus it becometh us to fulfill all righteousness. Then he suffered him.

And Jesus, when he was baptized, went up straightway out of the water: and, lo, the heavens were opened unto him, and he saw the Spirit of God descending like a dove, and lighting upon him.

Mark 1:9–10 And it came to pass in those days, that Jesus came from Nazareth of Galilee, and was baptized of John in Jordan.

And straightway coming up out of the water, he saw the heavens opened, and the Spirit like a dove descending upon him.

Book of Mormon

2 Nephi 31:5–7, 9 And now, if the Lamb of God, he being holy, should have need to be baptized by water, to fulfill all righteousness, O then, how much more need have we, being unholy, to be baptized, yea, even by water!

And now, I would ask of you, my beloved brethren, wherein the Lamb of God did fulfill all righteousness in being baptized by water?

Know ye not that he was holy? But notwithstanding he being holy, he showeth unto the children of men that, according to the flesh he humbleth himself before the Father, and witnesseth unto the Father that he would be obedient unto him in keeping his commandments. . . .

And again, it showeth unto the children of men the straitness of the path, and the narrowness of the gate, by which they should enter, he having set the example before them.

(G) Baptism by water—by immersion

New Testament

Because baptism by immersion is representative of Christ's death, burial, and resurrection, he set the example and was baptized by immersion. Key phrases in the various accounts of Jesus' baptism and the baptism of others indicate that his baptism was indeed by immersion:

Matthew 3:16	And Jesus, when he was baptized, went up straightway out of the water.
Mark 1:5	And there went out unto him all the land of Judæa, and they of Jerusalem, and were all baptized of him in the river of Jordan, confessing their sins.
John 3:23	And John also was baptizing in Aenon near to Salim, because there was much water there: and they came, and were baptized.
Acts 8:38–39	And he commanded the chariot to stand still: and they went down both into the water, both Philip and the eunuch; and he baptized him. And when they were come up out of the water, the Spirit of the Lord caught away Philip.

Paul is even more explicit in his epistle to the Romans:

Romans 6:4–5	Therefore we are buried with him by baptism into death: that like as Christ was raised up from the dead by the glory of the Father, even so we also should walk in newness of life. For if we have been planted together in the likeness of his death, we shall be also in the likeness of his resurrection.
Colossians 2:12	Buried with him in baptism, wherein also ye are risen with him through the faith of the operation of God, who hath raised him from the dead.

Book of Mormon

Mosiah 18:13–16	And when he had said these words, the Spirit of the Lord was upon him, and he said: Helam, I baptize thee, having authority from the Almighty God, as a testimony that ye have entered into a covenant to serve him until you are dead as to the mortal body; and may the Spirit of the Lord be poured out upon you; and may he grant unto you eternal life, through the redemption of Christ, whom he has prepared

from the foundation of the world.

And after Alma had said these words, both Alma and Helam were buried in the water; and they arose and came forth out of the water rejoicing, being filled with the Spirit.

And again Alma took another, and went forth a second time into the water, and baptized him according to the first, only he did not bury himself again in the water.

And after this manner he did baptize every one that went forth to the place of Mormon . . . and they were baptized in the waters of Mormon, and were filled with the grace of God.

3 Nephi 11:23–26 Verily I say unto you, that whoso repenteth of his sins through your words, and desireth to be baptized in my name, on this wise shall ye baptize them—Behold, ye shall go down and stand in the water, and in my name shall ye baptize them.

And now behold, these are the words which ye shall say, calling them by name, saying:

Having authority given me of Jesus Christ, I baptize you in the name of the Father, and of the Son, and of the Holy Ghost. Amen.

And then shall ye immerse them in the water, and come forth again out of the water.

3 Nephi 19:11–13 And it came to pass that Nephi went down into the water and was baptized.

And he came up out of the water and began to baptize. And he baptized all those whom Jesus had chosen.

And it came to pass when they were all baptized and had come up out of the water, the Holy Ghost did fall upon them, and they were filled with the Holy Ghost and with fire.

Doctrine and Covenants

D&C 13:1 Upon you my fellow servants, in the name of Messiah

I confer the Priesthood of Aaron, which holds the keys of the ministering of angels, and of the gospel of repentance, and of baptism by immersion for the remissions of sins.

D&C 20:72–74 Baptism is to be administered in the following manner unto all those who repent—

The person who is called of God and has authority from Jesus Christ to baptize, shall go down into the water with the person who has presented himself or herself for baptism, and shall say, calling him or her by name: Having been commissioned of Jesus Christ, I baptize you in the name of the Father, and of the Son, and of the Holy Ghost. Amen.

Then shall he immerse him or her in the water, and come forth again out of the water.

Pearl of Great Price

Moses 6:64 And it came to pass, when the Lord had spoken with Adam, our father, that Adam cried unto the Lord, and he was caught away by the Spirit of the Lord, and was carried down into the water, and was laid under the water, and was brought forth out of the water.

(H) Baptism for the dead

Because God is no respecter of persons, baptism is performed for those who have died in order that they might be judged according to those in the flesh.

New Testament

John 5:25, 28–29 Verily, verily, I say unto you, The hour is coming, and now is, when the dead shall hear the voice of the Son of God: and they that hear shall live. . . .

Marvel not at this: for the hour is coming, in the which all that are in the graves shall hear his voice,

And shall come forth; they that have done good, unto the resurrection of life; and they that have done evil, unto the resurrection of damnation.

1 Corinthians 15:29	Else what shall they do which are baptized for the dead, if the dead rise not at all? why are they then baptized for the dead?
1 Peter 4:6	For for this cause was the gospel preached also to them that are dead, that they might be judged according to men in the flesh, but live according to God in the spirit.

Doctrine and Covenants

D&C 124:29–31	For a baptismal font there is not upon the earth, that they, my saints, may be baptized for those who are dead— For this ordinance belongeth to my house, and cannot be acceptable to me, only in the days of your poverty, wherein ye are not able to build a house unto me, But I command you, all ye my saints, to build a house unto me; and I grant unto you a sufficient time to build a house unto me; and during this time your baptisms shall be acceptable unto me.
D&C 127:5–7	And again, I give unto you a word in relation to the baptism for your dead. Verily, thus saith the Lord unto you concerning your dead: When any of you are baptized for your dead, let there be a recorder, and let him be eye-witness of your baptisms; let him hear with his ears, that he may testify of a truth, saith the Lord; That in all your recordings it may be recorded in heaven; whatsoever you bind on earth, may be bound in heaven; whatsoever you loose on earth, may be loosed in heaven.
D&C 128:12–13	Herein is glory and honor, and immortality and eternal life—The ordinance of baptism by water, to be immersed therein in order to answer to the likeness of the dead, that one principle might accord

with the other; to be immersed in the water and come forth out of the water is in the likeness of the resurrection of the dead in coming forth out of their graves; hence, this ordinance was instituted to form a relationship with the ordinance of baptism for the dead, being in likeness of the dead.

Consequently, the baptismal font was instituted as a similitude of the grave, and was commanded to be in a place underneath where the living are wont to assemble, to show forth the living and the dead, and that all things may have their likeness, and that they may accord one with another—that which is earthly conforming to that which is heavenly, as Paul hath declared (to the Corinthians).

In the Doctrine and Covenants, 1 Peter 4:6 is quoted:

D&C 138:10 — For for this cause was the gospel preached also to them that are dead, that they might be judged according to men in the flesh, but live according to God in the spirit.

D&C 138:32–33 — Thus was the gospel preached to those who had died in their sins, without a knowledge of the truth, or in transgression, having rejected the prophets.

These were taught faith in God, repentance from sin, vicarious baptism for the remission of sins, the gift of the Holy Ghost by the laying on of hands.

(I) Infant baptism

Children, when they reach the age of accountability (eight years old) are to be baptized, but infants need no baptism. Baptism is for the remission of sins, and little children cannot sin: Satan has no power over them.

New Testament

Matthew 19:14 — But Jesus said, Suffer little children, and forbid them not, to come unto me: for of such is the kingdom of heaven.

Mark 9:36–37 — And he took a child, and set him in the midst of them: and when he had taken him in his arms, he said unto them,

Whosoever shall receive one of such children in my name, receiveth me: and whosoever shall receive me, receiveth not me, but him that sent me.

Mark 10:13–16 And they brought young children to him, that he should touch them: and his disciples rebuked those that brought them.

But when Jesus saw it, he was much displeased, and said unto them, Suffer the little children to come unto me, and forbid them not: for of such is the kingdom of God.

Verily I say unto you, Whosoever shall not receive the kingdom of God as a little child, he shall not enter therein.

And he took them up in his arms, put his hands upon them, and blessed them.

Book of Mormon

Mosiah 3:16, 18 And even if it were possible that little children could sin they could not be saved [by the law of Moses]; but I say unto you they are blessed; for behold, as in Adam, or by nature, they fall, even so the blood of Christ atoneth for their sins. . . .

For behold he judgeth, and his judgment is just; and the infant perisheth not that dieth in his infancy; but men drink damnation to their own souls except they humble themselves and become as little children, and believe that salvation was, and is, and is to come, in and through the atoning blood of Christ, the Lord Omnipotent.

Mosiah 15:25 And little children also have eternal life.

Moroni 8:11–15, 19–20, 22

And their little children need no repentance, neither baptism. Behold, baptism is unto repentance to the fulfilling the commandments unto the remission of sins.

But little children are alive in Christ, even from the foundations of the world; if not so, God is a partial God, and also a changeable God, and a respecter to persons; for how many little children have died without baptism!

Wherefore, if little children could not be saved without baptism, these must have gone to an endless hell.

Behold I say unto you that he that supposeth that little children need baptism is in the gall of bitterness and in the bonds of iniquity; for he hath neither faith, hope, nor charity; wherefore, should he be cut off while in the thought, he must go down to hell.

For awful is the wickedness to suppose that God saveth one child because of baptism, and the other must perish because he hath no baptism. . . .

Little children cannot repent; wherefore, it is awful wickedness to deny the pure mercies of God unto them, for they are all alive in him, because of his mercy.

And he that saith that little children need baptism denieth the mercies of Christ, and setteth at naught the atonement of him and the power of his redemption. . . .

For behold that all little children are alive in Christ, and also all they that are without the law. For the power of redemption cometh on all them that have no law; wherefore, he that is not condemned, or he that is under no condemnation, cannot repent; and unto such baptism availeth nothing.

Doctrine and Covenants

D&C 18:42 — For all men must repent and be baptized, and not only men, but women, and children who have arrived at the years of accountability.

D&C 20:71 — No one can be received into the church of Christ unless he has arrived unto the years of accountabil-

	ity before God, and is capable of repentance.
D&C 29:46–47	But behold, I say unto you, that little children are redeemed from the foundation of the world through mine Only Begotten; Wherefore, they cannot sin, for power is not given unto Satan to tempt little children, until they begin to become accountable before me.
D&C 68:27	And their children shall be baptized for the remission of their sins when eight years old, and receive the laying on of the hands.
D&C 137:10	And I also beheld that all children who die before they arrive at the years of accountability are saved in the celestial kingdom of heaven.

PEARL OF GREAT PRICE

Moses 6:54	Hence came the saying abroad among the people, that the Son of God hath atoned for original guilt, wherein the sins of the parents cannot be answered upon the heads of the children, for they are whole from the foundation of the world.

Chapter 13

One Must Have Authority to Act in God's Name

TENET: A person must be called of God and given authority by God through his called and anointed servants before acting in his name. No man is to take this honor upon himself.

Old Testament

Moses was called by God to bring the children of Israel out of Egypt.

Exodus 3:10, 12 — Come now therefore, and I will send thee unto Pharaoh, that thou mayest bring forth my people the children of Israel out of Egypt. . . .

And he said, Certainly I will be with thee; and this shall be a token unto thee, that I have sent thee: When thou hast brought forth the people out of Egypt, ye shall serve God upon this mountain.

Aaron was also called of God to be a mouthpiece for Moses.

Exodus 7:2 — Thou shalt speak all that I command thee: and Aaron thy brother shall speak unto Pharaoh, that he send the children of Israel out of his land.

People who were called to serve were also anointed to serve. *Anoint* is defined as "to rub oil or ointment on, to put oil on in a ceremony of making sacred or consecrating to high office."[1]

Exodus 28:41 — And thou shalt put them [the garments] upon Aaron thy brother, and his sons with him; and shalt anoint them, and consecrate them, and sanctify them, that they may minister unto me in the priest's office.

The Levites were called to perform the service of the tabernacle.

Numbers 3:5–7 And the Lord spake unto Moses, saying,

Bring the tribe of Levi near, and present them before Aaron the priest, that they may minister unto him.

And they shall keep his charge, and the charge of the whole congregation before the tabernacle of the congregation, to do the service of the tabernacle.

Numbers 11:16–17, 24–25

And the Lord said unto Moses, Gather unto me seventy men of the elders of Israel, whom thou knowest to be the elders of the people, and officers over them; and bring them unto the tabernacle of the congregation, that they may stand there with thee.

And I will come down and talk with thee there: and I will take of the spirit which is upon thee, and will put it upon them; and they shall bear the burden of the people with thee, that thou bear it not thyself alone. . . .

And Moses went out, and told the people the words of the Lord, and gathered the seventy men of the elders of the people, and set them round about the tabernacle.

And the Lord came down in a cloud, and spake unto him, and took of the spirit that was upon him, and gave it unto the seventy elders: and it came to pass, that, when the spirit rested upon them, they prophesied, and did not cease.

Prophets were sent to call the people to repentance.

2 Chronicles 24:19 Yet he sent prophets to them, to bring them again unto the Lord; and they testified against them: but they would not give ear.

Ezekiel 2:7	And thou shalt speak my words unto them, whether they will hear, or whether they will forbear: for they are most rebellious.

New Testament

Christ's apostles did not choose themselves to be apostles. They were called by Christ to the apostleship and were given priesthood power to act in his name.

Matthew 10:1	And when he had called unto him his twelve disciples, he gave them power against unclean spirits, to cast them out, and to heal all manner of sickness and all manner of disease.
Matthew 21:23–24	And when he was come into the temple, the chief priests and the elders of the people came unto him as he was teaching, and said, By what authority doest thou these things? and who gave thee this authority? And Jesus answered and said unto them, I also will ask you one thing, which if ye tell me, I in like wise will tell you by what authority I do these things.
Mark 1:22	And they were astonished at his doctrine: for he taught them as one that had authority, and not as the scribes.
Mark 13:34	For the Son of Man is as a man taking a far journey, who left his house, and gave authority to his servants, and to every man his work, and commanded the porter to watch.
Luke 9:1	Then he called his twelve disciples together, and gave them power and authority over all devils, and to cure diseases.
Luke 19:17	And he said unto him, Well, thou good servant: because thou hast been faithful in a very little, have thou authority over ten cities.
Luke 22:29–30	And I appoint unto you a kingdom, as my Father hath appointed unto me;

	That ye may eat and drink at my table in my kingdom, and sit on thrones judging the twelve tribes of Israel.
John 5:26–27	For as the Father hath life in himself; so hath he given to the Son to have life in himself; And hath given him authority to execute judgment also, because he is the Son of man.
John 15:16	Ye have not chosen me, but I have chosen you, and ordained you, that ye should go and bring forth fruit, and that your fruit should remain: that whatsoever ye shall ask of the Father in my name, he may give it you.
John 20:21	Then said Jesus to them again, Peace be unto you: as my Father hath sent me, even so send I you.
Acts 13:3	And when they had fasted and prayed, and laid their hands on them, they sent them away.
Hebrews 5:1, 4–5	For every high priest taken from among men is ordained for men in things pertaining to God, that he may offer both gifts and sacrifices for sins. . . . And no man taketh this honour unto himself, but he that is called of God, as was Aaron. So also Christ glorified not himself to be made an high priest; but he that said unto him, Thou art my Son, to day have I begotten thee.

Book of Mormon

The same principle, a man must be called of God and given authority from him to act in his name, applied to the Nephites and Lamanites as recorded in the Book of Mormon.

1 Nephi 2:22	And inasmuch as thou shalt keep my commandments, thou shalt be made a ruler and a teacher over they brethren.
2 Nephi 5:26	And it came to pass that I, Nephi, did consecrate Jacob and Joseph, that they should be priests and teachers over the land of my people.

Those who perform baptisms must have authority from God to do so.

Mosiah 18:13	And when he had said these words, the Spirit of the Lord was upon him, and he said: Helam, I baptize thee, having authority from the Almighty God, as a testimony that ye have entered into a covenant to serve him until you are dead as to the mortal body; and may the Spirit of the Lord be poured out upon you; and may he grant unto you eternal life, through the redemption of Christ, whom he has prepared from the foundation of the world.
Mosiah 21:33	And it came to pass that king Limhi and many of his people were desirous to be baptized; but there was none in the land that had authority from God.
Alma 4:4	And they began to establish the church more fully; yea, and many were baptized in the waters of Sidon and were joined to the church of God; yea, they were baptized by the hand of Alma, who had been consecrated the high priest over the people of the church, by the hand of his father Alma.
Alma 49:30	Yea, and there was continual peace among them, and exceedingly great prosperity in the church because of their heed and diligence which they gave unto the word of God, which was declared unto them by Helaman, and Shiblon, and Corianton, and Ammon and his brethren, yea, and by all those who had been ordained by the holy order of God, being baptized unto repentance, and sent forth to preach among the people.
3 Nephi 11:24–25	And now behold, these are the words which ye shall say, calling them by name, saying: Having authority given me of Jesus Christ, I baptize you in the name of the Father, and of the Son, and of the Holy Ghost. Amen.
3 Nephi 12:1	Jesus had spoken these words unto Nephi, and to those who had been called (now the number of them who had been called, and received power and

authority to baptize was twelve).

3 Nephi 18:26–27	And now it came to pass that when Jesus had spoken these words, he turned his eyes again upon the disciples whom he had chosen, and said unto them: Behold verily, verily, I say unto you, I give unto you another commandment, and then I must go unto my Father that I may fulfill other commandments which he hath given me.

Doctrine and Covenants

That same authority to act in God's name was bestowed upon Joseph Smith and Oliver Cowdery in these latter days by messengers sent from God.

D&C 13:1	Upon you my fellow servants, in the name of Messiah I confer the Priesthood of Aaron, which holds the keys of the ministering of angels, and of the gospel of repentance, and of baptism by immersion for the remission of sins.
D&C 20:2–3	Which commandments were given to Joseph Smith, Jun., who was called of God, and ordained an apostle of Jesus Christ, to be the first elder of this church; And to Oliver Cowdery, who was also called of God, an apostle of Jesus Christ, to be the second elder of the church, and ordained under his hand.
D&C 20:72–74	Baptism is to be administered in the following manner unto all those who repent— The person who is called of God and has authority from Jesus Christ to baptize, shall go down into the water with the person who has presented himself or herself for baptism, and shall say, calling him or her by name: Having been commissioned of Jesus Christ, I baptize you in the name of the Father, and of the Son, and of the Holy Ghost. Amen. Then shall he immerse him or her in the water, and come forth again out of the water.

The Lord called Emma Smith to fulfill certain tasks:

D&C 25:3	Behold, thy sins are forgiven thee, and thou art an elect lady, whom I have called.
D&C 27:8	Which John I have sent unto you, my servants, Joseph Smith, Jun., and Oliver Cowdery, to ordain you unto the first priesthood which you have received, that you might be called and ordained even as Aaron.
D&C 42:11	Again I say unto you, that it shall not be given to any one to go forth to preach my gospel, for to build up my church except he be ordained by some one who has authority, and it is known to the church that he has authority and has been regularly ordained by the heads of the church.
D&C 63:62	For behold, verily I say, that many there be who are under this condemnation, who use the name of the Lord, and use it in vain, having not authority.
D&C 68:8	Go ye into all the world, preach the gospel to every creature, acting in the authority which I have given you, baptizing in the name of the Father, and of the Son, and of the Holy Ghost.
D&C 76:52	That by keeping the commandments they might be washed and cleansed from all their sins, and receive the Holy Spirit by the laying on of the hands of him who is ordained and sealed unto this power.
D&C 107:20	The power and authority of the lesser, or Aaronic Priesthood, is to hold the keys of the ministering of angels, and to administer in outward ordinances, the letter of the gospel, the baptism of repentance for the remission of sins, agreeable to the covenants and commandments.
D&C 112:21	And again, I say unto you, that whosoever ye shall send in my name, by the voice of your brethren, the Twelve, duly recommended and authorized by you, shall have power to open the door of my kingdom unto any nation whithersoever ye shall send them.

D&C 128:9	It may seem to some to be a very bold doctrine that we talk of—a power which records or binds on earth and binds in heaven. Nevertheless, in all ages of the world, whenever the Lord has given a dispensation of the priesthood to any man by actual revelation, or any set of men, this power has always been given. Hence, whatsoever those men did in authority, in the name of the Lord, and did it truly and faithfully, and kept a proper and faithful record of the same, it became a law on earth and in heaven, and could not be annulled, according to the decrees of the great Jehovah.

Pearl of Great Price

Moses 8:19	And the Lord ordained Noah after his own order, and commanded him that he should go forth and declare his Gospel unto the children of men, even as it was given unto Enoch.
Abraham 1:1–4	I Abraham, saw that it was needful for me to obtain another place of residence; And, finding there was greater happiness and peace and rest for me, I sought for the blessings of the fathers, and the right whereunto I should be ordained to administer the same . . . I became a rightful heir, a High Priest, holding the right belonging to the fathers. It was conferred upon me from the fathers. . . . I sought for mine appointment unto the Priesthood according to the appointment of God unto the fathers concerning the seed.

Joseph Smith recorded his calling from the Lord to usher in this dispensation of the fullness of times:

JS—H 1:30, 33	While I was thus in the act of calling upon God, I discovered a light appearing in my room, which continued to increase until the room was lighter than at noonday, when immediately a personage appeared at my bedside, standing in the air, for his feet did

> not touch the floor. . . .
>
> He called me by name, and said unto me that he was a messenger sent from the presence of God to me, and that his name was Moroni; that God had a work for me to do.

Moroni proceeded to explain what the Lord was calling Joseph to do.

JS—H 1:68–69

> We still continued the work of translation, when, in the ensuing month [May 1829], we on a certain day went into the woods to pray and inquire of the Lord respecting baptism for the remission of sins, that we found mentioned in the translation of the plates. While we were thus employed, praying and calling upon the Lord, a messenger from heaven [John the Baptist] descended in a cloud of light, and having laid his hands upon us, he ordained us, saying:
>
> Upon you my fellow servants, in the name of Messiah, I confer the Priesthood of Aaron, which holds the keys of the ministering of angels, and of the gospel of repentance, and of baptism by immersion for the remission of sins; and this shall never be taken again from the earth until the sons of Levi do offer again an offering unto the Lord in righteousness.

Shortly thereafter, sometime in June, Joseph Smith and Oliver Cowdery were ordained to the Melchizedek Priesthood by Peter, James, and John. The exact date is unknown. The location was somewhere between Harmony, Pennsylvania, and Colesville, New York, on the Susquehanna River.[2]

Notes

1. *Webster's New World Dictionary*, 2nd college ed. (Cleveland, OH: World Publishing, 1976), 56 .
2. Joseph Fielding Smith, *Essentials in Church History,* 19th ed. (Salt Lake City: Deseret Book, 1964), 69.

Chapter 14

Tithing

TENET: (A) People throughout the scriptures have been commanded to pay tithing; (B) The Old Testament, New Testament, Book of Mormon, and Doctrine and Covenants all indicate that we are to pay tithing; (C) Tithing means one-tenth of the annual produce of one's land or of one's annual income paid to the Church; (D) Condemnation accompanies the absence of paying tithing; (E) Blessings are promised those who pay their tithing; (F) Paying tithing does not excuse us from living the rest of God's commandments.

Old Testament

Genesis 14:20 — And blessed be the most high God, which hath delivered thine enemies into thy hand. And he [Abram] gave him [Melchizedek] tithes of all.

Genesis 28:22 — And this stone, which I [Jacob] have set for a pillar, shall be God's house: and of all that thou shalt give me I will surely give the tenth unto thee.

Leviticus 27:30, 32 — And all the tithe of the land, whether of the seed of the land, or of the fruit of the tree, is the Lord's: it is holy unto the Lord. . . .

And concerning the tithe of the herd, or of the flock, even of whatsoever passeth under the rod, the tenth shall be holy unto the Lord.

Numbers 18:26	Thus speak unto the Levites, and say unto them, When ye take of the children of Israel the tithes which I have given you from them for your inheritance, then ye shall offer up an heave offering of it for the Lord, even a tenth part of the tithe.
Proverbs 3:9–10	Honour the Lord with thy substance, and with the first-fruits of all thine increase: So shall thy barns be filled with plenty, and thy presses shall burst out with new wine.
Nehemiah 10:38	And the priest the son of Aaron shall be with the Levites, when the Levites take tithes: and the Levites shall bring up the tithe of the tithes unto the house of our God, to the chambers, into the treasure house.
Malachi 3:7–11	Even from the days of your fathers ye are gone away from mine ordinances, and have not kept them. Return unto me, and I will return unto you, saith the Lord of hosts. But ye said, Wherein shall we return? Will a man rob God? Yet ye have robbed me. But ye say, Wherein have we robbed thee? In tithes and offerings. Ye are cursed with a curse; for ye have robbed me, even this whole nation. Bring ye all the tithes into the storehouse, that there may be meat in mine house, and prove me now herewith, saith the Lord of hosts, if I will not open you the windows of heaven, and pour you out a blessing, that there shall not be room enough to receive it. And I will rebuke the devourer for your sakes, and he shall not destroy the fruits of your ground; neither shall your vine cast her fruit before the time in the field, saith the Lord of hosts.

New Testament

It appears from New Testament scriptures that the people didn't have a problem with paying their tithing. The problem was, apparently, that they did pay their tithing but omitted living the rest of the commandments. Christ taught that it is requisite that we live according to his teachings as well as pay tithing.

Matthew 23:23 Woe unto you, scribes and Pharisees, hypocrites! for ye pay tithe of mint and anise and cummin, and have omitted the weightier matters of the law, judgment, mercy, and faith: these ought ye to have done, and not to leave the other undone!

Luke 18:10–14 Two men went up into the temple to pray; the one a Pharisee, and the other a publican.

The Pharisee stood and prayed thus with himself, God, I thank thee, that I am not as other men are, extortioners, unjust, adulterers, or even as this publican.

I fast twice in the week, I give tithes of all that I possess.

And the publican, standing afar off, would not lift up so much as his eyes unto heaven, but smote upon his breast, saying, God be merciful to me a sinner.

I tell you, this man went down to his house justified rather than the other: for every one that exalteth himself shall be abased; and he that humbleth himself shall be exalted.

In his epistle to the Hebrews, Paul reminded the people that Abraham paid tithes—ten percent of all he had—to Melchizedek:

Hebrews 7:2, 4 To whom also Abraham gave a tenth part of all. . . .

Now consider how great this man was, unto whom even the patriarch Abraham gave the tenth of the spoils.

Book of Mormon

The Book of Mormon reinforces the teachings of the Old Testament regarding the commandment to pay tithing with their accompanying condemnation if we fail to do so and the promised blessings if we do.

Referring to the Old Testament, Alma reminded the people that Abraham paid tithes to Melchizedek:

Alma 13:15 — And it was this same Melchizedek to whom Abraham paid tithes; yea, even our father Abraham paid tithes of one–tenth part of all he possessed.

When Christ appeared to the people in America following his resurrection, he chastised them and promised the same condemnation or blessings regarding the payment of tithes as he did to the people of the Old Testament. His words echoed those recorded in Malachi 3:7–11.

3 Nephi 24:7–11 — Even from the days of your fathers ye are gone away from mine ordinances, and have not kept them. Return unto me, and I will return unto you, saith the Lord of hosts. But ye say: Wherein shall we return?

Will a man rob God? Yet ye have robbed me. But ye say: Wherein have we robbed thee? In tithes and offerings.

Ye are cursed with a curse; for ye have robbed me, even this whole nation.

Bring ye all the tithes into the storehouse, that there may be meat in my house; and prove me now herewith, saith the Lord of Hosts, if I will not open you the windows of heaven, and pour you out a blessing, that there shall not be room enough to receive it.

And I will rebuke the devourer for your sakes, and he shall not destroy the fruits of your ground; neither shall your vine cast her fruit before the time in the fields, saith the Lord of Hosts.

Doctrine and Covenants

The law of tithing was again revealed by the Savior to Joseph Smith on September 11, 1831.

D&C 64:23 — Behold, now it is called today until the coming of the Son of Man, and verily it is a day of sacrifice, and a day for the tithing of my people; for he that is tithed shall not be burned at his coming.

The Lord was even more explicit in his instructions regarding tithing in a revelation which the Prophet Joseph Smith received July 8, 1838.

D&C 119:1–7

Verily, thus saith the Lord, I require all their surplus property to be put into the hands of the bishop of my church in Zion,

For the building of mine house, and for the laying of the foundation of Zion and for the priesthood, and for the debts of the Presidency of my Church.

And this shall be the beginning of the tithing of my people.

And after that, those who have thus been tithed shall pay one-tenth of all their interest annually; and this shall be a standing law unto them forever, for my holy priesthood, saith the Lord.

Verily I say unto you, it shall come to pass that all those who gather unto the land of Zion shall be tithed of their surplus properties, and shall observe this law, or they shall not be found worthy to abide among you.

And I say unto you, if my people observe not this law, to keep it holy, and by this law sanctify the land of Zion unto me, that my statutes and my judgments may be kept thereon, that it may be most holy, behold, verily I say unto you, it shall not be a land of Zion unto you.

And this shall be an ensample unto all the stakes of Zion. Even so. Amen.

Chapter 15

Priesthood

TENET: Priesthood is more than an organization of clergy who minister within their respective churches:

> As pertaining to eternity, priesthood is the eternal power and authority of Deity by which all things exist; by which they are created, governed, and controlled; by which the universe and worlds without number have come rolling into existence; by which the great plan of creation, redemption, and exaltation operates throughout immensity. It is the power of God. . . .
>
> As pertaining to man's existence on this earth, priesthood is the power and authority of God delegated to man on earth to act in all things for the salvation of men. It is the power by which the gospel is preached; by which the ordinances of salvation are performed so that they will be binding on earth and in heaven; by which men are sealed up unto eternal life, being assured of the fulness of the Father's kingdom hereafter; and by which in due course the Lord will govern the nations of the earth and all that pertains to them.[1]

There are two priesthoods: the Aaronic or Levitical Priesthood (after the order of Aaron) and the Melchizedek, or higher, priesthood (which includes the lesser priesthood).

There are various offices within those priesthoods, and each office has certain responsibilities that pertain to it, according to the level of priesthood authority God has delegated to that office. The offices of the Aaronic (or lesser) Priesthood are priest, teacher, and deacon. The offices of the Melchizedek (or higher) Priesthood are Apostle, Seventy, High Priest, and Elder.

(A) Aaronic Priesthood

Aaron and his sons and others of the tribe of Levi were ordained and consecrated to officiate in the ordinances pertaining to the Levitical, or Aaronic Priesthood.

Old Testament

Exodus 28:1	And take thou unto thee Aaron thy brother, and his sons with him, from among the children of Israel; that he may minister unto me in the priest's office.
Numbers 3:5–8	And the Lord spake unto Moses, saying, Bring the tribe of Levi near, and present them before Aaron the priest, that they may minister unto him. And they shall keep his charge, and the charge of the whole congregation before the tabernacle of the congregation, to do the service of the tabernacle. And they shall keep all the instruments of the tabernacle of the congregation, and the charge of the children of Israel, to do the service of the tabernacle.
Numbers 8:10–11	And thou shalt bring the Levites before the Lord: and the children of Israel shall put their hands upon the Levites: And Aaron shall offer the Levites before the Lord for an offering of the children of Israel, that they may execute the service of the Lord.
Numbers 18:6–7	And I, behold, I have taken your brethren the Levites from among the children of Israel: to you they are given as a gift for the Lord, to do the service of the tabernacle of the congregation. Wherefore thou and thy sons with thee shall keep your priest's office for every thing of the altar, and within the vail; and ye shall serve: I have given

your priest's office unto you as a service of gift.

Numbers 25:10–13 And the Lord spake unto Moses, saying,

Phinehas, the son of Eleazar, the son of Aaron the priest, hath turned my wrath away from the children of Israel, while he was zealous for my sake among them, that I consumed not the children of Israel in my jealousy.

Wherefore say, Behold, I give unto him my covenant of peace:

And he shall have it, and his seed after him, even the covenant of an everlasting priesthood; because he was zealous for his God, and made an atonement for the children of Israel.

Joshua 18:7 But the Levites have no part among you; for the priesthood of the Lord is their inheritance.

2 Kings 23:4 And the king commanded Hilkiah the high priest [in the Melchizedek priesthood], and the priests of the second order [the Aaronic priesthood], and the keepers of the door, to bring forth out of the temple of the Lord all the vessels that were made for Baal, and for the grove, and for all the host of heaven.

2 Chronicles 15:3 Now for a long season Israel hath been without the true God, and without a teaching priest, and without law.

Hezekiah counseled his sons to be faithful in fulfilling their priesthood callings.

2 Chronicles 29:11 My sons, be not now negligent: for the Lord hath chosen you to stand before him, to serve him, and that ye should minister unto him, and burn incense.

Nehemiah 8:2–3 And Ezra the priest brought the law before the congregation both of men and women, and all that could hear with understanding. . . .

And he read therein . . . and the ears of all the people were attentive unto the book of the law.

Nehemiah 13:29–30 Remember them, O my God, because they have defiled the priesthood, and the covenant of the priesthood, and of the Levites.

Thus cleansed I them from all strangers and appointed the wards of the priests and the Levites, everyone in his business.

Ezekiel 44:15 But the priests the Levites, the sons of Zadok, that kept the charge of my sanctuary when the children of Israel went astray from me, they shall come near to me to minister unto me, and they shall stand before me to offer unto me the fat and the blood, saith the Lord God.

The Lord condemned church leaders who pollute their callings and those who profess to hold the priesthood but are false prophets.

Micah 3:11–12 The heads thereof judge for reward, and the priests teach for hire, and the prophets thereof divine for money: yet will they lean upon the Lord, and say, Is not the Lord among us? none evil can come upon us.

Therefore shall Zion for your sake be plowed as a field, and Jerusalem shall become heaps, and the mountain of the house as the high places of the forest.

Zephaniah 3:4 Her prophets are light and treacherous persons: her priests have polluted the sanctuary, they have done violence to the law.

Malachi prophesied that in the latter days the Lord would:

Malachi 3:3 Sit as a refiner and purifier of silver: and he shall purify the sons of Levi, and purge them as gold and silver, that they may offer unto the Lord an offering in righteousness [they will exercise their Aaronic priesthood calling in righteousness].

New Testament

People do not receive the priesthood by simply claiming to speak for God or by starting a church or by teaching gospel principles: they must be called by God and be ordained by one in authority in order to receive the power of the priesthood.

Hebrews 5:4 — No man taketh this honour unto himself, but he that is called of God, as was Aaron.

Hebrews 7:5 — And verily they that are of the sons of Levi, who receive the office of the priesthood, have a commandment to take tithes of the people according to the law, that is, of their brethren, though they come out of the loins of Abraham.

In his epistle to the Hebrews, Paul reminded them that there were two priesthoods: the Levitical priesthood (or Aaronic priesthood) and a higher priesthood after the order of Melchizedek).

Hebrews 7:11 — If therefore perfection were by the Levitical priesthood, (for under it the people received the law,) what further need was there that another priest should rise after the order of Melchisedec, and not be called after the order of Aaron?

Book of Mormon

The Lord taught the Nephites the same thing he had taught Malachi centuries earlier regarding the sons of Levi honoring their priesthood callings in the latter days.

3 Nephi 24:3 — And he shall sit as a refiner and purifier of silver; and he shall purify the sons of Levi, and purge them as gold and silver, that they may offer unto the Lord an offering in righteousness.

Doctrine and Covenants

On May 15, 1829, an angel, who announced himself as John the Baptist, conferred the Aaronic Priesthood on Joseph Smith and Oliver Cowdery.

D&C 13:1 — Upon you my fellow servants, in the name of Messiah I confer the Priesthood of Aaron, which holds the keys of the ministering of angels, and of the gospel of repentance, and of baptism by immersion for the remission of sins; and this shall never be taken again from the earth, until the sons of Levi do offer again an offering unto the Lord in righteousness.

D&C 27:5, 7–8 Behold, this is wisdom in me; wherefore, marvel not, for the hour cometh that I will drink of the fruit of the vine with you on the earth, and with. . . .

John the son of Zacharias. . . .

Which John I have sent unto you, my servants, Joseph Smith, Jun., and Oliver Cowdery, to ordain you unto the first priesthood which you have received, that you might be called and ordained even as Aaron.

D&C 68:14–18 There remain hereafter, in the due time of the Lord, other bishops to be set apart unto the church, to minister even according to the first;

Wherefore they shall be high priests who are worthy, and they shall be appointed by the First Presidency of the Melchizedek Priesthood, except they be literal descendants of Aaron.

And if they be literal descendants of Aaron they have a legal right to the bishopric, if they are the firstborn among the sons of Aaron;

For the firstborn holds the right of the presidency over this priesthood, and the keys or authority of the same.

No man has a legal right to this office, to hold the keys of this priesthood, except he be a literal descendant and the firstborn of Aaron.

When the Lord took Moses out of the midst of the Israelites, he also took the Melchizedek Priesthood but left the Aaronic Priesthood upon the earth.

D&C 84:26–28, 30 And the lesser priesthood continued, which priesthood holdeth the key of the ministering of angels and the preparatory gospel;

Which gospel is the gospel of repentance and of baptism, and the remission of sins, and the law of carnal commandments, which the Lord in his wrath caused to continue with the house of Aaron among the children of Israel until John, whom God raised up, being filled with the Holy Ghost from his mother's womb.

For he was baptized while he was yet in his childhood, and was ordained by the angel of God at the time he was eight days old unto his power, to overthrow the kingdom of the Jews, and to make straight the way of the Lord before the face of his people, to prepare them for the coming of the Lord, in whose hand is given all power. . . .

And again, the offices of teacher and deacon are necessary appendages, belonging to the lesser priesthood, which priesthood was confirmed upon Aaron and his sons.

D&C 107:1, 6, 13–16, 20–21

There are, in the church, two priesthoods, namely, the Melchizedek and Aaronic, including the Levitical Priesthood. . . .

But there are two divisions or grand heads—one is the Melchizedek Priesthood, and the other is the Aaronic or Levitical Priesthood. . . .

The second priesthood is called the Priesthood of Aaron, because it was conferred upon Aaron and his seed, throughout all their generations.

Why it is called the lesser priesthood is because it is an appendage to the greater, or the Melchizedek Priesthood, and has power in administering outward ordinances.

The bishopric is the presidency of this priesthood, and hold the keys or authority of the same.

No man has a legal right to this office, to hold the keys of his priesthood, except he be a literal descendant of Aaron. . . .

The power and authority of the lesser, or Aaronic Priesthood, is to hold the keys of the ministering of angels, and to administer in outward ordinances, the letter of the gospel, the baptism of repentance for the remission of sins, agreeable to the covenants and commandments.

Of necessity there are presidents, or presiding officers growing out of, or appointed of or from among those who are ordained to the several offices in these two priesthoods.

D&C 132:59 Verily, if a man be called of my Father, as was Aaron, by mine own voice, and by the voice of him that sent me, and I have endowed him with the keys of the power of my priesthood, if he do anything in my name, and according to my law and by my word, he will not commit sin, and I will justify him.

Pearl of Great Price

JS—H 1:68–70 While we [Joseph Smith and Oliver Cowdery] were thus employed, praying and calling upon the Lord, a messenger from heaven descended in a cloud of light, and having laid his hands upon us, he ordained us, saying:

Upon you my fellow servants, in the name of Messiah, I confer the Priesthood of Aaron, which holds the keys of the ministering of angels, and of the gospel of repentance, and of baptism by immersion for the remission of sins; and this shall never be taken again from the earth until the sons of Levi do offer again an offering unto the Lord in righteousness.

He said this Aaronic Priesthood had not the power of laying on hands for the gift of the Holy Ghost, but that this should be conferred on us hereafter.

(B) Melchizedek Priesthood

The Melchizedek Priesthood is called after Melchizedek because he was such a great high priest and to avoid using the name of Deity too frequently. Prior to Melchizedek, the higher priesthood was called the Holy Priesthood, after the Order of the Son of God. The Melchizedek Priesthood includes the Aaronic Priesthood and holds the keys of all the spiritual blessings of the Church. From the time of Adam, whenever the Lord has established his Church upon the earth, it has been through revelation with high priests, prophets, apostles, and teachers.

Old Testament

Genesis 14:18 — And Melchizedek king of Salem brought forth bread and wine: and he was the priest of the most high God.

Exodus 19:6 — And ye shall be unto me a kingdom of priests, and an holy nation.

1 Samuel 2:35 — And I will raise me up a faithful priest, that shall do according to that which is in mine heart and in my mind: and I will build him a sure house; and he shall walk before mine anointed for ever.

Psalm 110:4 — The Lord hath sworn, and will not repent, Thou art a priest for ever after the order of Melchizedek.

Zechariah was commanded by the Lord to crown Joshua, the high priest, in similitude of Christ.

Zechariah 6:11–13 — Then take silver and gold, and make crowns, and set them upon the head of Joshua the son of Josedech, the high priest;

And speak unto him, saying, Thus speaketh the Lord of hosts, saying, Behold the man whose name is the BRANCH; and he shall grow up out of his place, and he shall build the temple of the Lord:

Even he shall build the temple of the Lord; and he shall bear the glory, and shall sit and rule upon his throne; and he shall be a priest upon his throne: and the counsel of peace shall be between them both.

New Testament

Hebrews 5:1–6 — For every high priest taken from among men is ordained for men in things pertaining to God, that he may offer both gifts and sacrifices for sins:

Who can have compassion on the ignorant, and on them that are out of the way; for that he himself also is compassed with infirmity.

And by reason hereof he ought, as for the people,

so also for himself, to offer for sins.

And no man taketh this honour unto himself, but he that is called of God, as was Aaron.

So also Christ glorified not himself to be made an high priest; but he that said unto him, Thou art my Son, to day have I begotten thee.

As he saith also in another place, Thou art a priest for ever after the order of Melchisedec.

JST, Hebrews 7:1–3 For this Melchisedec, king of Salem, priest of the most high God, who met Abraham returning from the slaughter of the kings, and blessed him;

To whom also Abraham gave a tenth part of all; first being by interpretation King of righteousness, and after that also King of Salem, which is, King of peace;

For this Melchizedek was ordained a priest after the order of the Son of God, which order was without father, without mother, without descent, having neither beginning of days, nor end of life. And all those who are ordained unto this priesthood are made like unto the Son of God, abiding a priest continually.

Hebrews 7:11–17, 19, 24–28

If therefore perfection were by the Levitical priesthood, (for under it the people received the law,) what further need was there that another priest should rise after the order of Melchisedec, and not be called after the order of Aaron?

For the priesthood being changed, there is made of necessity a change also of the law.

For he of whom these things are spoken pertaineth to another tribe, of which no man gave attendance at the altar.

For it is evident that our Lord sprang out of Juda; of which tribe Moses spake nothing concerning priesthood.

And it is yet far more evident; for that after the

similitude of Melchisedec there ariseth another priest,

Who is made, not after the law of a carnal commandment, but after the power of an endless life.

For he testifieth, Thou art a priest for ever after the order of Melchisedec. . . .

For the law made nothing perfect, but the bringing in of a better hope did; by the which we draw nigh unto God. . . .

But his man, because he continueth ever, hath an unchangeable priesthood.

Wherefore he is able also to save them to the uttermost that come unto God by him, seeing he ever liveth to make intercession for them.

For such an high priest became us, who is holy, harmless, undefiled, separate from sinners, and made higher than the heavens;

Who needeth not daily, as those high priests, to offer up sacrifice, first for his own sins, and then for the people's: for this he did once, when he offered up himself.

For the law maketh men high priests which have infirmity; but the word of the oath, which was since the law, maketh the Son, who is consecrated for evermore.

John revealed to the people that Christ:

Revelation 1:6 Hath made us kings and priests unto God and his Father.

Revelation 5:10 And hast made us unto our God kings and priests: and we shall reign on the earth.

John's revelation also acknowledged that the Melchizedek Priesthood, God's power invested in man to act in his name while here on the earth, is an eternal priesthood.

Revelation 20:6 Blessed and holy is he that hath part in the first resurrection: on such the second death hath no power, but they shall be priests of God and of Christ, and shall reign with him a thousand years.

BOOK OF MORMON

2 Nephi 5:26	And it came to pass that I, Nephi, did consecrate Jacob and Joseph, that they should be priests and teachers over the land of my people.
Jacob 1:17–18	Wherefore I, Jacob, gave unto them these words as I taught them in the temple, having first obtained mine errand from the Lord. For I, Jacob, and my brother Joseph had been consecrated priests and teachers of this people, by the hand of Nephi.
Jarom 1:11	Wherefore, the prophets, and the priests, and the teachers, did labor diligently, exhorting with all long-suffering the people to diligence; teaching the law of Moses, and the intent for which it was given; persuading them to look forward unto the Messiah, and believe in him to come as though he already was. And after this manner did they teach them.
Mosiah 6:3	And again, it came to pass that when king Benjamin had made an end of all these things, and had consecrated his son Mosiah to be a ruler and a king over his people, and had given him all the charges concerning the kingdom, and also had appointed priests to teach the people, that thereby they might hear and know the commandments of God, and to stir them up in remembrance of the oath which they had made, he dismissed the multitude, and they returned, every one, according to their families, to their own houses.
Mosiah 18:18–20	And it came to pass that Alma, having authority from God, ordained priests; even one priest to every fifty of their number did he ordain to preach unto them, and to teach them concerning the things pertaining to the kingdom of God. And he commanded them that they should teach nothing save it were the things which he had taught, and which had been spoken by the mouth of

the holy prophets.

Yea, even he commanded them that they should preach nothing save it were repentance and faith on the Lord, who had redeemed his people.

Mosiah 18:24

And he also commanded them that the priests whom he had ordained should labor with their own hands for their support.

Mosiah 23:16–17

And now, Alma was their high priest, he being the founder of their church.

And it came to pass that none received authority to preach or to teach except it were by him from God. Therefore he consecrated all their priests and all their teachers; and none were consecrated except they were just men.

Mosiah 25:21–22

Therefore they did assemble themselves together in different bodies, being called churches; every church having their priests and their teachers, and ever priest preaching the word according as it was delivered to him by the mouth of Alma.

And thus, notwithstanding there being many churches they were all one church, yea, even the church of God; for there was nothing preached in all the churches except it were repentance and faith in God.

Mosiah 26:7–8

And it came to pass that they [church members who committed sin] were brought before the priests, and delivered up unto the priests by the teachers; and the priests brought them before Alma, who was the high priest.

Now king Mosiah had given Alma the authority over the church.

Alma 4:7

Now this was the cause of much affliction to Alma, yea, and to many of the people whom Alma had consecrated to be teachers, and priests, and elders over the church.

Alma 6:1

And now it came to pass that after Alma had made an end of speaking unto the people of the church, which was established in the city of Zarahemla, he ordained priests and elders, by laying on his hands according to the order of God, to preside and watch over the church.

Alma explained the eternal nature and significance of the priesthood.

Alma 13:1–4, 6–9, 13–16

And I would that ye should remember that the Lord God ordained priests, after his holy order, which was after the order of his Son, to teach these things unto the people.

And those priests were ordained after the order of his Son, in a manner that thereby the people might know in what manner to look forward to his Son for redemption.

And this is the manner after which they were ordained—being called and prepared from the foundation of the world according to the foreknowledge of God, on account of their exceeding faith and good works. . . .

And thus they have been called to this holy calling on account of their faith. . . .

And thus being called by this holy calling, and ordained unto the high priesthood of the holy order of God, to teach his commandments unto the children of men, that they also might enter into his rest—

This high priesthood being after the order of his Son, which order was from the foundation of the world; or in other words, being without beginning of days or end of years, being prepared from eternity to all eternity, according to his foreknowledge of all things—

Now they were ordained after this manner—being called with a holy calling, and ordained with a holy ordinance, and taking upon them the high priesthood of the holy order, which calling, and ordinance, and high priesthood, is without beginning or end—

Thus they become high priests forever, after the order of the Son. . . .

And now, my brethren, I would that ye should humble yourselves before God, and bring forth fruit meet for repentance. . . .

Yea, humble yourselves even as the people in the days of Melchizedek, who was also a high priest after this same order which I have spoken, who also took upon him the high priesthood forever.

And it was this same Melchizedek to whom Abraham paid tithes; yea, even our father Abraham paid tithes of one-tenth part of all he possessed.

Now these ordinances were given after this manner, that thereby the people might look forward on the Son of God, it being a type of his order, or it being his order, and this that they might look forward to him for a remission of their sins, that they might enter into the rest of the Lord.

Alma 15:13 — And Alma established a church in the land of Sidom, and consecrated priests and teachers in the land, to baptize unto the Lord whosoever were desirous to be baptized.

Alma 45:22 — Therefore, Helaman [the son of Alma] and his brethren went forth to establish the church again in all the land, yea, in every city throughout all the land which was possessed by the people of Nephi. And it came to pass that they did appoint priests and teachers throughout all the land, over all the churches.

Before Moroni, the last writer of the Book of Mormon, hid up the records of his people, he recorded important information regarding the priesthood for those who would eventually receive those records. He recorded Christ's instructions to the twelve disciples chosen from among the Nephites:

Moroni 2:1–2 — The words of Christ, which he spake unto his disciples, the twelve whom he had chosen, as he laid his hands upon them—

And he called them by name, saying: Ye shall call on the Father in my name, in mighty prayer; and after ye have done this ye shall have power [priesthood power] that to him upon whom ye shall lay your hands, ye shall give the Holy Ghost; and in my name shall ye give it, for thus do mine apostles.

Moroni also recorded the manner in which priesthood power was given to righteous men.

Moroni 3:1–4

The manner which the disciples, who were called the elders of the church, ordained priests and teachers—

After they had prayed unto the Father in the name of Christ, they laid their hands upon them, and said:

In the name of Jesus Christ I ordain you to be a priest, (or, if he be a teacher) I ordain yo to be a teacher, to preach repentance and remission of sins through Jesus Christ, by the endurance of faith on his name to the end. Amen.

And after this manner did they ordain priests and teachers, according to the gifts and callings of God unto men; and they ordained them by the power of the Holy Ghost, which was in them.

Doctrine and Covenants

The promise given in Malachi in the Old Testament was repeated in the Doctrine and Covenants on September 21, 1823.

D&C 2:1–3

Behold, I will reveal unto you the Priesthood [the power by which that which is sealed on earth is sealed in heaven], by the hand of Elijah the prophet, before the coming of the great and dreadful day of the Lord.

And he shall plant in the hearts of the children the promises made to the fathers, and the hearts of the children shall turn to their fathers.

If it were not so, the whole earth would be utterly wasted at his coming.

In a revelation given to the Prophet Joseph Smith in November of 1831, more clarification regarding the priesthood was given.

D&C 68:19–20 But, as a high priest of the Melchizedek Priesthood has authority to officiate in all the lesser offices he may officiate in the office of bishop when no literal descendant of Aaron can be found, provided he is called and set apart and ordained unto this power, under the hands of the First presidency of the Melchizedek Priesthood.

And a literal descendant of Aaron, also, must be designated by this Presidency, and found worthy, and anointed, and ordained under the hands of this Presidency, otherwise they are not legally authorized to officiate in their priesthood.

On September 22–23, 1832, Joseph Smith received another revelation regarding the priesthood. Referring to the children of Israel after they were led out of Egypt, the Lord said:

D&C 84:24–27, 29 But they hardened their hearts and could not endure his presence; therefore, the Lord in his wrath, for his anger was kindled against them, swore that they should not enter into his rest while in the wilderness, which rest is the fulness of his glory.

Therefore, he took Moses out of their midst, and the Holy Priesthood also;

And the lesser priesthood continued, which priesthood holdeth the key of the ministering of angels and the preparatory gospel;

Which gospel is the gospel of repentance and of baptism, and the remission of sins, and the law of carnal commandments, which the Lord in his wrath caused to continue with the house of Aaron among the children of Israel until John, whom God raised up, being filled with the Holy Ghost from his mother's womb. . . .

And again, the offices of elder and bishop are necessary appendages belonging unto the high priesthood.

And again, the offices of teacher and deacon are necessary appendages belonging to the lesser priesthood, which priesthood was confirmed upon Aaron and his sons.

Pearl of Great Price

In the Pearl of Great Price we have additional scripture that attests to the eternal nature of the priesthood.

Moses 6:7–8 Now this same Priesthood, which was in the beginning, shall be in the end of the world also.

Now this prophecy Adam spake, as he was moved upon by the Holy Ghost.

The Prophet Joseph Smith recorded in his history that the messenger (John the Baptist) who conferred the Aaronic Priesthood upon him and Oliver Cowdery in May 1829 indicated that:

JS—H 1:72 He acted under the direction of Peter, James and John, who held the keys of the Priesthood of Melchizedek, which Priesthood, he said, would in due time be conferred on us.

Peter, James, and John subsequently conferred the Melchizedek Priesthood upon Joseph and Oliver in June of 1829. The exact date is unknown, but the location was somewhere between Harmony, Pennsylvania, and Colesville, New York, on the Susquehanna River.

Notes

1. Bruce R. McConkie, *Mormon Doctrine*, 2nd ed. (Salt Lake City: Bookcraft, 1966), 594.

Chapter 16

Marriage, Homosexuality, and Plural Marriage

TENET: Marriage is ordained of God. God delights in the chastity of his children and abhors all forms of sexual immorality. The prophets throughout the ages understood this and condemned sexual sins. God instructed his people to have one wife only, unless he specifically authorized an individual or group of individuals to have additional wives for his own purposes.

(A) Marriage

The scriptures teach that marriage is ordained of God.

Old Testament

Genesis 2:18, 24	And the Lord God said, It is not good that the man should be alone; I will make him an help meet for him. . . . Therefore shall a man leave his father and his mother, and shall cleave unto his wife: and they shall be one flesh.

The eternal nature of marriage (as well as other statutes) as ordained of God is reaffirmed in Ecclesiastes.

Ecclesiastes 3:14	I know that, whatsoever God doeth, it shall be for ever: nothing can be put to it, nor any thing taken from it: and God doeth it, that men should fear before him.

New Testament

Marriage, as instituted by God in the Garden of Eden, was meant to be eternal. It was not to be just "until death do us part" (such temporal marriages will not exist in the next life because the contract is voided when one of the partners dies) nor to be ended with divorce. The Savior conferred upon Peter the sealing powers of the priesthood.

Matthew 16:19 And I will give unto thee the keys of the kingdom of heaven: and whatsoever thou shalt bind on earth shall be bound in heaven: and whatsoever thou shalt loose on earth shall be loosed in heaven.

Christ reaffirmed the importance of the sealing power.

Matthew 18:18 Verily I say unto you, Whatsoever ye shall bind on earth shall be bound in heaven: and whatsoever ye shall lose on earth shall be loosed in heaven.

Matthew 19:4–6 And he [Jesus] answered and said unto them, Have ye not read, that he which made them at the beginning made them male and female,

And said, for this cause shall a man leave father and mother and shall cleave to his wife: and they twain shall be one flesh?

Wherefore they are no more twain, but one flesh. What therefore God hath joined together, let not man put asunder.

The Sadducees queried Jesus about the fate of the woman whose husband had died and she was subsequently married to each of the six remaining brothers.

Matthew 22:23–30 That same day came to him the Sadducees, which say that there is no resurrection, and asked him,

Saying, Master, Moses said, if a man die, having no children, his brother shall marry his wife, and raise up seed unto his brother.

Now there were with us seven brethren: and the first, when he had married a wife, deceased, and, having no issue, left his wife unto his brother:

Likewise the second also, and the third, unto the seventh.

> And last of all the woman died also.
> Therefore in the resurrection whose wife shall she be of the seven? for they all had her.
> Jesus answered and said unto them, Ye do err, not knowing the scriptures, nor the power of God.
> For in the resurrection they neither marry, nor are given in marriage, but are as the angels of God in heaven.

His answer pointed out that her temporal marriages ended with the death of each spouse. Thus, she would have no husband in the next life. If a celestial marriage is not performed in this life, that marriage will not be binding in the next life.

Mark 10:6–9

> But from the beginning of the creation God made them male and female.
> For this cause shall a man leave his father and mother, and cleave to his wife;
> And they twain shall be one flesh: so then they are no more twain, but one flesh.
> What therefore God hath joined together, let not man put asunder.

There is a time and a season for all things, and Paul, responding to some questions about marriage, pointed out that it would be best if men remained single while serving as missionaries:

1 Corinthians 7:32–33

> But I would have you without carefulness [cares]. He that is unmarried careth for the things that belong to the Lord, how he may please the Lord:
> But he that is married careth for the things that are of the world, how he may please his wife.

However, he provided a caveat:

1 Corinthians 7:2

> Nevertheless, to avoid fornication, let every man have his own wife, and let every woman have her own husband.

In Paul's epistle to the Ephesians, he compared his counsel to husbands and wives to be one flesh to the members of the church being one with

Christ. Then he admonished them:

Ephesians 5:33 — Nevertheless let every one of you in particular so love his wife even as himself; and the wife see that she reverence her husband.

In his epistle to Timothy, Paul described the latter-day apostasy that would occur.

1 Timothy 4:1–3 — Now the Spirit speaketh expressly, that in the latter times some shall depart from the faith, giving heed to seducing spirits, and doctrines of devils;

Speaking lies in hypocrisy; having their conscience seared with a hot iron;

Forbidding to marry.

In Hebrews, we are reminded by Paul that:

Hebrews 13:4 — Marriage is honourable in all, and the bed undefiled: but whoremongers and adulterers God will judge.

Book of Mormon

The Book of Mormon prophets were no less explicit in declaring that marriage was a commandment of the Lord.

1 Nephi 7:1 — And now I would that ye might know, that after my father, Lehi, had made an end of prophesying concerning his seed, it came to pass that the Lord spake unto him again, saying that it was not meet for him, Lehi, that he should take his family into the wilderness alone; but that his sons should take daughters to wife, that they might raise up seed unto the Lord in the land of promise.

1 Nephi 16:7–8 — And it came to pass that I, Nephi, took one of the daughters of Ishmael to wife; and also, my brethren took of the daughters of Ishmael to wife; and also Zoram took the eldest daughter of Ishmael to wife.

And thus my father had fulfilled all the commandments of the Lord which had been given unto him.

The sealing power was also conferred upon God's people here in the Americas.

Helaman 10:6–7	Behold, thou art Nephi, and I am God. Behold, I declare it unto thee in the presence of mine angels, that ye shall have power over this people, and shall smite the earth with famine, and with pestilence, and destruction, according to the wickedness of this people. Behold, I give unto you power, and whatsoever ye shall seal on earth should be sealed in heaven; and whatsoever ye shall loose on earth shall be loosed in heaven; and thus shall ye have power among this people.
4 Nephi 1:10–11	And now, behold, it came to pass that the people of Nephi did wax strong, and did multiply exceedingly fast, and became an exceedingly fair and delightsome people. And they were married, and given in marriage, and were blessed according to the multitude of the promises which the Lord had made unto them.

Doctrine and Covenants

On February 9, 1831, the Lord stressed to a prophet in these latter days the sanctity of marriage.

D&C 42:22	Thou shalt love thy wife with all thy heart, and shalt cleave unto her and none else.

A month later, in March 1831, Joseph Smith was given a revelation wherein the Lord declared:

D&C 49:15	And again, verily I say unto you, that whoso forbiddeth to marry is not ordained of God, for marriage is ordained of God unto man.

Joseph Smith, Jun, in 1843, counseled the members of the Church:

D&C 131:1–4	In the celestial glory there are three heavens or degrees; And in order to obtain the highest, a man must enter into this order of the priesthood (meaning the new and everlasting covenant of marriage);

And if he does not, he cannot obtain it.

He may enter into the other, but that is the end of his kingdom; he cannot have an increase.

Continuing that message, the Lord revealed to Joseph Smith as early as 1831, the following:

D&C 132:19 And again, verily I say unto you, if a man marry a wife by my word, which is my law, and by the new and everlasting covenant, and it is sealed unto them by the Holy Spirit of promise, by him who is anointed, unto whom I have appointed this power and the keys of this priesthood; and it shall be said unto them—Ye shall come forth in the first resurrection; and if it be after the first resurrection, in the next resurrection; and shall inherit thrones, kingdoms, principalities, and powers, dominions, all heights and depths—then shall it be written in the Lamb's Book of Life, that he shall commit no murder whereby to shed innocent blood, and if ye abide in my covenant, and commit no murder whereby to shed innocent blood, it shall be done unto them in all things whatsoever my servant hath put upon them, in time, and through all eternity; and shall be of full force when they are out of the world; and they shall pass by the angels, and the gods, which are set there, to their exaltation and glory in all things, as hath been sealed upon their heads, which glory shall be a fulness and a continuation of the seeds forever and ever.

Pearl of Great Price

In the Pearl of Great Price, scriptures echo those of the Bible and other scriptures and provide another witness that God ordained marriage from the very beginning.

Moses 3:23–24 And Adam said: This I know now is bone of my bones, and flesh of my flesh; she shall be called Woman, because she was taken out of man.

Therefore shall a man leave his father and his

mother, and shall cleave unto his wife; and they shall be one flesh.

Abraham 5:14, 16–18

And the Gods said: Let us make an help meet for the man, for it is not good that the man should be alone, therefore we will form an help meet for him. . . .

And of the rib which the Gods had taken from man, formed they a woman, and brought her unto the man.

And Adam said: This was bone of my bones, and flesh of my flesh; now she shall be called Woman, because she was taken out of man;

Therefore shall a man leave his father and his mother, and shall cleave unto his wife, and they shall be one flesh.

(B) Homosexuality and other sexual sins

Just as the scriptures are clear that marriage is ordained of God, they are also explicit in their condemnation of sexual sins. The dictionary defines sodomy as "any sexual intercourse held to be abnormal, as bestiality; specifically, anal intercourse between two male persons."[1] Sodom and Gomorrah were destroyed by the Lord because of their gross wickedness and their practice of sodomy.

Old Testament

Genesis 13:13

But the men of Sodom were wicked and sinners before the Lord exceedingly.

Genesis 19:4–7

But before they lay down, the men of the city, even the men of Sodom, compassed the house round, both old and young, all the people from every quarter:

And they called unto Lot, and said unto him, Where are the men which came in to thee this night? bring them out unto us, that we may know them.

And Lot went out at the door unto them, and shut the door after him,

And said, I pray you, brethren, do not so wickedly.

To "know them," in this context, means to have sexual intercourse with them. Mary used the same term—know—in her response to the angel indicating she had never had sex, and therefore did not understand how she could become pregnant: "Then said Mary unto the angel, How shall this be, seeing I know not a man?" (Luke 1:34).

Reuben, Jacob's firstborn son, lost the birthright because of sexual sin:

Genesis 35:22	And it came to pass, when Israel dwelt in that land, that Reuben went and lay with Bilhah his father's concubine: and Israel heard it.
Genesis 49: 1, 3–4	And Jacob called unto his sons, and said, Gather yourselves together, that I may tell you that which shall befall you in the last days. . . . Reuben, thou art my firstborn, my might, and the beginning of my strength, the excellency of dignity, and the excellency of power: Unstable as water, thou shalt not excel; because thou wentest up to they father's bed; then defiledst thou it: he went up to my couch.

The Lord is very direct in his instruction and condemnation regarding homosexual activity.

Leviticus 18:22	Thou shalt not lie with mankind, as with womankind [same-sex relationships]: It is abomination.

There are several different sexual sins, and the Lord enumerates a host of them in Leviticus, including adultery, incest, homosexuality, and bestiality.

Leviticus 20:10–21	And the man that committeth adultery with another man's wife, even he that committeth adultery with his neighbour's wife, the adulterer and the adulteress shall surely be put to death. And the man that lieth with his father's wife hath uncovered his father's nakedness: both of them shall surely be put to death; their blood shall be upon them. And if a man lie with his daughter in law, both of them shall surely be put to death: they have wrought confusion; their blood shall be upon them.

> If a man also lie with mankind, as he lieth with a woman [homosexual engagement], both of them have committed an abomination: they shall surely be put to death; their blood shall be upon them.
>
> And if a man take a wife and her mother, it is wickedness: they shall be burnt with fire, both he and they that there be no wickedness among you.
>
> And if a man lie with a beast, he shall surely be put to death: and ye shall slay the beast.
>
> And if a woman approach unto any beast, and lie down thereto, thou shalt kill the woman, and the beast: they shall surely be put to death; their blood shall be upon them.
>
> And if a man shall take his sister, his father's daughter or his mother's daughter, and see her nakedness, and she see his nakedness, it is a wicked thing; and they shall be cut off in the sight of their people: he hath uncovered his sister's nakedness; he shall bear his iniquity.
>
> And if a man shall lie with a woman having her sickness, and shall uncover her nakedness; he hath discovered her fountain, and she hath uncovered the fountain of her blood: and both of them shall be cut off from among their people.
>
> And thou shalt not uncover the nakedness of thy mother's sister, nor of thy father's sister: for he uncovereth his near kin: they shall bear their iniquity.
>
> And if a man shall lie with his uncle's wife, he hath uncovered his uncle's nakedness: they shall bear their sin; they shall die childless.
>
> And if a man shall take his brother's wife, it is an unclean thing: he hath uncovered his brother's nakedness; they shall be childless [also see 18:6–24].

While the penalties for these sins are not applied in our day and age, God will undoubtedly hold us accountable at the day of judgment.

Deuteronomy 23:17 There shall be no whore of the daughters of Israel, nor a sodomite of the sons of Israel.

A wicked situation similar to the one in Sodom occurred in Gibeah.

Judges 19:22–23 Behold, the men of the city . . . beset the house round about . . . saying, Bring forth the man that came into thine house, that we may know him [have sex with him].

And the man, the master of the house, went out unto them, and said unto them, Nay, my brethren, nay, I pray you, do not so wickedly.

Jeremiah recorded:

Jeremiah 23:14 I have seen also in the prophets of Jerusalem an horrible thing: they commit adultery, and walk in lies: they strengthen also the hands of evildoers, that none doth return from his wickedness: they are all of them unto me as Sodom, and the inhabitants thereof as Gomorrah.

New Testament

Sexual sins are also condemned in the New Testament. In the Sermon on the Mount, Jesus said:

Matthew 5:27–28 Ye have heard that it was said by them of old time, Thou shalt not commit adultery:

But I say unto you, That whosoever looketh on a woman to lust after her hath committed adultery with her already in his heart.

Jesus listed adultery and fornication among evil things that proceed forth from the heart.

Matthew 15:19 For out of the heart proceed evil thoughts, murders, adulteries, fornications.

In the epistle of Paul to the Romans, Paul wrote:

Romans 1:26–27, 29, 31

For this cause God gave them up unto vile affections: for even their women did change the natural use into that which is against nature [lesbian activity]:

And likewise also the men, leaving the natural use of the woman, burned in their lust one toward

> another; men with men, working that which is unseemly, and receiving in themselves that recompence of their error which was meet. . . .
>
> Being filled with all unrighteousness, fornication, wickedness, covetousness. . . .
>
> Without understanding, covenantbreakers, without natural affection.

Paul condemned the fornication that was prevalent among the Corinthians:

1 Corinthians 5:1, 4–5, 9

> It is reported commonly that there is fornications among you, and such fornication as is not so much as named among the Gentiles, that one should have his father's wife. . . .
>
> In the name of our Lord Jesus Christ, when ye are gathered together, and my spirit, with the power of our Lord Jesus Christ,
>
> To deliver such an one unto Satan for the destruction of the flesh, that the spirit may be saved in the day of the Lord Jesus. . .
>
> I wrote unto you in an epistle not to company with fornicators.

Paul addressed that same subject in his epistle to the Corinthians.

1 Corinthians 6:9, 18

> Know ye not that the unrighteous shall not inherit the kingdom of God? Be not deceived: neither fornicators, nor idolaters, nor adulterers, nor effeminate, nor abusers of themselves with mankind. . . .
>
> Flee fornication. Every sin that a man doeth is without the body; but he that committeth fornication sinneth against his own body.

Paul counseled missionaries to remain single; however, he also counseled:

1 Corinthians 7:2

> Nevertheless, to avoid fornication, let every man have his own wife, and let every woman have her own husband.

To the Galatians, Paul wrote:

Galatians 5:19	Now the works of the flesh are manifest which are these; Adultery, fornication, uncleanness, lasciviousness.

Paul also wrote the Colossians:

Colossians 3:5–6	Mortify therefore your members which are upon the earth; fornication, uncleanness, inordinate affection, evil concupiscence, and covetousness, which is idolatry: For which things' sake the wrath of God cometh on the children of disobedience.

To Timothy, Paul wrote:

1 Timothy 1:9–10	Knowing this, that the law is not made for a righteous man, but to the lawless and disobedient. . . . For whoremongers, for them that defile themselves with mankind.

Prophesying that sexual sins (as well as other sins) would exist in the last days, Paul wrote to Timothy:

2 Timothy 3:1–3	This know also, that in the last days perilous times shall come. For men shall be lovers of their own selves. . . . Without natural affection.

Apostle Peter also wrote regarding those who follow the lustful pursuit of the flesh:

2 Peter 2:9–10	The Lord knoweth how to deliver the godly out of temptations, and to reserve the unjust unto the day of judgment to be punished: But chiefly them that walk after the flesh in the lust of uncleanness.

Jude, the brother of James, again calls our attention to the wickedness of Sodom and Gomorrha:

Jude 1:7	Even as Sodom and Gomorrha, and the cities about them in like manner, giving themselves over to fornication, and going after strange flesh, are set forth

for an example, suffering the vengeance of eternal fire.

Book of Mormon

The sins committed by the people in Sodom were acknowledged and condemned by Nephi.

2 Nephi 13:9 — The show of their countenance doth witness against them, and doth declare their sin to be even as Sodom, and they cannot hide it. Wo unto their souls, for they have rewarded evil unto themselves.

Jacob, son of Lehi, condemned sexual sins:

Jacob 3:12 — And now I, Jacob, spake many more things unto the people of Nephi, warning them against fornication and lasciviousness, and every kind of sin, telling them the awful consequences of them.

Wicked King Noah put down all the righteous priests and replaced them with wicked men.

Mosiah 11:6, 14 — Yea, and thus they were supported in their laziness, and in their idolatry, and in their whoredoms, by the taxes which king Noah had put upon his people; thus did the people labor exceedingly to support iniquity. . . .

And it came to pass that he placed his heart upon his riches, and he spent his time in riotous living with his wives and his concubines; and so did also his priests spend their time with harlots.

The dictionary defines *whoredom* as prostitution or fornication and *whoremonger* as a man who fornicates or associates with whores, specifically a pimp.[2]

Alma chastised his son Corianton for committing a sexual sin.

Alma 39:3, 5 — And this is not all, my son, Thou didst do that which was grievous unto me; for thou didst forsake the ministry, and did go over into the land of Siron among the borders of the Lamanites, after the harlot Isabel. . . .

Know ye not, my son, that these things are an abomination in the sight of the Lord; yea, most abominable above all sins save it be the shedding of innocent blood or denying the Holy Ghost?

Alma's son Helaman warned against sexual sins:

Helaman 8:26 — Yea, even at this time ye are ripening, because of your murders and your fornication and wickedness, for everlasting destruction; yea, and except ye repent it will come unto you soon.

When Christ appeared to the Nephites following his resurrection, he taught the Nephites the same things he taught in the Sermon on the Mount:

3 Nephi 12:27–28 — Behold, it is written by them of old time, that thou shalt not commit adultery;

But I say unto you, that whosoever looketh on a woman, to lust after her, hath committed adultery already in his heart.

Christ continually beckons his children to forego their sins, among which are sexual sins, and come unto him.

3 Nephi 30:1–2 — Hearken, O ye Gentiles, and here the words of Jesus Christ. . .

Turn, all ye Gentiles, from your wicked ways; and repent of your evil doings, of your lyings and deceivings, and of your whoredoms.

Corianton, a Jaredite king, committed sexual sins and reaped his punishment.

Ether 10:11 — And he did do justice unto the people, but not unto himself because of his many whoredoms; wherefore he was cut off from the presence of the Lord.

Doctrine and Covenants

In August of 1831 the Lord revealed to Joseph Smith this warning, which again points out that sexual sins are very grievous to the Lord.

D&C 63:17–18 — Wherefore, I, the Lord, have said that the fearful, and the unbelieving, and all liars, and whosoever

> loveth and maketh a lie, and the whoremonger, and the sorcerer, shall have their part in that lake which burneth with fire and brimstone, which is the second death.
>
> Verily I say, that they shall not have part in the first resurrection.

The consequence for committing sexual sins is great: Joseph Smith was shown a vision on February 16, 1832, wherein he saw the fate of those who engage in such activity.

D&C 76:102–103 Last of all, these all are they who will not be gathered with the saints, to be caught up unto the church of the Firstborn, and received into the cloud.

> These are they who are liars, and sorcerers, and adulterers, and whoremongers, and whosoever loves and makes a lie.

No one familiar with the scriptures should have any doubt that the Lord condemns sexual sins and that the consequences of such sins are very serious.

(C) Plural marriage

God instructed his people to have one wife only, unless he specifically authorized an individual or group of individuals to have additional wives for his own purposes. As a result, the scriptures have many examples where various people were justified in having multiple wives. There are also commandments indicating that people should have only one wife.

Old Testament

In Genesis 16 we read of Sarah giving Hagar to Abraham for a wife so she could have children by her. The Lord did not condemn this. In Genesis 29:15–28 we read of Jacob receiving both Leah and Rachel as his wives. Later, he received both Bilhah (Rachel's maid) and Zilpah (Leah's maid) as wives. Through these four wives descended the Twelve Tribes of Israel. God did not condemn Jacob for having multiple wives (see Genesis 30:4, 9, 26).

In Deuteronomy, the Lord warned kings about the danger of taking multiple wives:

Deuteronomy 17:17 Neither shall he multiply wives to himself, that his heart turn not away.

The Lord counseled those who had multiple wives:

Deuteronomy 21:15–16

> If a man have two wives, one beloved, and another hated, and they have born him children, both the beloved and the hated; and if the firstborn son be hers that was hated:
>
> Then it shall be, when he maketh his sons to inherit that which he hath, that he may not make the son of the beloved firstborn before the son of the hated, which is indeed the firstborn.

The Lord required that justice and fairness be practiced by men who had multiple wives. However, that ideal seemed very difficult to achieve, and wickedness resulted.

King David had multiple wives which the Lord did not condemn. However, he was condemned for taking wives he was not authorized to have; for example, he was condemned for taking Bathsheba, Uriah's wife.

2 Samuel 12:7–10 And Nathan said to David, Thou art the man. Thus saith the Lord God of Israel, I anointed thee king over Israel, and I delivered thee out of the hand of Saul;

> And I gave thee thy master's house, and thy master's wives into thy bosom, and gave thee the house of Israel and of Judah; and if that had been too little, I would moreover have given unto thee such and such things.
>
> Wherefore hast thou despised the commandment of the Lord, to do evil in his sight? thou hast killed Uriah the Hittite with the sword, and hast taken his wife to be thy wife. . . .
>
> Now therefore the sword shall never depart from thine house; because thou hast despised me, and hast taken the wife of Uriah the Hittite to be thy wife.

King Solomon had 700 wives and 300 concubines. However, he "loved many strange women," and when Solomon was old, "his wives turned away his heart after other gods" (1 Kings 11:1, 4).

1 Kings 11: 9 — And the Lord was angry with Solomon, because his heart was turned from the Lord God of Israel.

It appears that God was not so angry with Solomon for having multiple wives as for marrying strange women, women who he did not give to him, women who turned him from worshiping him to worshiping idols.

King Abijah (or Abijam) was the son of King Rehoboam and had fourteen wives (2 Chronicles 13:21).

Jehoiada the priest gave two wives to Joash, who lived righteously as long as Jehoiada was alive (2 Chronicles 24:2–3).

Isaiah prophesied that in the millennial day:

Isaiah 4:1–2 — Seven women shall take hold of one man, saying, We will eat our own bread, and wear our own apparel: only let us be called by thy name, to take away our reproach.

In that day shall the branch of the Lord be beautiful and glorious, and the fruit of the earth shall be excellent and comely for them that are escaped of Israel.

New Testament

The scriptures reveal that God expects his children to obey the laws of the land. This also extends to laws concerning marriage.

Paul wrote to Titus and instructed him:

Titus 3:1 — Put them [the members of the church] in mind to be subject to principalities and powers, to obey magistrates, to be ready to every good work.

Peter also instructed the people:

1 Peter 2:13–15 — Submit yourselves to every ordinance of man for the Lord's sake: whether it be to the king, as supreme;

Or unto governors, as unto them that are sent

by him for the punishment of evildoers, and for the praise of them that do well,

For so is the will of God, that with well doing ye may put to silence the ignorance of foolish.

Book of Mormon

Jacob, Nephi's younger brother, taught the people the word of the Lord regarding multiple wives:

Jacob 2:23–31

But the word of God burdens me because of your grosser crimes. For behold, thus saith the Lord: This people begin to wax in iniquity; they understand not the scriptures, for they seek to excuse themselves in committing whoredoms, because of the things which were written concerning David, and Solomon his son.

Behold, David and Solomon truly had many wives and concubines (and it led to their downfall), which thing was abominable before me, saith the Lord.

Wherefore, thus saith the Lord, I have led this people forth out of the land of Jerusalem, by the power of mine arm, that I might raise up unto me a righteous branch from the fruit of the loins of Joseph.

Wherefore, I the Lord God will not suffer that this people shall do like unto them of old.

Wherefore, my brethren, hear me, and hearken to the word of the Lord: For there shall not any man among you have save it be one wife; and concubines he shall have none;

For I, the Lord God, delight in the chastity of women. And whoredoms are an abomination before me; thus saith the Lord of Hosts.

Wherefore, this people shall keep my commandments, saith the Lord of Hosts, or cursed be the land for their sakes.

For if I will, saith the Lord of Hosts, raise up seed unto me, I will command my people; otherwise they shall hearken unto these things.

For behold, I, the Lord, have seen the sorrow, and heard the mourning of the daughters of my people in the land of Jerusalem, yea, and in all the lands of my people, because of the wickedness and abominations of their husbands.

Sexual sins also plagued the Jaredites.

Ether 10:5 And it came to pass that Riplakish did not do that which was right in the sight of the Lord, for he did have many wives and concubines, and did lay that upon men's shoulders which was grievous to be borne.

Doctrine and Covenants

In May 1831, the Lord gave this instruction regarding marriage:

D&C 49:16 Wherefore, it is lawful that he should have one wife, and they twain shall be one flesh, and all this that the earth might answer the end of its creation.

On July 12, 1843, the Lord gave Joseph Smith a revelation pertaining to the new and everlasting covenant, including the eternity of the marriage covenant, and the plurality of wives. (However, the Prophet had apparently known of these doctrines and principles as early as 1831.)

D&C 132:7 And verily I say unto you, that the conditions of this law are these: All covenants, contracts, bonds, obligations, oaths, vows, performances, connections, associations, or expectations, that are not made and entered into and sealed by the Holy Spirit of promise, of him who is anointed, both as well for time and for all eternity, and that too most holy, by revelation and commandment through the medium of mine anointed, whom I have appointed on the earth to hold this power (and I have appointed unto my servant Joseph to hold this power in the last days, and there is never but one on the earth at a time on whom this power and the keys of this priesthood are conferred), are of no efficacy, virtue, or force in and after the resurrection from the dead; for all contracts that are not made unto this end have an end when men are dead.

The Lord defended Abraham having multiple wives and indicated that David's and Solomon's sins were in that they took wives which he did not authorize.

D&C 132:37–39 Abraham received concubines, and they bore him children; and it was accounted unto him for righteousness, because they were given unto him, and he abode in my law; as Isaac also and Jacob did none other things than that which they were commanded; and because they did none other things than that which they were commanded, they have entered into their exaltation, according to the promises, and sit upon thrones, and are not angels but are gods.

David also received many wives and concubines, and also Solomon and Moses my servants, as also many others of my servants, from the beginning of creation until this time, and in nothing did they sin save in those things which they received not of me.

David's wives and concubines were given unto him of me, by the hand of Nathan, my servant, and others of the prophets who had the keys of this power; and in none of these things did he sin against me save in the case of Uriah and his wife; and, therefore he hath fallen from his exaltation, and received his portion; and he shall not inherit them out of the world, for I gave them unto another, saith the Lord.

The Lord further instructed:

D&C 132:61–62 And again, as pertaining to the law of the priesthood—if any man espouse a virgin, and desire to espouse another, and the first give her consent, and if he espouse the second, and they are virgins, and have vowed to no other man, then is he justified; he cannot commit adultery for they are given unto him; for he cannot commit adultery with that that belongeth unto him and to no one else.

And if he have ten virgins given unto him by this law, he cannot commit adultery, for they belong to him, and they are given unto him; therefore is he justified [July 12, 1843].

The Lord informed Joseph Smith that he suffered the constitution of the United States to be established and that it "should be maintained for the rights and protection of all flesh" (D&C 101:77).

The Prophet Joseph Smith also wrote:

D&C 134:1 We believe that governments were instituted of God for the benefit of man; and that he holds men accountable for their acts in relation to them, both in making laws and administering them, for the good and safety of society.

In keeping with the statements and revelations of Joseph Smith and New Testament prophets, and in compliance with the laws of the land, Wilford Woodruff made the following declaration in 1890:

> Inasmuch as laws have been enacted by Congress forbidding plural marriages, which laws have been pronounced constitutional by the court of last resort . . . . And I now publicly declare that my advice to the Latter-day Saints is to refrain from contracting any marriage forbidden by the law of the land. (Official Declaration 1)

Pearl of Great Price

Joseph Smith summarized the foregoing on government in a brief, concise statement.

Articles of Faith 1:12 We believe in being subject to kings, presidents, rulers, and magistrates, in obeying, honoring, and sustaining the law.

Teachings of the Prophet Joseph Smith:

> Gave instructions to try those persons who were preaching, teaching, or practicing the doctrine of plurality of wives; for, according to the law, I hold the keys of this power in the last days; for there is never but one on earth at a time on whom the power and its keys are conferred,

> and I have constantly said no man shall have but one wife at a time unless the Lord directs otherwise.[3]

More recently, Bruce R. McConkie, an apostle of our day, declared:

> All who pretend or assume to engage in plural marriage in this day, when the one holding the keys has withdrawn the power by which they are performed, are guilty of gross wickedness.[4]

It is clear from the scriptures that marriage is ordained of God; marriage was intended to be eternal but unless it is sealed upon earth by one having the sealing power it will not be sealed in heaven and the marriage contract will end upon death; that marriage is to be between one man and one woman unless the Lord directs otherwise; and that God abhors sexual immorality of all kinds. It is also evident that the Old Testament, New Testament, Book of Mormon, and Doctrine and Covenants all teach the same principles.

Notes

1. *Webster's New World Dictionary,* 2nd College ed. (Cleveland, OH: World Publishing, 1976), 994, 1353.
2. Ibid., 1624.
3. *Teachings of the Prophet Joseph Smith,* compiled by Joseph Fielding Smith (Salt Lake City: Deseret Book, 1968), 324.
4. Bruce R. McConkie, *Mormon Doctrine,* 2nd ed., (Salt Lake City: Bookcraft, 1966), 579.

Chapter 17

The Plan of Salvation

TENET. In our premortal state as spirit children of our Heavenly Father, we met in a grand council in heaven during which our Father in Heaven presented his plan of happiness which would enable us to progress and become like him. The plan provided for us to come to earth, gain a mortal body of flesh and blood, live by faith, and use the agency he granted us to make choices whereby we would learn the good from the evil. We would be tried and tested in all things. A Savior was to be provided so we could overcome the effects of our wrong choices through repentance and return back into his presence.

Heavenly Father inquired as to whom he should send to be the Savior. Two of his spirit children offered to be the Savior: Jehovah (Christ) and Lucifer (Satan). Christ was willing to follow the plan outlined by our Father, giving the glory to the Father. Lucifer wanted to amend the plan, not allow anyone to use their agency to make choices so that no one could sin, but he desired the glory for himself. The Father chose Christ to be the Savior. Satan rebelled and a war ensued. He and his followers were defeated and cast out of heaven.

(A) The Grand Council in Heaven

Old Testament

We receive a hint of that great council in heaven from the book of Job:

Job 38:1, 4, 7 Then the Lord answered Job out of the whirlwind. . . .

> Where wast thou when I laid the foundations of the earth? . . .
>
> When the morning stars sang together, and all the sons of God shouted for joy?

New Testament

Paul also makes reference to actions that were taken in the premortal life before the foundation of the world:

Ephesians 1:3–5, 11–12

> Blessed be the God and Father of our Lord Jesus Christ, who hath blessed us with all spiritual blessings in heavenly places in Christ:
>
> According as he hath chosen us in him before the foundation of the world, that we should be holy and without blame before him in love:
>
> Having predestinated us unto the adoption of children by Jesus Christ to himself, according to the good pleasure of his will. . . .
>
> In whom also we have obtained an inheritance, being predestinated according to the purpose of him who worketh all things after the counsel of his own will:
>
> That we should be to the praise of his glory, who first trusted in Christ.

Book of Mormon

Alma reminded the Nephites that "the plan of redemption . . . was laid from the foundation of the world" and that "there was a plan of redemption laid, which shall bring to pass the resurrection of the dead, of which has been spoken" (Alma 12:25).

Alma also reminded his people that God knew us and knew our righteousness in the premortal life.

Alma 13:3

> And this is the manner after which they were ordained—being called and prepared from the foundation of the world according to the foreknowledge of God, on account of their exceeding faith and good works.

Alma 42:26 — And thus God bringeth about the great and eternal purposes, which were prepared from the foundation of the world. And thus cometh about the salvation and the redemption of men, and also their destruction and misery.

Doctrine and Covenants

While Joseph Smith was incarcerated in Liberty Jail in Missouri, he took the occasion to write down certain prophecies and other information. He makes reference to that "which was ordained in the midst of the Council of the Eternal God of all other gods before this world was" (D&C 121:32).

Years later, on October 18, 1918, another prophet, President Joseph F. Smith, had a vision. Referring to those who had died and whom the Lord had visited after his crucifixion and prior to his resurrection, he wrote:

D&C 138:55–56 — I observed that they were also among the noble and great ones who were chosen in the beginning to be rulers in the Church of God.

Even before they were born, they, with many others, received their first lessons in the world of spirits and were prepared to come forth in the due time of the Lord to labor in his vineyard for the salvation of the souls of men.

Pearl of Great Price

The Lord instructed Abraham regarding the premortal existence and the plan for man's happiness.

Abraham 3:22–23 — Now the Lord had shown unto me, Abraham, the intelligences that were organized before the world was; and among all these there were many of the noble and great ones;

And God saw these souls that they were good, and he stood in the midst of them, and he said: These I will make my rulers; for he stood among those that were spirits, and he saw that they were good; and he said unto me: Abraham, thou art one of them; thou wast chosen before thou wast born.

The scriptures may use various terms—"Where wast thou when I laid the foundations of the earth? When the morning stars sang together, and all the sons of God shouted for joy?"; "According as he hath chosen us in him before the foundation of the world"; "Having predestinated us"; "In whom also we have obtained an inheritance, being predestinated according to the purpose of him who worketh all things after the counsel of his own will"; "there was a plan of redemption laid"; "which was ordained in the midst of the Council of the Eternal God of all other gods before this world was"—but they all provide evidence that in the premortal existence there was a council held in heaven where certain important decisions were made.

(B) God gave his children their agency

In order for God to judge his children and to reward them for their righteousness and give them just punishment for their disobedience, it was imperative for him to give us our agency so we could make wise or foolish choices. Without our agency, we could not progress and become like our Father in Heaven.

Old Testament

In the Garden of Eden, God gave Adam and Eve their agency and told them, "Of every tree of the garden thou mayest freely eat" (Genesis 2:16). However, he then instructed them not to eat of the tree of knowledge of good and evil because they would suffer death if they did. Nevertheless, they were given their agency and were allowed to choose for themselves.

Moses reminded the children of Israel that if they used their agency to obey the commandments they would be blessed but that if they chose not to keep the commandments they would be cursed (Deuteronomy 11:27–28).

Deuteronomy 30:19 I call heaven and earth to record this day against you, that I have set before you life and death, blessing and cursing: therefore choose life, that both thou and thy seed may live:

New Testament

It is because God gave us our agency (the ability to choose to act for ourselves) that we can—and will—be held accountable for our words and deeds.

Matthew 12:36–37 But I say unto you, That every idle word that men

	shall speak, they shall give account thereof in the day of judgment. For by thy words thou shalt be justified, and by thy words thou shalt be condemned.
Revelation 20:12	And I saw the dead, small and great, stand before God; and the books were opened: and another book was opened, which is the book of life: and the dead were judged out of those things which were written in the books, according to their works.

Book of Mormon

The Nephites were taught the importance of agency.

2 Nephi 2:16	Wherefore, the Lord God gave unto man that he should act for himself.
2 Nephi 2:27	Wherefore, men are free according to the flesh; and all things are given them which are expedient unto man. And they are free to choose liberty and eternal life, through the great mediation of all men, or to choose captivity and death, according to the captivity and power of the devil.

Helaman, the son of Alma, reminded his people:

Helaman 14:30–31	God hath given unto you a knowledge and he hath made you free. He hath given unto you that ye might know good from evil, and he hath given unto you that ye might choose life or death.

Doctrine and Covenants

The Lord reiterated in these latter days that he had given man his agency.

D&C 29:35	Behold, I gave unto him [Adam] that he should be an agent unto himself [September 1830].

The Lord again declared to Joseph Smith:

D&C 98:8	I, the Lord God, make you free, therefore ye are free indeed [August 6, 1833].

The Lord again reminded the people that he gave them agency to act for themselves:

D&C 101:78 That every man may act in doctrine and principle pertaining to futurity, according to the moral agency which I have given unto him, that every man may be accountable for his own sins in the day of judgment [December 16, 1833].

Pearl of Great Price

The Lord told Moses that man had been given his agency to act for himself.

Moses 7:32 And in the Garden of Eden, gave I unto man his agency.

Man's agency to act for himself is central to the plan of happiness as designed by God. Without agency, there could be no plan: man could not learn to make wise choices and demonstrate our willingness to follow the Savior's teachings.

(C) Christ was chosen to be the Savior: satan rebelled and waged war

Satan desired to deny us our agency and sought to exalt himself above God.

Old Testament

Isaiah 14:12–15 How art thou fallen from heaven, O Lucifer, son of the morning! how art thou cut down to the ground, which didst weaken the nations!

For thou hast said in thine heart, I will ascend into heaven, I will exalt my throne above the stars of God: I will sit also upon the mount of the congregation, in the sides of the north:

I will ascend above the heights of the clouds; I will be like the most High.

Yet thou shalt be brought down to hell, to the sides of the pit.

New Testament

Luke 10:18 And he [Jesus] said unto them, I beheld Satan as lightning fall from heaven.

The Apostle Peter also reminded the people that:

2 Peter 2:4	God spared not the angels that sinned, but cast them down to hell, and delivered them into chains of darkness, to be reserved unto judgment.

Jude taught the same doctrine:

Jude 1:6	And the angels which kept not their first estate, but left their own habitation, he hath reserved in everlasting chains under darkness unto the judgment of the great day.
Revelation 12:7–9	And there was war in heaven: Michael and his angels fought against the dragon; and the dragon fought and his angels, And prevailed not; neither was their place found any more in heaven. And the great dragon was cast out, that old serpent, called the Devil, and Satan, which deceiveth the whole world: he was cast out into the earth, and his angels were cast out with him.

Book of Mormon

2 Nephi 2:17	And I, Lehi, according to the things which I have read, must needs suppose that an angel of God, according to that which is written, had fallen from heaven; wherefore, he became a devil, having sought that which was evil before God.

Doctrine and Covenants

D&C 29:36–40	And it came to pass that Adam, being tempted of the devil—for, behold, the devil was before Adam, for he rebelled against me, saying, Give me thine honor, which is my power; and also a third part of the hosts of heaven turned he away from me because of their agency; And they were thrust down and thus came the devil and his angels; And, behold, there is a place prepared for them

from the beginning, which place is hell.

And it must needs be that the devil should tempt the children of men, or they could not be agents unto themselves; for if they never should have bitter they could not know the sweet—

Wherefore, it came to pass that the devil tempted Adam, and he partook of the forbidden fruit and transgressed the commandment, wherein he became subject to the will of the devil, because he yielded unto temptation.

On February 16, 1832, Joseph Smith the Prophet and Sidney Rigdon received a vision regarding important points pertaining to the salvation of man, including this excerpt regarding the fall of Satan.

D&C 76:25–28 And this we saw also, and bear record, that an angel of God who was in authority in the presence of God, who rebelled against the Only Begotten Son whom the Father loved and who was in the bosom of the Father, was thrust down from the presence of God and the Son.

And was called Perdition, for the heavens wept over him—he was Lucifer, a son of the morning.

And we beheld, and lo, he is fallen! is fallen, even a son of the morning!

And while we were yet in the Spirit, the Lord commanded us that we should write the vision; for we beheld Satan, that old serpent, even the devil, who rebelled against God, and sought to take the kingdom of our God and his Christ.

Pearl of Great Price

Moses 4:1–4 And I, the Lord God, spake unto Moses, saying: That Satan, whom thou hast commanded in the name of mine Only Begotten, is the same which was from the beginning, and he came before me, saying—Behold, here am I, send me, I will be thy son, and I will redeem all mankind, that one soul shall not be lost, and surely I will do it; wherefore give me thine honor.

But, behold, my Beloved Son, which was my Beloved and Chosen from the beginning, said unto me—Father, thy will be done, and the glory be thine forever.

Wherefore, because that Satan rebelled against me, and sought to destroy the agency of man, which I, the Lord God, had given him, and also, that I should give unto him mine own power; by the power of mine Only Begotten, I caused that he should be cast down;

And he became Satan, yea, even the devil, the father of all lies, to deceive and to blind men, and to lead them captive at his will, even as many as would not hearken unto my voice.

Abraham 3:24–28 And there stood one among them that was like unto God, and he said unto those who were with him: We will go down, for there is space there, and we will take of these materials, and we will make an earth whereon these may dwell;

And we will prove them herewith, to see if they will do all things whatsoever the Lord their God shall command them;

And they who keep their first estate shall be added upon; and they who keep not their first estate shall not have glory in the same kingdom with those who keep their first estate; and they who keep their second estate shall have glory added upon their heads for ever and ever.

And the Lord said: Whom shall I send? And one answered like unto the Son of Man: Here am I, send me. And another answered and said: Here am I, send me. And the Lord said: I will send the first.

And the second was angry, and kept not his first estate; and, at that day, many followed after him.

The Old Testament, New Testament, Book of Mormon, Doctrine and Covenants, and Pearl of Great Price all speak of Satan falling from heaven, of the war in heaven, and of those who followed Satan also being cast out of heaven. These all testify to the reality of the council that was held in the premortal existence and of the plan that was presented for our happiness.

Chapter 18

The Sabbath Day

TENET: When God created the heavens and earth and all that is in them, he rested on the seventh day and hallowed it.

Genesis 2:2–3 — And on the seventh day God ended his work which he had made; and he rested on the seventh day from all his work which he had made. And God blessed the seventh day, and sanctified it: because that in it he had rested from all his work which God created and made.

Because God sanctified the seventh day, he commanded his children to honor the Sabbath day and keep it holy. There is condemnation for those who do not honor the Sabbath day. There are blessings promised to those who do.

Christ taught that the gospel surpassed the law of Moses and that "the Son of Man is Lord even of the sabbath day" (Matthew 12:8).

(A) We are commanded to keep the Sabbath day holy.

Old Testament

Exodus 20:8–11 — Remember the sabbath day, to keep it holy.

Six days shalt thou labour, and do all thy work:

But the seventh day is the sabbath of the Lord thy God: in it thou shalt not do any work, thou, nor thy son, nor thy daughter, thy manservant, nor thy maidservant, nor thy cattle, nor thy stranger that is within thy gates:

For in six days the Lord made heaven and earth, the sea, and all that in them is, and rested the seventh day: wherefore the Lord blessed the sabbath day, and hallowed it.

Exodus 23:12 Six days thou shalt do thy work, and on the seventh day thou shalt rest: that thine ox and thine ass may rest, and the son of thy handmaid, and the stranger, may be refreshed.

Exodus 35:2 Six days shall work be done, but on the seventh day there shall be to you an holy day, a sabbath of rest to the Lord.

Leviticus 23:3 Six days shall work be done: but the seventh day is the sabbath of rest, an holy convocation; ye shall do no work therein: it is the sabbath of the Lord in all your dwellings.

Deuteronomy 5:12–14

Keep the sabbath day to sanctify it, as the Lord thy God hath commanded thee.

Six days thou shalt labour, and do all thy work:

But the seventh day is the sabbath of the Lord thy God: in it thou shalt not do any work, thou, nor thy son, nor thy daughter, nor thy manservant, nor thy maidservant, nor thine ox, nor thine ass, nor any of thy cattle, nor thy stranger that is within thy gates; that thy manservant and thy maidservant may rest as well as thou.

The Levites praised the Lord for giving them the sabbath and other blessings and acknowledged his goodness toward Israel.

Nehemiah 9:13–14 Thou camest down also upon mount Sinai, and spakest with them from heaven, and gavest them right judgments, and true laws, good statutes and commandments:

	And madest known unto them thy holy sabbath, and commandest them precepts, statutes, and laws, by the hand of Moses thy servant.
Jeremiah 17:21–22	Thus saith the Lord; Take heed to yourselves, and bear no burden on the sabbath day, nor bring it in by the gates of Jerusalem; Neither carry forth a burden out of your houses on the sabbath day, neither do ye any work, but hallow ye the sabbath day, as I commanded your fathers.

New Testament

Luke 23:56	And they returned, and prepared spices and ointments; and rested the sabbath day according to the commandment.
Hebrews 4:4	For he spake in a certain place of the seventh day on this wise, And God did rest the seventh day from all his works.

Book of Mormon

Jarom 1:5	And now, behold, two hundred years had passed away, and the people of Nephi had waxed strong in the land. They observed to keep the law of Moses and the sabbath day holy unto the Lord.
Mosiah 13:16–19	Remember the sabbath day, to keep it holy. Six days shalt thou labor, and do all thy work; But the seventh day, the sabbath of the Lord thy God, thou shalt not do any work, thou, nor thy son, nor thy daughter, thy man-servant, nor thy maid-servant, nor thy cattle, nor thy stranger that is within thy gates; For in six days the Lord made heaven and earth, and the sea, and all that in them is; wherefore the Lord blessed the sabbath day, and hallowed it.

Alma commanded those who believed and were baptized:

Mosiah 18:23	That they should observe the sabbath day, and keep it holy.

Doctrine and Covenants

D&C 59:9–13 — And that thou mayest more fully keep thyself unspotted from the world, thou shalt go to the house of prayer and offer up thy sacraments upon my holy day;

For verily this is a day appointed unto you to rest from your labors, and to pay thy devotions unto the Most High;

Nevertheless thy vows shall be offered up in righteousness on all days and at all times;

But remember that on this, the Lord's day, thou shalt offer thine oblations and thy sacraments unto the Most High, confessing thy sins unto thy brethren, and before the Lord.

And on this day thou shalt do none other thing, only let thy food be prepared with singleness of heart that thy fasting may be perfect, or, in other words, that thy joy may be full.

D&C 68:29 — And the inhabitants of Zion shall also observe the Sabbath day to keep it holy.

Pearl of Great Price

Moses 3:2–3 — And on the seventh day I, God, ended my work, and all things which I had made; and I rested on the seventh day from all my work, and all things which I had made were finished, and I God, saw that they were good;

And I, God, blessed the seventh day, and sanctified it; because that in it I had rested from all my work which I, God, had created and made.

Abraham recorded that from the beginning, the Gods planned for the seventh day to be a day of rest and sanctified it.

Abraham 5:2–3 — And the Gods said among themselves: On the seventh time we will end our work, which we have counseled; and we will rest on the seventh time from all our work which we have counseled.

And the Gods concluded upon the seventh time, because that on the seventh time they would rest from all their works which they (the Gods] counseled among themselves to form; and sanctified it. And thus were their decisions at the time that they counseled among themselves to form the heavens and the earth.

(B) The significance of the Sabbath day

The Lord commanded Man to honor the Sabbath day for specific reasons. (Note: reasons are underlined for easier identification.)

Old Testament

Exodus 31:12–13

And the Lord spake unto Moses, saying,

Speak thou also unto the children of Israel, saying, Verily my sabbaths ye shall keep: for it is a sign between me and you throughout your generations; that ye may know that I am the Lord that doth sanctify you.

Exodus 31:16–17

Wherefore the children of Israel shall keep the sabbath, to observe the sabbath throughout their generations, for a perpetual covenant.

It is a sign between me and the children of Israel for ever: for in six days the Lord made heaven and earth, and on the seventh day he rested, and was refreshed.

Deuteronomy 5:15

And remember that thou wast a servant in the land of Egypt, and that the Lord thy God brought thee out thence through a mighty hand and by a stretched out arm: therefore the Lord thy God commanded thee to keep the sabbath day.

Ezekiel 20:12

Moreover also I gave them my sabbaths, to be a sign between me and them, that they might know that I am the Lord that sanctify them.

Doctrine and Covenants

In the New Testament, in the Revelation of John, we know that Christ's apostle was shown a more extensive understanding of the significance of God's sanctifying the seventh day. Just as God sanctified the seventh day, at the beginning of the Millennium—at the beginning of the seventh thousand years—he will sanctify the earth. He revealed that significance to Joseph Smith the Prophet in March 1832.

D&C 77:12 Q. What are we to understand by the sounding of the trumpets, mentioned in the 8th chapter of Revelation?

A. We are to understand that as God made the world in six days, and the seventh day he finished his work, and sanctified it, and also formed man out of the dust of the earth, even so, in the beginning of the seventh thousand years will the Lord God sanctify the earth, and complete the salvation of man, and judge all things, and shall redeem all things, except that which he hath not put into his power, when he shall have sealed all things, unto the end of all things; and the sounding of the trumpets of the seven angels are the preparing and finishing of his work, in the beginning of the seventh thousand years—the preparing of the way before the time of his coming.

(C) Consequences of not keeping the Sabbath day holy

Because the children of Israel were especially prone to slip back into wicked practices, the Mosaic Law was a strict schoolmaster to teach them to obey Heavenly Father's commandments, and failure to observe the sabbath day reaped immediate negative consequences. (Note: consequences are **bolded** for easier identification.)

Old Testament

The children of Israel were commanded to gather just enough manna to last for that day, with the exception that on Saturday they were to gather enough for the sabbath as well, but no more.

Exodus 16:19–20 And Moses said, Let no man leave of it till the morning.

Notwithstanding they hearkened not unto Moses; but some of them left of it until the morning, and **it**

	bred worms, and stank: and Moses was wroth with them.
Exodus 31:14–15	Ye shall keep the sabbath therefore; for it is holy unto you: every one that defileth it shall surely be **put to death**: for whosoever doeth any work therein, that soul shall be **cut off from among his people**. Six days may work be done; but in the seventh is the sabbath of rest, holy to the Lord: whosoever doeth any work in the sabbath day, he shall surely be **put to death**.
Exodus 35:2	Whosoever doeth work therein shall be **put to death**.
Numbers 15:32–36	And while the children of Israel were in the wilderness, they found a man that gathered sticks upon the sabbath day. And they that found him gathering sticks brought him unto Moses and Aaron, and unto all the congregation. And they put him in ward, because it was not declared what should be done to him. And the Lord said unto Moses, The man shall be surely **put to death**: all the congregation shall **stone him with stones** without the camp. And all the congregation brought him without the camp, and **stoned him with stones, and he died**; as the Lord commanded Moses.
Nehemiah 13:15	In those days saw I in Judah some treading wine presses on the sabbath, and bringing in sheaves, and lading asses; as also wine, grapes, and figs, and all manner of burdens, which they brought into Jerusalem on the sabbath day: and **I testified against them** in the day wherein they sold victuals.
Jeremiah 17:21, 27	Thus saith the Lord; Take heed to yourselves, and bear no burden on the sabbath day, nor bring it in by the gates of Jerusalem. . . . But if ye will not hearken unto me to hallow the sabbath day, and not to bear a burden, even entering

in at the gates of Jerusalem on the sabbath day, then will **I kindle a fire in the gates thereof, and it shall devour the palaces of Jerusalem, and it shall not be quenched**.

Ezekiel 20:13, 15–16 But the house of Israel rebelled against me in the wilderness: they walked not in my statutes, and they despised my judgments, which if a man do, he shall even live in them; and my sabbaths they greatly polluted: then I said, **I would pour out my fury upon them in the wilderness, to consume them**. . . .

Yet also I lifted up my hand unto them in the wilderness, that **I would not bring them into the land which I had given them**, flowing with milk and honey, which is the glory of all lands;

Because they despised my judgments, and walked not in my statutes, but polluted my sabbaths: for their heart went after their idols.

New Testament

Matthew 24:20–21 But pray ye that your flight be not in the winter, neither on the sabbath day:

For then shall be **great tribulation**, such as was not since the beginning of the world to this time, no, nor ever shall be.

While the punishments meted out during Old Testament times are not meted out today, we will certainly ultimately suffer negative consequences for our failure to obey the Lord's command to keep the Sabbath day holy.

(D) Blessings are promised to those who keep the Sabbath day holy

Old Testament

In contrast to that which occurred when the people gathered more manna than they were commanded to gather, when they did as instructed, they were blessed. (Note: blessings are *italicized* for easier identification.)

Exodus 16:22–24 And it came to pass that on the sixth day they gathered twice as much bread, two omers for one man:

and all the rulers of the congregation came and told Moses.

And he said unto them, This is that which the Lord hath said, Tomorrow is the rest of the holy sabbath unto the Lord: bake that which ye will bake to day, and seethe that ye will seethe; and that which remaineth over lay up for you to be kept until the morning.

And they laid it up till the morning, as Moses bade: and *it did not stink, neither was there any worm therein.*

Isaiah 56:2–7

Blessed is the man that doeth this, and the son of man that layeth hold on it; that keepeth the sabbath from polluting it, and keepeth his hand from doing any evil.

Neither let the son of the stranger, that hath joined himself to the Lord, speak, saying The Lord hath utterly separated me from his people; neither let the eunuch say, Behold, I am a dry tree.

For thus saith the Lord unto the eunuchs that keep my sabbaths, and choose the things that please me, and take hold of my covenant;

Even unto them will I give in mine house and within my walls a place and a name better than of sons and of daughters: I will give them an everlasting name, that shall not be cut off.

Also the sons of the stranger, that join themselves to the Lord, to serve him, and to love the name of the Lord, to be his servants, every one that keepeth the sabbath from polluting it, and taketh hold of my covenant;

Even them *will I bring to my holy mountain, and make them joyful in my house of prayer: their burnt offerings and their sacrifices shall be accepted upon mine altar*; for mine house shall be called an house of prayer for all people.

Isaiah 58:13–14

If thou turn away thy foot from the sabbath, from

doing thy pleasure on my holy day; and call the sabbath a delight, the holy of the Lord honourable; and shalt honour him, not doing thine own ways, nor finding thine own pleasure, nor speaking thine own words:

Then shalt thou delight thyself in the Lord; and I will cause thee to ride upon the high places of the earth, and feed thee with the heritage of Jacob thy father: for the mouth of the Lord hath spoken it.

Jeremiah 17:24–25 And it shall come to pass, if ye diligently hearken unto me, saith the Lord, to bring in no burden through the gates of this city on the sabbath day, but hallow the sabbath day, to do no work herein;

Then shall there enter into the gates of this city kings and princes sitting upon the throne of David, riding in chariots and on horses, they, and their princes, the men of Judah, and the inhabitants of Jerusalem: and this city shall remain for ever.

Doctrine and Covenants

In these latter days, the Lord also revealed to the Prophet Joseph Smith that both temporal and spiritual blessings would come to those who keep the sabbath day holy.

D&C 59:10, 13, 16–19

For verily this is a day appointed unto you to rest from your labors, and to pay thy devotions unto the Most High. . . .

And on this day thou shalt do none other thing, only let thy food be prepared with singleness of heart that thy fasting may be perfect, or in other words, that thy joy may be full. . . .

Verily I say, that inasmuch as ye do this, *the fulness of the earth is yours, the beasts of the field and the fowls of the air, and that which climbeth upon the trees and walketh upon the earth;*

Yea, and the herb, and the good things which come of the earth, whether for food or for raiment, or for houses, or for barns, or for orchards, or for gardens, or for wineyards;

Yea, all things which come of the earth, in the season thereof, are made for the benefit and the use of man, both to please the eye and to gladden the heart;

Yea, for food and for raiment, for taste and for smell, to strengthen the body and to enliven the soul.

Spiritual as well as temporal blessing come from keeping the Sabbath day holy.

(E) The Son of Man is Lord of the Sabbath day

Christ preached and showed by his own actions that, contrary to the letter of the law as practiced by the children of Israel as they lived under the law of Moses, certain sabbath behavior was acceptable.

New Testament

Matthew 12:10–13 And, behold, there was a man which had his hand withered. And they asked him, saying, Is it lawful to heal on the sabbath days? that they might accuse him.

And he said unto them, What man shall there be among you, that shall have one sheep, and if it fall into a pit on the sabbath day, will he not lay hold on it, and lift it out?

How much then is a man better than a sheep? Wherefore it is lawful to do well on the sabbath days.

Then saith he to the man, Stretch forth thine hand. And he stretched it forth; and it was restored whole, like as the other.

Mark 2:23–28 And it came to pass, that he went through the corn fields on the sabbath day; and his disciples began, as they went, to pluck the ears of corn.

And the Pharisees said unto him, Behold, why do they on the sabbath day that which is not lawful?

And he said unto them, Have ye never read what

David did, when he had need, and was an hungered, he, and they that were with him?

How he went into the house of God in the days of Abiathar the high priest, and did eat the shewbread, which is not lawful to eat but for the priests, and gave also to them which were with him?

And he said unto them, The sabbath was made for man, and not man for the sabbath:

Therefore the Son of man is Lord also of the sabbath.

The incident involving the man with the withered hand was also recorded by Mark and Luke.

Mark 3:4–5

And he saith unto them, Is it lawful to do good on the sabbath days, or to do evil? to save life, or to kill? But they held their peace.

And when he had looked round about on them with anger, being grieved for the hardness of their hearts, he saith unto the man, Stretch forth thine hand. And he stretched it out: and his hand was restored whole as the other [see Luke 14:1–5].

The incident of Christ's disciples plucking corn on the sabbath is also retold in Luke 6:1–5. The incident of Christ healing the man's withered hand on the sabbath is retold in Luke 6:6–10.

Luke 13:10–16

And he was teaching in one of the synagogues on the sabbath.

And, behold, there was a woman which had a spirit of infirmity eighteen years, and was bowed together, and could in no wise lift up herself.

And when Jesus saw her, he called her to him, and said unto her, Woman, thou art loosed from thine infirmity.

And he laid his hands on her: and immediately she was made straight, and glorified God.

And the ruler of the synagogue answered with indignation, because that Jesus had healed on the sabbath day, and said unto the people, There are six days in which men ought to work: in them therefore come and be healed, and not on the sabbath day.

The Lord then answered him, and said, Thou hypocrite, doth not each one of you on the sabbath loose his ox or his ass from the stall, and lead him away to watering?

And ought not this woman, being a daughter of Abraham, whom Satan hath bound, lo, these eighteen years, be loosed from this bond on the sabbath day?

John 5:2, 5–9 Now there is at Jerusalem by the sheep market a pool, which is called in the Hebrew tongue Bethesda, having five porches. . . .

And a certain man was there, which had an infirmity thirty and eight years.

When Jesus saw him lie, and knew that he had been now a long time in that case, he saith unto him, Wilt thou be made whole?

The impotent man answered him, Sir, I have no man, when the water is troubled, to put me into the pool: but while I am coming, another steppeth down before me.

Jesus saith unto him, Rise, take up thy bed, and walk.

And immediately the man was made whole, and took up his bed, and walked: and on the same day was the sabbath.

Jesus not only healed on the sabbath, but also instructed the man to pick us his bed, and walk. The Jews chided the man because, they said, "It is not lawful for thee to carry thy bed" (John 5:10).

John 7:21–24 Jesus answered and said unto them, I have done one work, and ye all marvel.

Moses therefore gave unto you circumcision; (not because it is of Moses, but of the fathers;) and ye on the sabbath day circumcise a man.

If a man on the sabbath day receive circumcision, that the law of Moses should not be broken;

are ye angry at me, because I have made a man every whit whole on the sabbath day.

Judge not according to the appearance, but judge righteous judgment.

John 9:6–7, 14 When he had thus spoken, he spat on the ground, and made clay of the spittle, and he anointed the eyes of the blind man with the clay,

And said unto him, Go, wash in the pool of Siloam. . . . He went his way therefore, and washed, and came seeing. . . .

And it was the sabbath day when Jesus made the clay, and opened his eyes.

The apostles demonstrated that other activities were also acceptable on the sabbath day, activities such as preaching the gospel.

Acts 13:42, 44–46 And when the Jews were gone out of the synagogue, the Gentiles besought that these words might be preached to them the next sabbath. . . .

And the next sabbath day came almost the whole city together to hear the word of God.

But when the Jews saw the multitudes, they were filled with envy, and spake against those things which were spoken by Paul, contradicting and blaspheming.

Then Paul and Barnabas waxed bold, and said, It was necessary that the word of God should first have been spoken to you: but seeing ye put it from you, and judge yourselves unworthy of everlasting life, lo, we turn to the Gentiles.

Again referring to Paul, the scriptures record:

Acts 18:4 And he reasoned in the synagogue every sabbath, and persuaded the Jews and the Greeks.

The gospel of Jesus Christ surpassed the law of Moses. In his second epistle to the Corinthians, Paul reminded them that Christ had "made us able ministers of the new testament; not of the letter, but of the spirit: for the letter killeth, but the spirit giveth life" (2 Corinthians 3:6).

It is clear from the scriptures that we are commanded to keep the Sabbath day holy; that certain activities are not acceptable on the Sabbath day, but that other activities are. It is also clear that keeping the Sabbath day holy brings blessings and not keeping the Sabbath day holy brings condemnation.

Conclusion

Truth is established by the mouths of two or more witnesses. That was true anciently and is true today. The truth of Christ's divinity, his atonement, and his teachings is established by the mouth of two witnesses: those witnesses are the stick of Judah (the Bible) and the stick of Joseph (the Book of Mormon: Another Testament of Jesus Christ). As recorded in Ezekiel 37:19, they are to be "one in thine hand."